THE HASKINS SOCIETY JOURNAL

STUDIES IN MEDIEVAL HISTORY

The Charles Homer Haskins Society
Officers and Councillors for 2012

THE HASKINS SOCIETY JOURNAL

STUDIES IN MEDIEVAL HISTORY

EDITED BY WILLIAM NORTH AND LAURA L. GATHAGAN

Volume 24
2012

THE BOYDELL PRESS

First published 2013
The Boydell Press, Woodbridge

ISBN 978–1–84383–830–2

ISSN 0963–4959

The Boydell Press is an imprint of Boydell & Brewer Ltd
PO Box 9, Woodbridge, Suffolk IP12 3DF, UK
and of Boydell & Brewer Inc.
668 Mt Hope Avenue, Rochester, NY 14620–2731, USA
website: www.boydellandbrewer.com

A CIP catalogue record for this book is available
from the British Library

The publisher has no responsibility for the continued existence or accuracy of
URLs for external or third-party internet websites referred to in this book,
and does not guarantee that any content on such websites is,
or will remain, accurate or appropriate.

Papers used by Boydell & Brewer Ltd are natural, recyclable products
made from wood grown in sustainable forests

Printed in Great Britain by
CPI Group (UK) Ltd, Croydon, CR0 4YY

Contents

Figures

Editor's Note

This volume of the *Haskins Society Journal* includes papers read at the 30th Annual Conference of the Charles Homer Haskins Society at Boston College in November 2011, papers read at earlier Haskins conferences, and individual paper submissions. The papers by Howard Clarke and Monika Otter were featured papers at the Haskins Conference, and Susanna Throop's essay received the 2011 Bethell Prize, which was judged by Howard C. Clarke of University College, Dublin. It forms the regular volume for 2012. The Editor and Assistant Editor would like to offer thanks to the contributors and anonymous reviewers, and to Caroline Palmer and the excellent staff at Boydell & Brewer Ltd for their help and patience during the production of this volume.

The *Haskins Society Journal* is an international refereed journal, and its contents are not limited to papers read at the Society's own conference or at the sessions which it sponsors at Leeds, Kalamazoo, or other venues. Papers on topics in the many fields and periods of the medieval past to which Charles Homer Haskins contributed, including but not limited to Anglo-Saxon, viking, Norman, and Angevin history as well as the history of the neighboring peoples and territories, are welcome from any scholar. Authors intending to submit are asked to consult the Society's website (www.haskinssociety.org) or write to the Editor (Dr Laura L. Gathagan, Department of History, SUNY Cortland, P.O. Box 2000 Cortland, NY 13045–0900, USA; email: laura.gathagan@cortland.edu) or Assistant Editor (Dr William North, Department of History, Carleton College, 1 North College Street, Northfield, MN 55057, USA; email: wnorth@carleton.edu).

William North, Editor

Abbreviations

AASS	*Acta Sanctorum* (67 vols., Antwerp/Brussels/Paris 1643–1884)
AHR	*American Historical Review*
ANS	*Anglo-Norman Studies* (formerly *Proceedings of the Battle Conference on Anglo-Norman Studies*)
ASC	Anglo-Saxon Chronicle; normally cited from *Two of the Saxon Chronicles Parallel*, ed. Charles Plummer (2 vols., Oxford, 1892–99), with year and MS
ASE	*Anglo-Saxon England*
Bede, *EH*	Bede, *Ecclesiastical History of the English People*, ed. and trans. B. Colgrave and R.A.B. Mynors (Oxford, rev. ed. 1991)
BHL	*Bibliotheca Hagiographica Latina*, Subsidia Hagiographica 6 (2 vols., Bruxelles, 1898–1901)
Bk. of Fees	*Liber feodorum: the Book of Fees, commonly called Testa de Nevill* (3 vols., London, 1920–31)
BL	British Library, London
Bracton	*Bracton on the Laws and Customs of England,* ed. and trans. Samuel E. Thorne (4 vols., Cambridge, MA, 1968–77)
Bracton's Note Book	*Bracton's Note Book: a Collection of Cases decided in the King's Courts during the Reign of Henry the Third,* ed. F.W. Maitland (3 vols., London, 1887)
CCM	*Cahiers de Civilisation Médiévale*
Cal. Chart. R.	*Calendar of the Charter Rolls, 1226–1516* (6 vols., London, 1903–27)
Cal. Docs. France, ed. Round	*Calendar of Documents preserved in France illustrative of the History of Great Britain and Ireland, I: A.D. 918–1206,* ed. J.H. Round (London, 1899)
Cal. Lib. R.	*Calendar of the Liberate Rolls preserved in the Public Record Office* (6 vols., London, 1916–64)
Cal. Pat.	*Calendar of the Patent Rolls preserved in the Public Record Office* (London, 1891 and in progress)
Camb. Hist. Jnl.	*Cambridge Historical Journal*

CCSL	Corpus Christianorum, series latina (Turnhout, 1953–)
CCCM	Corpus Christianorum, continuatio mediaevalis (Turnhout, 1971–)
Close R.	*Close Rolls of the Reign of Henry III preserved in the Public Record Office* (14 vols., London, 1902–38)
Complete Peerage	G.E. C[okayne], *The Complete Peerage of England, Scotland, Ireland, Great Britain, and the United Kingdom, Extant, Extinct, and Dormant,* new edn. by V. Gibbs and others (12 vols. in 13, London, 1910–59)
Cur. Reg. R.	*Curia Regis Rolls preserved in the Public Record Office* (17 vols., in progress, London, 1922–)
DB	*Domesday Book, seu liber censualis Wilhelmi primi regis Angliae,* [ed. Abraham Farley] (2 vols., London, 1783)
DNB	*Dictionary of National Biography,* ed. Leslie Stephen and Stephen Lee
Dudo, *History*	Eric Christiansen, trans., *Dudo of St Quentin: History of the Normans* (Woodbridge, 1998)
EcHR	*Economic History Review*
EHD	*English Historical Documents, I: c. 500–1042,* ed. Dorothy Whitelock (2nd edn., London, 1979); *II: 1042–1189,* ed. David C. Douglas and George W. Greenaway (2nd edn., London, 1981); *III: 1189–1327,* ed. Harry Rothwell (London, 1975)
EHR	*English Historical Review*
EME	*Early Medieval Europe*
EYC	*Early Yorkshire Charters,* ed. W. Farrer and C.T. Clay (13 vols.: vols. i–iii, Edinburgh, 1914–16; index to vols. I–iii, and vols. iv–xii, Yorkshire Archaeological Soc. Record Ser. Extra Ser. 1–10 [1935–65])
FSI	*Fonti per la Storia d'Italia*
Gesta Stephani	*Gesta Stephani,* ed. K.R. Potter and revised R.H.C. Davis (Oxford, 1976)
Glanvill	*The Treatise on the Laws and Customs of the Realm of England commonly called Glanvill,* ed. and trans. G.D.G. Hall with guide to further reading by M.T. Clanchy (Oxford, rev. ed. 1993)
GND, ed. van Houts	*The Gesta Normannum Ducum of William of Jumièges, Orderic Vitalis, and Robert of Torigni,* ed. and trans. Elisabeth M.C. van Houts (2 vols., Oxford, 1992–5)
Henry of Huntingdon, *Historia*	Henry, Archdeacon of Huntingdon, *Historia Anglorum: the History of the English People,* ed. and trans. Diana Greenway (Oxford, 1996)
Hist. Res.	*Historical Research* (formerly *Bulletin of the Institute of Historical Research*)

HSJ	*Haskins Society Journal*
JMH	*Journal of Medieval History*
JEH	*Journal of Ecclesiastical History*
John of Worcester,	*The Chronicle of John of Worcester,* ed. and trans. R.R.
Chronicle	Darlington, P. McGurk, and J. Bray (3 vols., Oxford, 1995–)
MGH	Monumenta Germaniae Historica
AA	*Auctores Antiquissimi*
Epp.	*Epistolae*
LdL	*Libelli de Lite*
SS	*Scriptores in folio*
SSRG	*Scriptores Rerum Germanicarum, separatim editi*
SSRG, n.s.	*Scriptores Rerum Germanicarum, nova series*
MS/MSS	Manuscript/Manuscripts
OV	*The Ecclesiastical History of Orderic Vitalis,* ed. Marjorie Chibnall (6 vols., Oxford, 1969–80)
PP	*Past and Present*
PBA	*Proceedings of the British Academy*
Pipe R.	*The Great Roll of the Pipe* (Pipe Roll Society), with regnal year
PL	*Patrologia latina cursus completus,* ed. J.-P. Migne (221 vols., Paris, 1844–64)
Rec. Com.	Record Commissioners
Recueil, ed. Fauroux	*Recueil des actes des ducs de Normandie de 911 à 1066,* ed. M. Fauroux (Caen, 1961)
Regesta	*Regesta regum Anglo-Normannorum, 1066–1154,* ed. H.W.C. Davis and others (4 vols., Oxford, 1913–69)
RHC	*Recueil des Historiens des Croisades*
Doc.Arm.	*Documents arméniennes* (2 vols., Paris, 1869–1906)
Gr.	*Historiens Grecs* (2 vols., Paris, 1875–1881)
Lois	*Lois* (2 vols., Paris, 1841–43)
Occid.	*Historiens Occidentaux* (5 vols. in 6, 1844–95)
Or.	*Historiens Orientaux* (5 vols., Paris, 1872–1906)
RIS	*Rerum Italicarum Scriptores*
Rot. de Lib.	*Rotuli de liberate ac de misis et praestitis, regnante Johanne,* ed. T.D. Hardy (London, 1844)
Rot. Hund.	*Rotuli hundredorum temp. Hen. III & Edw. I,* ed. W. Illingworth and J. Caley (2 vols., London, 1812–18)
Rot. Litt. Claus.	*Rotuli litterarum clausarum in turri Londinensi asservati, 1204–27,* ed. T.D. Hardy (2 vols., London, 1833–44)
Rot. Litt. Pat.	*Rotuli litterarum patentium in Turri Londinensi asservati (1201–16),* ed. T. D. Hardy (London, 1835)
RS	Rolls Series

Sawyer, *Charters*	P.H. Sawyer, *Anglo-Saxon Charters: an Annotated List and Bibliography* (London, 1968), with charter number
s.a. (no italics)	*sub anno/annis* [under the year/–s]
ser.	series
Settimane	*Settimane di Studio del Centro Italiano di Studi sull'Alto Medioevo*
Soc.	Society
Stubbs, *Charters*	*Select Charters and Other Illustrations of English Constitutional History from the Earliest Times to the Reign of Edward the First,* ed. William Stubbs (9th edn., revised H.W.C. Davis, Oxford, 1913)
s.v. (no italics)	*sub verbo*
Symeon, *Opera*	*Symeonis monachi opera omnia,* ed. Thomas Arnold, RS 75 (2 vols., London, 1882–85)
TNA	The National Archives, Kew, London
TRHS	*Transactions of the Royal Historical Society*
Univ.	University
unpub.	unpublished
VCH	*The Victoria History of the Counties of England* (in progress), with name of county
William of Malmesbury, *GP*	William of Malmesbury, *Gesta Pontificum Anglorum,* ed. and trans. R.M. Thomson and M. Winterbottom (2 vols., Oxford, 2007)
William of Malmesbury, *GR*	William of Malmesbury, *Gesta regum Anglorum,* ed. and trans. R.A.B. Mynors, R.M. Thomson, and M. Winterbottom (2 vols., Oxford, 1998–1999)
William of Malmesbury, *HN*	William of Malmesbury, *Historia novella,* ed. K.R. Potter and E. King (Oxford, 1998)
William of Poitiers, *Gesta*	William of Poitiers, *The Gesta Gvillelmi of William of Poitiers,* ed. and trans. R.H.C. Davis and M. Chibnall (Oxford, 1998)

1

'Those Five Knights which you Owe me in Respect of your Abbacy'. Organizing Military Service after the Norman Conquest: Evesham and Beyond*

Howard B. Clarke

The quotation will be familiar to many readers. It represents part of the famous writ of military summons directed by William the Conqueror to Æthelwig, the last Anglo-Saxon abbot of Evesham, in Worcestershire. The full text reads as follows in translation in volume II of *English Historical Documents*:

William, king of the English, to Æthelwig, abbot of Evesham, greeting. I order you to summon all those who are subject to your administration and jurisdiction that they bring before me at Clarendon on the octave of Pentecost all the knights they owe me duly equipped. You, also, on that day, shall come to me, and bring with you fully equipped those five knights which you owe me in respect of your abbacy. Witness Eudo the steward. At Winchester.[1]

As is well known, much was made of this little document by J.H. Round back in 1895, and many other scholars have followed in his wake.[2] It is the only scrap of record evidence to suggest that *servitia debita* were established early in the Conqueror's reign, and it has been made to bear an enormous burden of proof for the so-called introduction of 'feudalism' into England. The chaotic cartulary in which it survives has never been published in full, and the Latin text that most historians appear to have used is that produced by Round. Yet, in the five-and-a-half lines it occupies in the 1964 reprint of *Feudal England*,

*   I am grateful to Sarah Gearty, project manager and cartographic editor of the Irish Historic Towns Atlas project of the Royal Irish Academy, for drawing the maps.
[1]   *EHD* ii, 960.
[2]   Including H.M. Chew in her classic study *The English Ecclesiastical Tenants-in-Chief and Knight Service, especially in the Thirteenth and Fourteenth Centuries* (Oxford and London, 1932), 3, 75, 83–84, but excluding Susan Reynolds, *Fiefs and Vassals: the Medieval Evidence Reinterpreted* (Oxford, 1994), where it goes unmentioned.

Round succeeded in introducing not only feudalism but also no fewer than twenty-five errors and misimpressions in his transcription.[3] Furthermore, he referred the reader in a footnote to the wrong manuscript, although he did at least get the folio number right.[4]

In his discussion of the Evesham writ, Round found 'the vigour of its language' convincing.[5] Most historians (including myself)[6] have until recently accepted it at face value, though back in 1963 Messrs Richardson and Sayles expressed doubts:

We do not, in sober fact, know the purpose of the writ of summons; we do not know who were summoned or their numbers; we are not even certain of the year of the summons. The only certain fact, beyond those in the writ itself, is that it was issued before Æthelwig's death in 1077.... And if, instead of surmising with Round that the date of the writ is 1072, we surmise that its date lies between 1067 and 1070, which seems equally possible, how then do we interpret it and what becomes of Round's thesis? We cannot build upon such flimsy foundations.[7]

Yet, even one of their 'facts' is by no means certain, for the probability is that the good abbot died in February 1078.[8] Subsequently, John Gillingham discussed the difficulties in understanding the precise purpose of the document (assuming it to be authentic) and in ascertaining its date, David Bates queried its authenticity, and Nicholas Brooks firmly rejected it.[9] Clarendon always seemed more redolent of the reign of Henry II than that of the Conqueror and therefore of the date of this cartulary text. One possible context for the production of the document, whether or not based on an authentic original, is the arbitrary *donum* of 1159 when Evesham Abbey's assessment at 60 marks may have been thought to be out of line, especially in comparison to that of

---

[3]   J.H. Round, *Feudal England: Historical Studies on the Eleventh and Twelfth Centuries* (London, 1895; repr. 1964), 238 and note 251.
[4]   London, BL, MS Cotton Vespasian B xxiv, fol. 18.
[5]   Round, *Feudal England*, 238.
[6]   H.B. Clarke, '1066, 1169, and All That: the Tyranny of Historical Turning Points', in *European Encounters: Essays in Memory of Albert Lovett*, ed. Judith Devlin and H.B. Clarke (Dublin, 2003), 11–36 at 19–21, hinting at the possibility of forgery.
[7]   H.G. Richardson and G.O. Sayles, *The Governance of Mediaeval England from the Conquest to Magna Carta* (Edinburgh, 1963), 64–65.
[8]   H.B. Clarke, 'The Early Surveys of Evesham Abbey: an Investigation into the Problem of Continuity in Anglo-Norman England', PhD thesis (University of Birmingham, 1977), 32–33.
[9]   John Gillingham, *The English in the Twelfth Century: Imperialism, National Identity and Political Values* (Woodbridge, 2000; orig. published 1982), 195–96; *Regesta Regum Anglo-Normannorum: the Acta of William I, 1066–1087*, ed. David Bates (Oxford, 1998), no. 131; Nicholas Brooks, 'The Archbishopric of Canterbury and the So-Called Introduction of Knight-Service into England', *ANS* 34 (2012), 41–62 at 44. John Gillingham in a personal comment on the question of the writ's authenticity said that he thought that he had not 'emphatically rejected' it, as Brooks alleged, but had merely been timidly non-committal.

the neighbours at Pershore and Winchcombe.[10] It is worth noting, too, that three other texts accompany the writ on the recto of same folio, and that at least two and probably all three of them are open to suspicion. Moreover, the whole lot are written over a partially erased pre-Conquest charter in favour of Hereford Cathedral, which by the twelfth century was proving to be an embarrassment to the monks of Evesham in the context of a complicated squabble they were enjoying with the monks of Crowland.[11]

Round himself observed that there was nothing 'to be gained by forging a document which admits, by placing on record, the abbey's full liability'.[12] In this he was correct with regard to the reign of Henry II, for the *cartae baronum* of 1166 do indeed yield a *servitium debitum* of five knights for the abbot of Evesham. There is every reason to believe that Æthelwig had secured a favourable deal with his new master from the point of view of a medium-sized Benedictine house whose estates had been vastly increased by means of policies pursued by the same abbot. The reference in the writ to Æthelwig's area of jurisdiction is surely correct even if the word *ballia* is not.[13] Moreover, when Evesham Abbey fell upon harder times, Henry I saw fit to reduce its obligation to four-and-a-half knights in 1107.[14] A year after the battle of Tinchebrai, it had become clear that the need for a 'feudal army' was more likely to be felt on the Continent than in England, and scutage payments started to be seen as a more flexible and useful aid than any sort of body of fully equipped knights enfeoffed in the island kingdom.

These are merely hints of the background against which I wish to discuss the question of how tenants-in-chief went about the task of organizing their military service obligations. What sorts of fief did they create and for whom? Were fiefs compact estates or scattered bits and pieces? Were they located near the residence of the tenant-in-chief or at a remove? Can anything be said about the quality of the land from an agrarian point of view? Over the decades were the same lands granted out to successive knightly subtenants or were changes made? Finally – and I hope not too frivolously, given that the abbey's reputation as a source of reliable historical information has taken another hit – can anything be said in order to salvage the reputation of those Worcestershire Benedictines who were apparently so predisposed to engage in forgery on an almost heroic scale?[15] Before attempting to answer such

---

[10] David Knowles, *The Monastic Order in England: a History of its Development from the Times of St Dunstan to the Fourth Lateran Council 940–1216* (Cambridge, 1966), 712.
[11] For the Crowland perspective, see Sandra Raban, *The Estates of Thorney and Crowland: a Study in Medieval Monastic Land Tenure* (Cambridge, 1977), 28–29.
[12] Round, *Feudal England*, 238.
[13] The dictionary reference *c.* 1072 is apparently based on the presumed date of the writ: R.E. Latham, *Revised Medieval Latin Word-List from British and Irish Sources* (London, 1965), 42.
[14] *Regesta*, ii, no. 831; Chew, *Ecclesiastical Tenants-in-Chief*, 9 and note 4, 98–99.
[15] For a detailed study of some of the Evesham forgeries, see H.B. Clarke, 'Uses and Abuses of Foundation Legends: the Case of Evesham Abbey', in *The Medieval Imagination, Mirabile*

questions, I shall provide a brief overview of the nature of the core estates of Evesham Abbey. In so doing I shall use the word 'estate' to refer to a discrete area of agrarian resources comprising one or more 'manors' (*maneria*) or their pre-manorial equivalents.

The Evesham Abbey Estates

According to legend, and probably in truth, Evesham Abbey was founded by Æthelræd, king of the Mercians, in or about the year 701 in the time of Bishop Ecgwine of Worcester. Ecgwine's diocese corresponded to the tribal kingdom of the Hwicce, and Evesham occupied a central position in it. It was one of a striking number of monastic and quasi-monastic foundations in the Avon valley district (minster churches in John Blair's construct).[16] A site for the church and the core endowment were acquired during the years 701–709, comprising a compact territory on both banks of the Avon and a woodland outlier at Ombersley in the Severn valley (three 'estates'). There may have been intermittent contact with primitive urban centres at Alcester, Droitwich, and Worcester. When Ecgwine died in semi-retirement at Evesham on 30 December 717, Anglo-Saxon monasticism was at its zenith. Thereafter decline set in on a large scale, secularization became a powerful force, Vikings came and were absorbed, and a modest recovery was achieved in the first half of the eleventh century.[17]

The outcome at Evesham can be assessed for the year 1058, when Abbot Æthelwig (1058–1078) had taken over from his ailing predecessor Mannig. Three developments had occurred. First, more woodland resources had been secured in the Arden–Feckenham Forest district to the north. Second, an important estate had been assembled in the north-eastern Cotswolds that would later become focused on the borough of Stow-on-the-Wold. Third, thanks to the kinship of King Cnut with Abbot Ælfweard (1014–1044), an estate in western Northamptonshire comprising Badby and Newnham had been acquired, if only insecurely, for it had been lost by 1066. Then, in eight short years, Æthelwig embarked on a remarkable programme of opportunistic expansion (Figure 1). More manors (as we may now call them)[18] were added to the original core estates as well as to the Cotswold one. A new, though small, estate was added in the northern Cotswolds. His only apparent failure was in Northamptonshire. From whom did Æthelwig acquire these manors?

Dictu: Essays in Honour of Yolande de Pontfarcy Sexton, ed. Phyllis Gaffney and Jean-Michel Picard (Dublin, 2012), 123–145 at 132–43.

[16] John Blair, *The Church in Anglo-Saxon Society* (Oxford, 2005), 79–290.

[17] For an account of the early history of Evesham Abbey, with references, see Clarke, 'Early Surveys', 74–97.

[18] C.P. Lewis, 'The Invention of the Manor in Norman England', *ANS* 34 (2012), 123–150.

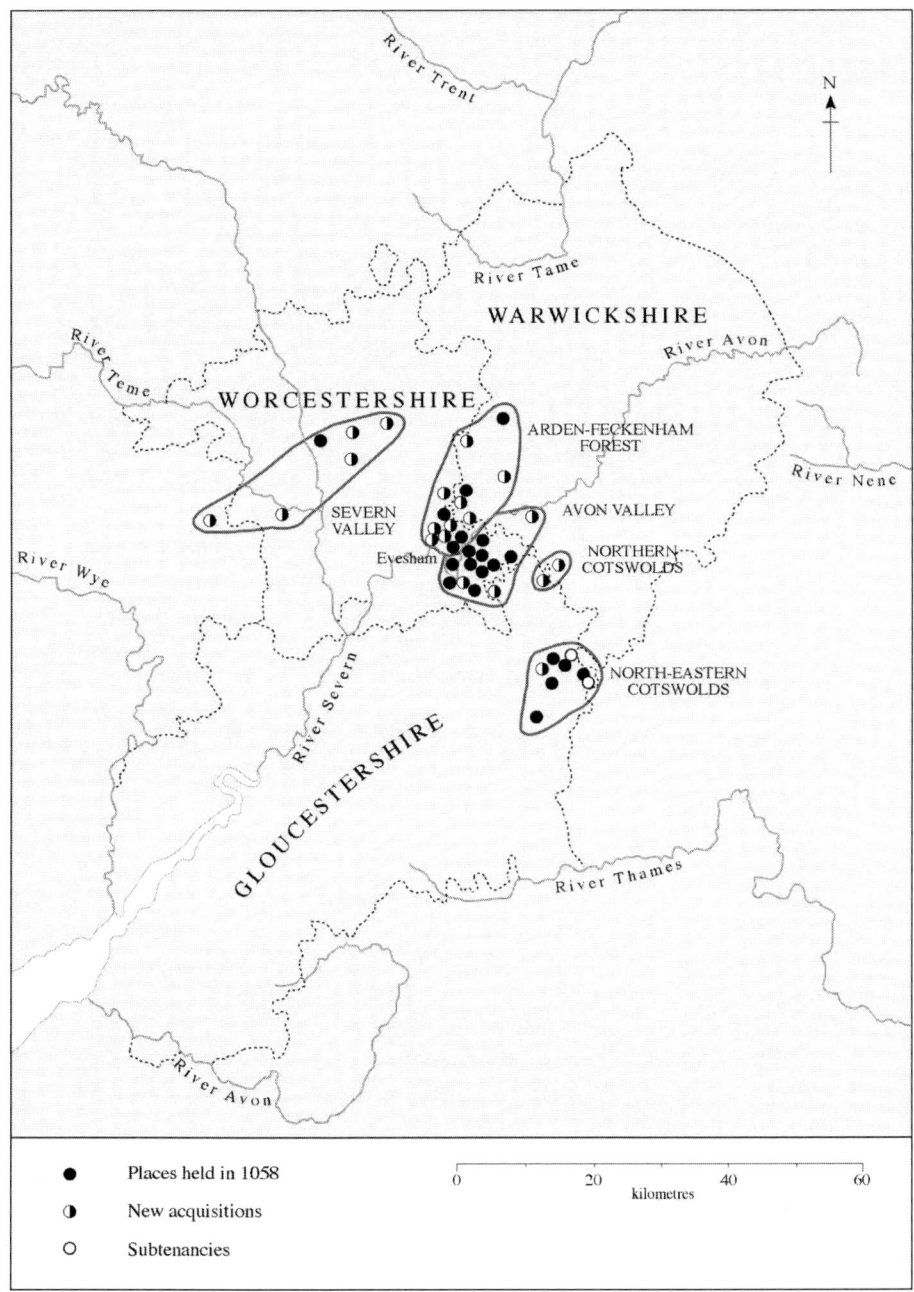

Figure 1. The estates of Evesham Abbey, 1066.

The short answer is independent thegns and lessees of the bishop of Worcester. Both categories were vulnerable because of the political uncertainties of King Edward's declining years and because of the (alleged) unworldliness of the new bishop, Wulfstan II, after 1062.[19] With cunning and persistence, Æthelwig seized his chance as the various opportunities presented themselves.[20]

During the Conqueror's reign an even more complex situation had evolved by 1078. Never before or afterwards were the possessions of Evesham Abbey so extensive. The most spectacular aspect of the period 1066–1078 was the addition of a further thirty-one manors to the existing estates. The topographical logic is impressive. The main effort to expand was directed upstream along the Avon valley and the hills immediately to the north. Including the lost 'Wivleshale', no fewer than eighteen of the places mentioned in the biographer's catalogue of acquisitions were in these districts, which belonged to the same economic region as Evesham itself. The second target for expansion was Oxfordshire, one of the counties within Æthelwig's bailiwick. Simultaneously, the estate in the north-eastern Cotswolds was being consolidated. Finally, the isolated manor of Litchborough in the Northamptonshire uplands was probably acquired at this time, perhaps to compensate for the loss of Badby and Newnham. If we again enquire from whom was so much property obtained, it is abundantly clear that the great majority were free men or thegns, who must have either died in the battles of 1066, forfeited their land, or sought the abbot's protection. Although few of these manors were worth large sums, their combined value was considerable: the total of £89 13s. was almost double that of the monastery's most valuable estate in 1066.[21]

Against this background we can understand that the bargain struck by Æthelwig with the Conqueror, if such it was, was a real one from the monks' point of view. They had plenty of thegnly holdings from which to choose for subinfeudation. We gain a partial picture of these thanks to the post-Domesday survey of confiscated and disputed manors called Evesham D, which records that three manors east of Ombersley had been subinfeudated to knights attached to Sheriff Urse in return for military service.[22] These had been acquired by Æthelwig before the Conquest, as Domesday Book confirms. They were Hampton Lovett, assessed at four hides; Upton

[19] Emma Mason, *St Wulfstan of Worcester c. 1008–1095* (Oxford, 1990), 85–86, 127–28, 139.
[20] For the details, see Clarke, 'Early Surveys', 97–104 and table 3. The evidence for the evolution of the Evesham estates has numerous layers of extreme complexity, partly owing to the forged charters, and only small selections of this material are reproduced in the following notes. Appendix A of 'Early Surveys', 372–521, attempts to resolve the issues, with cross-references forward to other discussions.
[21] Again for the details, see Clarke, 'Early Surveys', 104–10, map 10 and table 4.
[22] London, BL, MS Cotton Vespasian B xxiv, fol. 10v, Evesham D 3: 'Heamtun et Vptun et Wittun quidam milites Ursonis pro seruitio tenuerunt de ecclesia. Set post mortem abbatis [Æthelwig] Vrsone inuadente ipsas terras, nullum seruitium potuit habere'.

Warren, assessed at three hides; and Witton (in the salt town of Droitwich), assessed at half a hide. All were acquired by Urse after the abbot's death and all had declined in value by 1086. The holders are named as Robert (Parler), Herlebald, and Gunfrid respectively – perhaps three of the earliest known military subtenants of Evesham Abbey.[23] In addition it is possible that *c.* 1066 Æthelwig had gained control of Sheriff's Lench, in the hilly country about four miles (6.5 km) north of Evesham, but that shortly afterwards William FitzOsbern pressurized him into enfeoffing Gilbert FitzTurold with all four hides there and that, following the earl's death in battle in 1071, Æthelwig succeeded in recovering it and in retaining control for the rest of his lifetime.[24]

The territorial position laboriously built up by Æthelwig collapsed rapidly under his Norman successor, Walter of Cerisy-le-Forêt in western Normandy and the diocese of Bayeux.[25] This collapse was not seen as inevitable by contemporaries. Prior Dominic in the early twelfth century was inclined to attribute the losses suffered by his house to Walter's youth, lack of worldly wisdom and reliance on the counsel of young relatives.[26] In particular, the new abbot is accused of refusing the homage of the men commended to his predecessor and of attempting to take away their lands. Complaints reached the ears of Odo, bishop of Bayeux, who was acting in effect as regent in 1077–1080, during the king's absence from England. A moot of five county courts was convened at the Four Shire Stone near Moreton-in-Marsh (Gloucestershire),[27] at which forty-two of Æthelwig's fifty-one territorial acquisitions were forfeited.[28] Of these Walter managed to recover only five, with the result that by 1086 the structure of the monastic estates had again changed dramatically. These losses comprised thirty-three Domesday manors assessed at just over 128 hides and valued at more than £114 8*s.*[29] Without

---

[23] DB i. 177v; *Worcestershire* 26 §§ 15–17. Other early grantors of knights' fees were the abbots of Bury St Edmunds, St Albans and Tavistock: Chew, *Ecclesiastical Tenants-in-Chief*, 115–16.

[24] London, BL, MS Cotton Vespasian B xxiv, fols. 10v–11r, Evesham D 4; Clarke, 'Early Surveys', 481–84. Sheriff's Lench is the subject of two of the suspect documents on the same folio as the writ of military summons: *The Acta*, ed. Bates, nos. 136, 137.

[25] For the details, see Clarke, 'Early Surveys', 111–23 and table 5.

[26] The deeds of Abbot Walter are described in *Thomas of Marlborough: History of the Abbey of Evesham*, ed. and trans. Jane Sayers and Leslie Watkiss (Oxford, 2003), 176–81.

[27] The Four Shire Stone marks the former meeting point of Gloucestershire, Oxfordshire, Warwickshire and Worcestershire, in all of which Æthelwig had bought or otherwise acquired land. The fifth county represented may have been Northamptonshire, where Evesham Abbey had one manor, Litchborough, held freely by Leofnoth in the time of King Edward: DB i. 222v; *Northamptonshire* 13 § 1. A number of judicial inquiries were apparently instigated by Odo at this time: F.M. Stenton, *Anglo-Saxon England* (3rd edn., Oxford, 1971), 610.

[28] The house chronicler gives these figures as twenty-eight and thirty-six respectively: *History of the Abbey*, ed. Sayers and Watkiss, 176–77.

[29] The value of Dornford and 'Wivleshale' is unknown. Since the Conquest a certain amount

exception the lost manors had been acquired by Æthelwig, mainly after the Conquest.[30]

The principal beneficiaries of the judicial inquiry of *c.* 1078 were Bishop Odo, Sheriff Urse and other local magnates, along with a few smaller landholders identifiable as royal servants and English thegns. In the generation between 1058 and 1086 the Evesham monks had seen their temporalities, or feudal demesne, successively doubled and halved. But this was only part of the story of the Norman land settlement, which brought into question the relations not only between king and barons, but also between barons and their own tenants. In short, we have to examine the phenomenon of progressive subinfeudation, an important historical process that the rich (and reliable) Evesham documentation illuminates with unusual clarity.

Post-Conquest Subtenancies

Thomas of Marlborough's *Historia* refers briefly to Abbot Walter's nepotism and military enfeoffments, though both statements are alterations to the original text. The first Norman abbot is said to have appointed a clerk, a dean, and a steward from among his kinsmen, the existing steward having been removed. In the early thirteenth century it was believed that Walter had invested nearly all the abbey's knights with hereditary fees.[31] To supplement these comments we have the evidence of Domesday Book and three early surveys: Evesham E, Evesham J, and Evesham O. The subinfeudated properties can thus be catalogued fully, but the chronology of enfeoffment is much less certain. The Domesday survey is the only fixed point during Walter's abbacy; Evesham J was compiled *c.* 1104 (immediately following his death)[32] and Evesham E and Evesham O *c.* 1130. Regarding the obligation to provide five knights for the royal army, I have already suggested that Æthelwig himself may have used some of his acquisitions for this purpose. The loss of all these lands in and after 1078 meant that Walter was probably forced to make a fresh start with his military retainers (Figure 2). If the quota system really was in operation, the minimum of five knights would have had to be provided following Bishop Odo's judicial inquiry, a hypothesis confirmed by Domesday Book. After 1086 more subtenancies seem to have been created, willingly or unwillingly on the part of the abbot and unwillingly

---

of manorial rationalization had taken place, resulting in a smaller number of manors in the villages acquired by Æthelwig.

[30] The lost pre-Conquest acquisitions were Acton Beauchamp, Bransford, Hampton Lovett, Sheriff's Lench, Upton Warren and Witton, situated mainly in the Severn valley estate.

[31] *History of the Abbey*, ed. Sayers and Watkiss, 179–81.

[32] For a numbered edition, see H.B. Clarke, 'Evesham J and Evesham L: Two Early Twelfth-Century Manorial Surveys', *ANS* 30 (2008), 62–84 at 83–84.

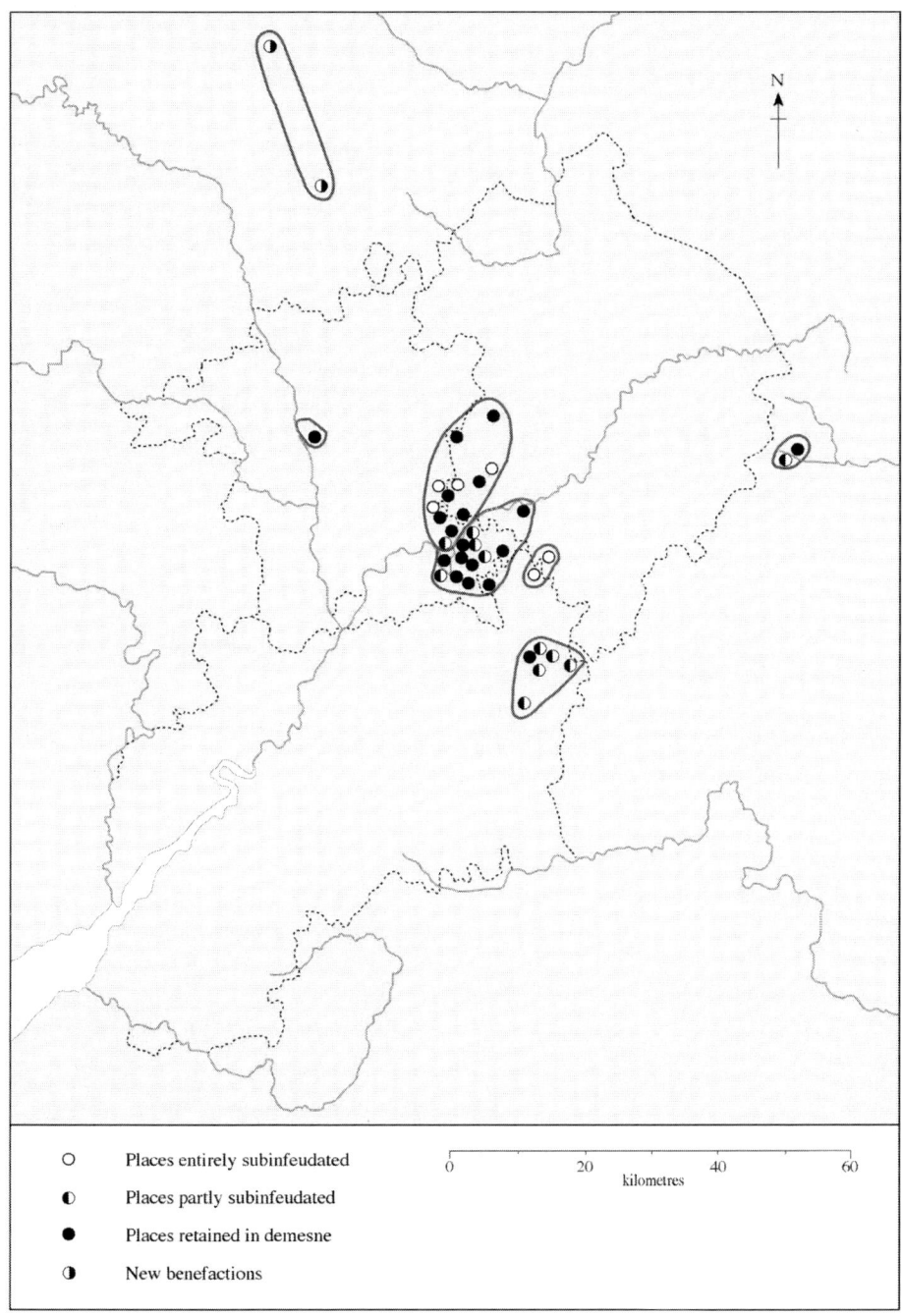

Figure 2. The subtenancies of Abbot Walter, 1078–1104.

on the part of his monks. In this way, the feudal geography of these monastic estates became increasingly complicated, impressing its pattern on a long future.

The scale of subinfeudation can be indicated only in terms of fiscal hides. In 1086 the abbey's demesne comprised just over 133 hides;[33] by 1104 fifty-eight hides, or approaching half, had been granted to subtenants, not all of them of knightly status. This statement should be qualified by another to the effect that the evidence of Domesday Book and the three Evesham surveys overlaps considerably but not completely; our knowledge of certain subtenancies is derived from only one of these sources. Where they do coincide, however, the degree of exact correspondence is impressive, for there are just one or two minor discrepancies in the details.[34] This suggests that our information is at least accurate. With the exception of Ombersley in the Severn valley, all of the monastery's estates were implicated to a greater or lesser extent in these early stages of subinfeudation. Six manors were entirely subinfeudated, four of these in Arden–Feckenham Forest along with the two small manors in the northern Cotswolds. Of these, all but one were in the hands of knights before 1086, presumably those five knights who were expected to serve in the royal army. By 1104 eleven other manors had been partially subinfeudated and on six of these the monks' demesne was less than half the hidated area. Least affected by early subfeudation were the bigger Cotswold manors.

On turning to examine the subtenants themselves, one group stands out prominently – Abbot Walter's relatives.[35] In combination, Walter's brothers Geoffrey and Ralph, his sister Albretha, and his nephews Hugh and William received twenty-nine hides, or exactly half the total, located on nine different manors. Of these, Ralph alone held 18¾ hides.[36] At the time of Walter's death in 1104, the wife of his other brother, Geoffrey, was holding land at Badby that had been recovered (possibly her husband was absent on the First Crusade or elsewhere, for Geoffrey is recorded as the current holder *c.* 1130).[37] Apart from Sheriff Urse, none of the known subtenants was a major landholder. Most of them seem to have belonged to the local squirearchy, possessing names of both Anglo-Scandinavian and northern French origins. Three subtenants are identified with particular villages: Godwine of Hook

---

[33] Including those retained in demesne at Adlestrop and Bengeworth: Clarke, 'Early Surveys', 401–10.

[34] For the discrepancy in the tax assessment of Lark Stoke, see Clarke, 'Early Surveys', table 6, note 5.

[35] Comparable examples are Thorold of Peterborough, Athelelm of Abingdon and Guimond of Tavistock: Chew, *Ecclesiastical Tenants-in-Chief*, 116–17.

[36] At Hidcote Boyce and Lark Stoke, Ralph was preceded as subtenant by two unnamed knights ('ii^obus militibus suis'), one of whom may have been Ralph himself: DB i. 166r; *Gloucestershire* 12 § 9.

[37] Evesham J 12; Evesham O 11. Although compiled *c.* 1130, Evesham E and Evesham O were not necessarily up to date in their details.

Norton, Hugh of Bretforton, and William of Donnington, the two last villages forming part of the abbey's estates.[38] The individual holdings ranged from five hides down to one virgate, averaging 1½ hides. Almost all of the larger subtenancies had been given to members of Walter's family. A few subtenants held in addition smaller amounts of land measured in acres or described as cottage tenements (*bordella*). Sometimes the grant had been carved out of the manorial demesne; sometimes it was villein land. Unfortunately, this information has not been preserved with sufficient regularity to permit meaningful generalization about the relative proportions. What is made clear by some entries in Evesham E and Evesham O is that the monastic chapter was opposed to Walter's policy of subinfeudation, though less consistently than to that of his two successors.

Almost the only memory of Abbot Robert of Jumièges, the probable next-but-one abbot of Evesham, in the early thirteenth century was the fact that he distributed many monastic lands to his kinsmen.[39] It was nevertheless an accurate memory to judge by Evesham E and Evesham O. Besides recording the subtenancies of the first Norman abbot, Walter, these surveys deal with those of his successors, Maurice and Robert. For most of these subtenancies Robert of Jumièges was responsible. Unlike Robert and Walter, Maurice before his election had been a monk at Evesham and may have been reluctant to alienate the property of his own house. He was remembered by a later generation as a builder, provider of ornaments for the church, and author of other good works.[40] Even so, the subtenancies created by all three abbots were set down in writing both topographically (Evesham E) and chronologically (Evesham O) *c.* 1130, perhaps in an effort to dissuade the new abbot from continuing along the road to ruin. After the death of Robert, however, the estates of Evesham Abbey escheated temporarily to the crown and it may equally have been in the interests of royal officers to commission a survey of the entire fief.

The amount of land sublet by Abbots Maurice and Robert, approximately 23½ hides, was considerably less than in the case of Maurice's predecessor.[41] One obvious factor here is that less land was available to be granted to subtenants. Most of the new subtenancies were created in the Avon valley and Arden–Feckenham Forest districts. By 1130 the majority of forest manors had been entirely subinfeudated: according to Domesday Book these were among the abbey's least valuable assets in terms of leasehold income. At

---

[38] Evesham E 25, 27; Evesham J 11; Evesham O 6, 15. Chew, *Ecclesiastical Tenants-in-Chief*, 29, refers to 'the ruralization of the lesser tenants which followed rapidly upon the completion of the Conquest'.

[39] *History of the Abbey*, ed. Sayers and Watkiss, 180–81.

[40] *History of the Abbey*, ed. Sayers and Watkiss, 180–81.

[41] There is an element of approximation in this and related figures: Clarke, 'Early Surveys', table 8.

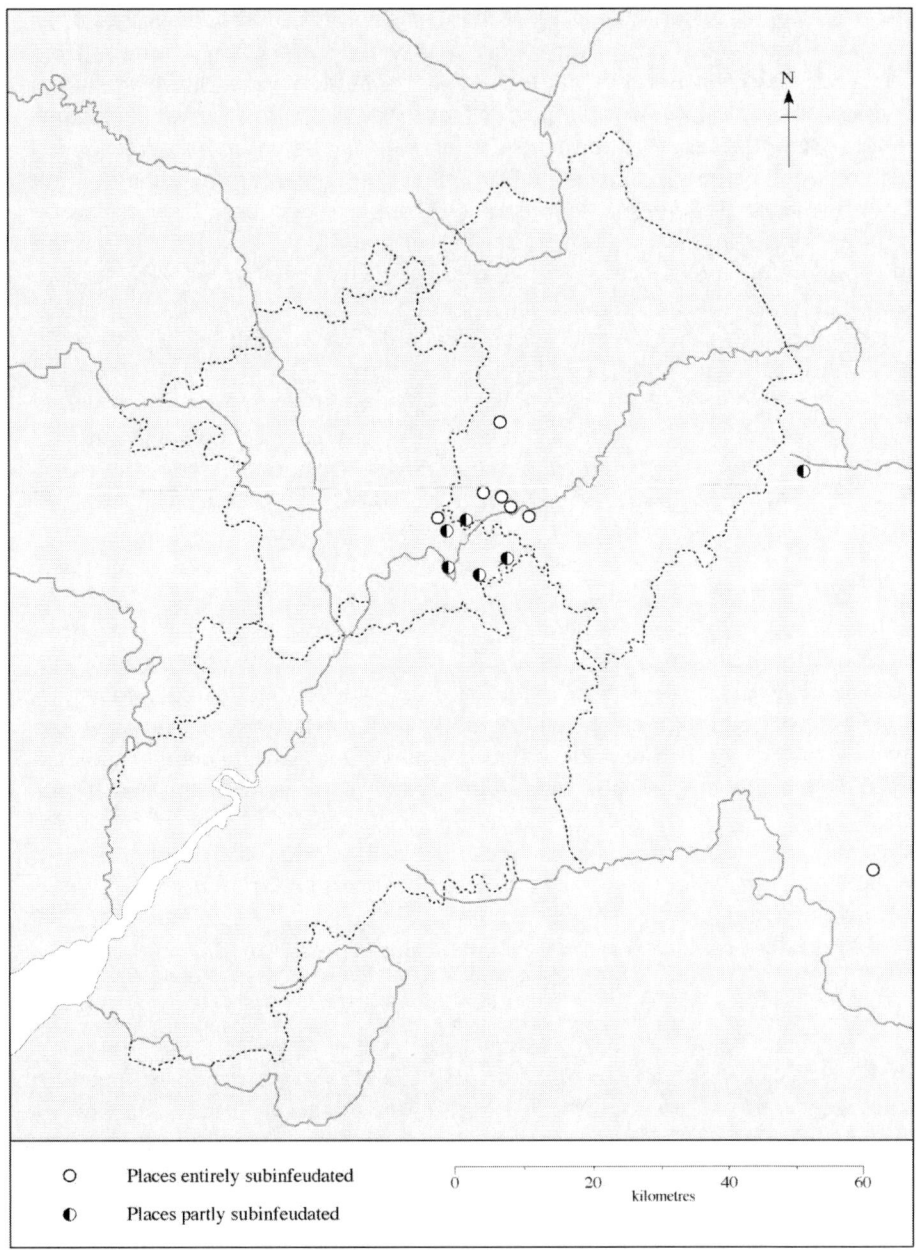

Figure 3. The subtenancies of Abbots Maurice and Robert, 1104–29.

Evesham itself, half the fiscal hidage was now in other hands.[42] At Badby, where seven hides had been alienated already, a further twelve acres were given to the local parish church in exchange for all tithes, an arrangement that was, in the end, unsuccessful for the tithes had been withheld.[43] Church Lench had originally been granted to Urse for his lifetime only.[44] Evesham O has William I de Beauchamp (1131–1170) holding it by gift of Abbot Robert, but does not record whether Walter de Beauchamp, Urse's son-in-law and William's father, had ever held this manor.[45] Including Church Lench, seven of the thirteen manors were wholly subinfeudated by Abbots Maurice and Robert (Figure 3). In size their grants ranged from five hides down to twelve acres and averaged 1¼ hides, a slightly lower figure than for those of Abbot Walter.

If the thirteenth-century chronicler is correct in accusing Abbot Robert of distributing monastic land to his relations, we might guess that one of their number was William the seneschal. He was given three virgates at Abbots Salford and five at Badsey.[46] A second William held the office of chamberlain, together with one virgate of demesne land at Evesham itself, granted without the chapter's consent.[47] Another officer, Pain the clerk, received one hide of villein land at Church Honeybourne from Abbot Maurice and five messuages in Evesham from his successor.[48] Apart from William de Beauchamp, most of the remaining subtenants were officers in aristocratic households or members of the gentry. Ralph of Oversley, near Alcester, held two subtenancies in the same area: 3¼ hides at Ardens Grafton and five at Wixford.[49] William of Seacourt, in Berkshire, was another important subtenant, with four messuages in Evesham, one hide at Hillborough and four hides at Weston-on-Avon, all granted by Abbot Robert.[50] William had married the sister of Simon Dispenser, a royal steward who was given Oldberrow in the Forest of Arden by the same abbot.[51] In three instances we are told that the subtenancy was

---

[42] Evesham E 1, 8, 9; Evesham O 16, 19, 31.

[43] Evesham J 12; Evesham O 18.

[44] London, BL, MS Cotton Vespasian B xxiv, fol. 11r, Evesham D 5: 'Aliam uillam que Chyrchlench uocatur de dominio abbas Walterius sibi eo tenore concessit, ut eo uiuente prefatam terram pro seruitio teneret et post mortem eius ad ecclesiam rediret'; Evesham J 10.

[45] Evesham O 27.

[46] Evesham E 24; Evesham O 33, 34.

[47] Evesham E 1; Evesham O 19. This entry comes first in Evesham E and in Abbot Robert's section of Evesham O, perhaps reflecting a degree of kinship between the two men.

[48] Evesham E 3, 14; Evesham O 17, 21.

[49] Evesham E 12, 13; Evesham O 28. For details of the complex connection between Ardens Grafton and Wixford, see Clarke, 'Early Surveys', 486, 493–95.

[50] Evesham E 2, 10, 11; Evesham O 20, 25, 26.

[51] Evesham E 16; Evesham O 29. William of Seacourt was the son of the Domesday subtenant of this Abingdon manor, Askell, whose lands were confiscated in the reign of William Rufus: *VCH Berkshire*, iv, 422. William seems to have owed the restoration of his fortunes partly to the fact that his widowed mother, Ansfrida, was a mistress of Henry I: *Historia Ecclesie*

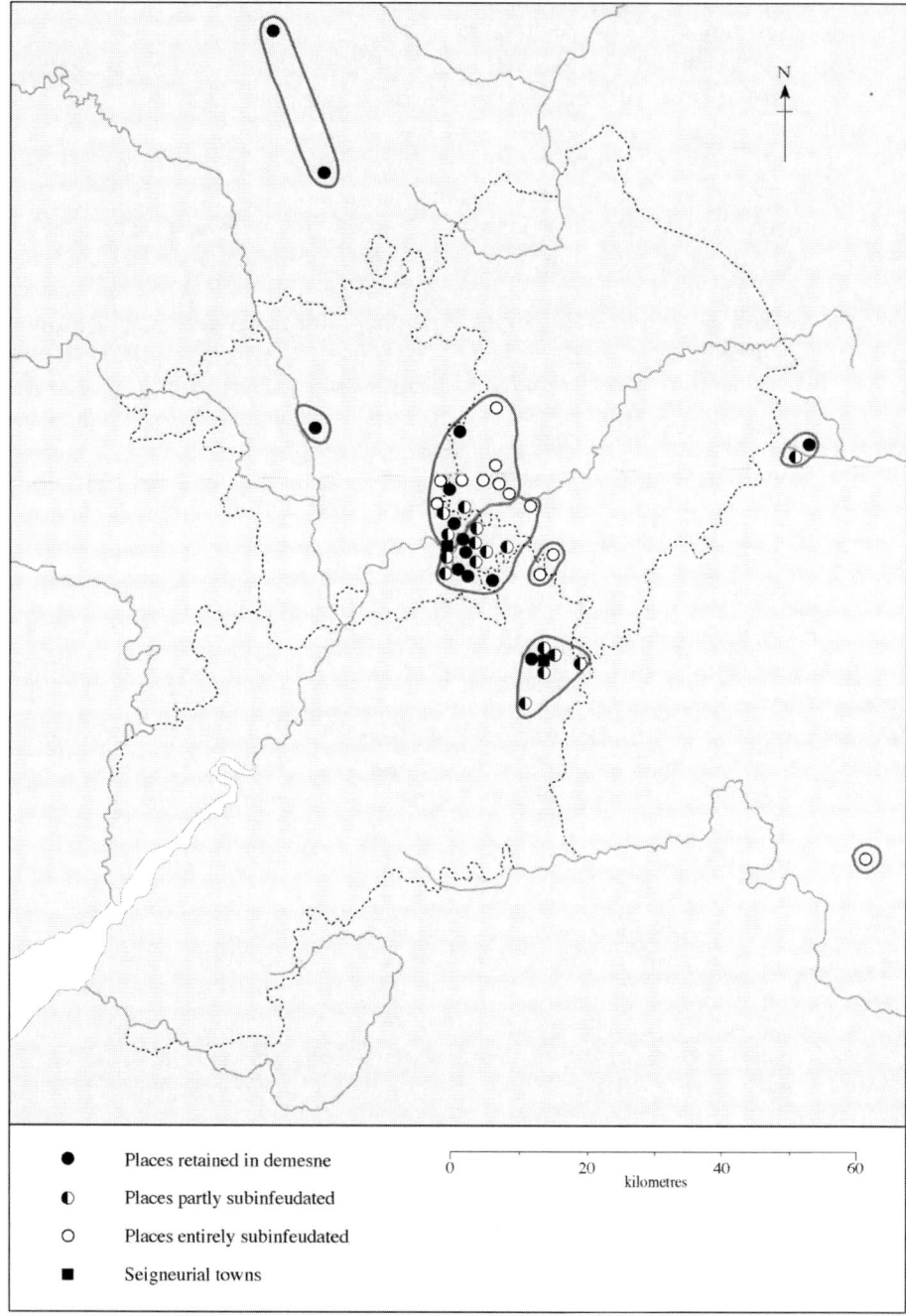

Figure 4. Demesne manors and subinfeudation, *c.* 1130

being held at farm. William Silvan was the lessee of Golder in Oxfordshire for 10s. a year, though according to Evesham E he was refusing to hand over the money.[52] The farms at Oldberrow and Wixford were worth £1 5s. and £4 respectively.[53] With the exception of the church of Badby's twelve acres, we do not know on what precise terms these subtenancies were granted. The lack of consent on the part of the chapter indicates that most of these grants were not deemed judicious or profitable by the monks, who must have been more than usually reluctant to alienate the monastic patrimony after the experiences of Abbot Walter's early years.

The surveys Evesham E and Evesham O, backed up by Domesday Book, reveal that perhaps as many as 77½ hides had been subinfeudated between 1078 and 1130. What these surveys do not record, with few exceptions, is the changes that occurred at subtenurial level during this period of over half a century. One exception is the passing of Church Lench from Sheriff Urse to his grandson through the female line, William de Beauchamp. Although most of Abbot Walter's subtenancies may have been created after 1086, some of his subtenants must have died well before 1130. These surveys, therefore, deal primarily with the formation of subtenancies rather than with their subsequent evolution. Very possibly, all or most of these holdings continued to be subinfeudated in 1130, in which case a reasonably accurate picture of the distribution of the abbey's feudal demesne and subinfeudated land late in the reign of Henry I can be mapped (Figure 4). The general impression is clear enough. Whereas the less valuable forest and upland estates had been completely or heavily subinfeudated, the erosion of feudal demesne on the more valuable lowland estates was only partial. Similar principles of subinfeudation can be discerned in a very different landscape around Peterborough, as Edmund King has demonstrated.[54] The impact of the Norman Conquest on the estates of Evesham Abbey was thus two-fold. First, soon after the death of Abbot Æthelwig, the dramatically extended territorial position built up since 1058 collapsed, and the monks were thrown back on more limited and traditional resources. Second, much of the patrimony was willingly or unwillingly subinfeudated in return for cash or services, while the basic structure of the estates remained unchanged.

Abbendonensis. The History of the Church of Abingdon, ed. and trans. John Hudson (2 vols., Oxford, 2002–2007), ii, 52–53 and note 127, 180–81.

[52] Evesham E 17; Evesham O 32.

[53] Evesham E 12, 16; Evesham O 28, 29.

[54] Edmund King, *Peterborough Abbey, 1086–1310: a Study in the Land Market* (Cambridge, 1973), 16–18.

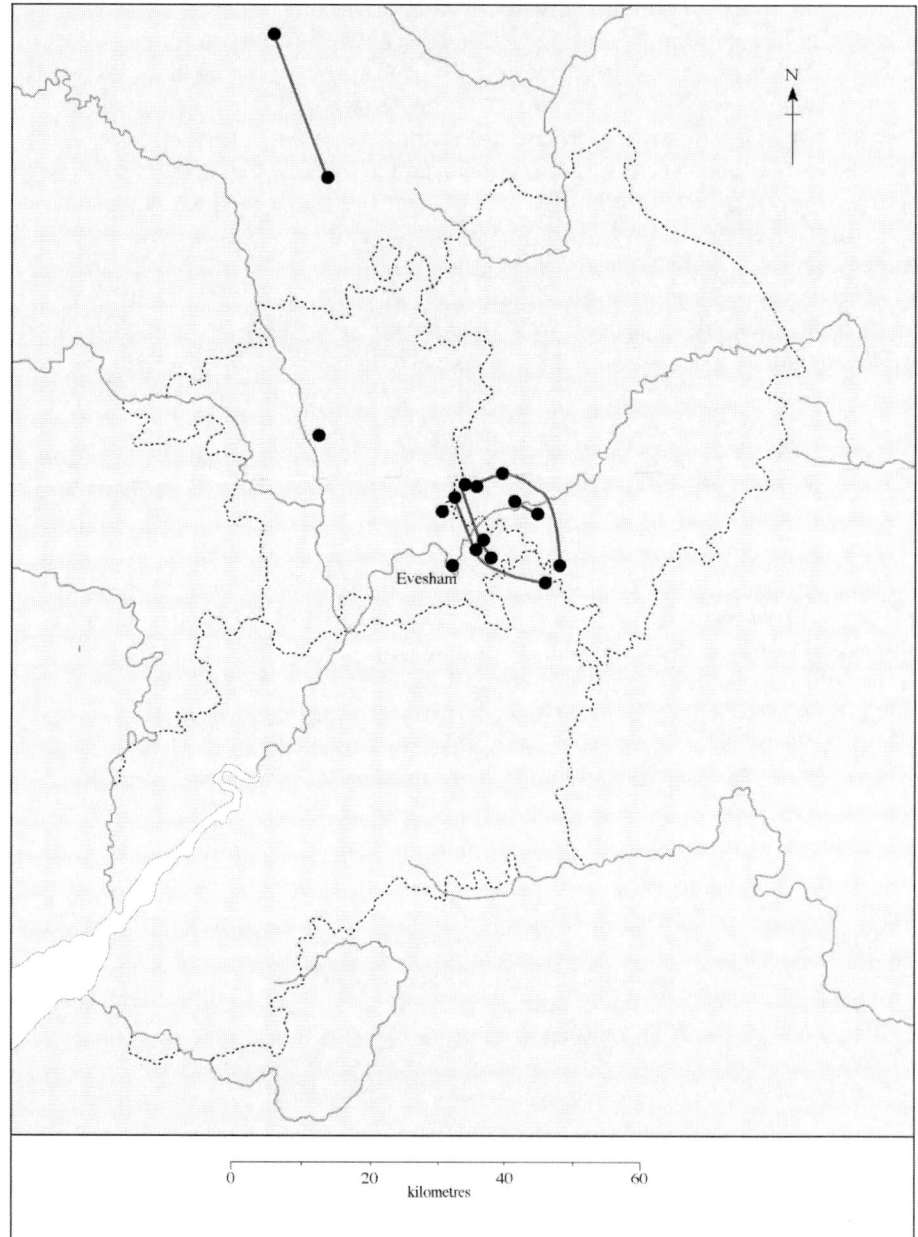

Figure 5. Knights' fees, 1166.

The Angevin Legacy

The internal development of the Evesham estates between 1130 and 1160 is obscure. Only one of the early surveys (Evesham B) falls within the period, and this is concerned with two lay fiefs.[55] The decades that witnessed St Bernard at the height of his powers and influence were unfavourable to Benedictine monasteries of the old observance. New benefactions tended to enrich the new orders. By contrast traditional communities were foundering into financial crisis and suffering from loss of identity, problems that overtook Cluny under Pons of Melgueil and Peter the Venerable. At Evesham, the mid-twelfth century seems to have been marked by stagnation rather than crisis. Apart from a few transactions relating to watermills, most of the surviving documents highlight the monks' peripheral interests in Lancashire, Middlesex, Staffordshire, and the city of London.[56] More distant still was Evesham's daughter-house at Odense in Denmark, where monks suffered persecution during a long period of civil war that lasted from 1131 to 1157. Back in 1135 x 1139 arrangements had been made between Abbot Reginald of Evesham and Bishop Riculf of Odense to govern mutual conduct, prayer, residence, and visitation.[57] Relations with Odense provide an illustration of how the years of dynastic uncertainty, civil war, and reconstruction from 1130 to 1160 were a time of unspectacular progress and developing contacts with a wider world, interspersed with moments of high drama.

We move forward, then, to the abbacy of Adam (1161–1189) and to the reign of Henry II. Educated in the schools of Paris, Adam got to know John of Salisbury and was himself capable of sophisticated writing.[58] Under the rule of this Cluniac monk, Evesham Abbey achieved a greater degree of maturity and serenity than at any time since the days of Abbot Mannig in the mid-eleventh century. Thomas of Marlborough's prose takes on an aura of contemporaneity: some events he claims to have witnessed himself.[59] Nevertheless his portrait of the abbacy is still only partial and centred on the Evesham estates; much that is known from other sources goes unmentioned or is passed over quickly. For example, in 1163 x 1164 Simon, son of William of Coughton and grandson of Abbot Walter's brother, Ralph, was granted

---

[55] London, BL, MS Cotton Vespasian B xxiv, fol. 8r, those of William I de Beauchamp and Roger I de Tony. I hope to publish an analysis of this text elsewhere.

[56] Clarke, 'Early Surveys', 143–45.

[57] London, BL, MSS Cotton Vespasian B xxiv, fols. 22r–v, 48v (two copies); Harley 3763, fols. 88v–89r, printed in Lauritz Weibull (ed.), *Diplomatarium Danicum*, I raekke, 2 bind, *1053–1169* (Copenhagen, 1963), no. 66; discussed in Peter King, 'English Influence on the Church at Odense in the Early Middle Ages', *JEH* 13 (1962), 145–155 at 152–53.

[58] D.C. Cox, 'The Literary Remains of Adam, Abbot of Evesham (1161–1189)', *Journal of Medieval Latin* 20 (2010), 113–166.

[59] Adam's biography is to be found in *History of the Abbey*, ed. Sayers and Watkiss, 184–89.

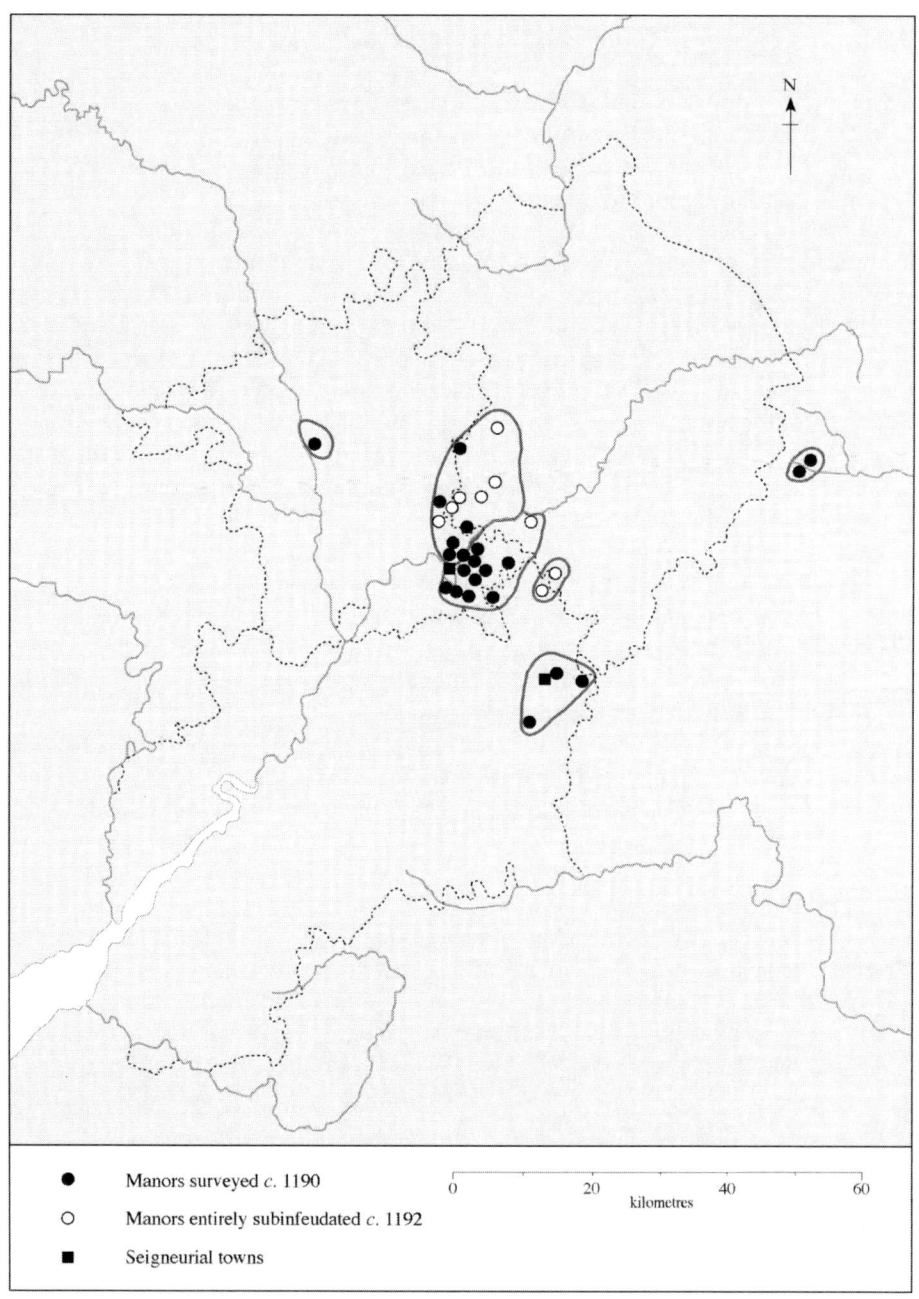

Figure 6. The estates of Evesham Abbey and the extents of *c.* 1190.

Loynton and Wrottesley in Staffordshire in hereditary fee.[60] As part of the bargain Simon and his brother, Ralph, quitclaimed their lands in Abbots Morton, Evesham, Little Hampton, and Norton.[61] Adam was presumably endeavouring to recover feudal demesne locally at the expense of subinfeudating inconveniently distant manors. According to the *Historia*, the mills at Loynton and Wrottesley were put to farm, as were those at Farington and Howick, near Penwortham in Lancashire.[62] Rationalization of estates was one option in the age of the earliest manorial extents.[63]

For our purposes one of the most informative sources for the abbacy of Adam is the 1166 inquiry into knights' fees – what has been termed 'the feudal basis of coercive power'.[64] This document enables us to produce a more or less complete picture of the abbey's subtenants holding by military service. The abbot's *carta* does not record how many hides each knight held or where his land was situated.[65] The location of the fees has therefore been deduced from other sources, chiefly a late survey called Evesham G (Figure 5). The fees created in the old enfeoffment (before 1135) numbered four-and-a-half, the quota recorded in Henry I's charter of 1107. There was clearly a marked degree of continuity at subtenurial level. Ralph of Coughton and Ralph of Kinwarton represented two branches of the family descended from Abbot Walter's brother of the same name. The former held land at Bretforton, Middle Littleton, and Weethley; the latter at Kinwarton, Lark Stoke, and Weethley.[66] William de Beauchamp was the grandson of Sheriff Urse to whom Church Lench had originally been granted.[67] Hillborough and Weston-on-Avon had been subinfeudated to William of Seacourt by Abbot Robert.[68] Hidcote Boyce had been in knightly hands by 1086, but the fee of which it was now part was apparently of later formation.[69] The new enfeoffment consisted of half a knight's fee held by Richard of Ombersley and located in the manor from which he derived his name.[70] The combined

---

[60] The destroyed original is printed in George Wrottesley, *History of the Family of Wrottesley at Wrottesley, Co. Stafford* (Exeter, 1903), 8–9. The dating limits are worked out in R.W. Eyton, 'The Staffordshire Cartulary: Series I', in *Collections for a History of Staffordshire*, William Salt Archaeological Society, 2 (London, 1881), 191.

[61] Ralph's quitclaim is to be found in London, BL, MS Cotton Vespasian B xxiv, fol. 35r. See also Clarke, 'Early Surveys', 444, 495.

[62] *History of the Abbey*, ed. Sayers and Watkiss, 188–89.

[63] Outlined in Clarke, 'Evesham J and Evesham L', 79–82.

[64] T.N. Bisson, *The Crisis of the Twelfth Century: Power, Lordship, and the Origins of European Government* (Princeton and Oxford, 2009), 300.

[65] *The Red Book of the Exchequer*, ed. Hubert Hall, RS 99 (3 vols., London, 1896), i, 301–2; trans. in *EHD* ii, 912.

[66] Evesham G 3, 4.

[67] Evesham G 2.

[68] Evesham E 10, 11; Evesham O 25, 26.

[69] DB i. 166r; *Gloucestershire* 12 § 9; Evesham G 6.

[70] Evesham G 7.

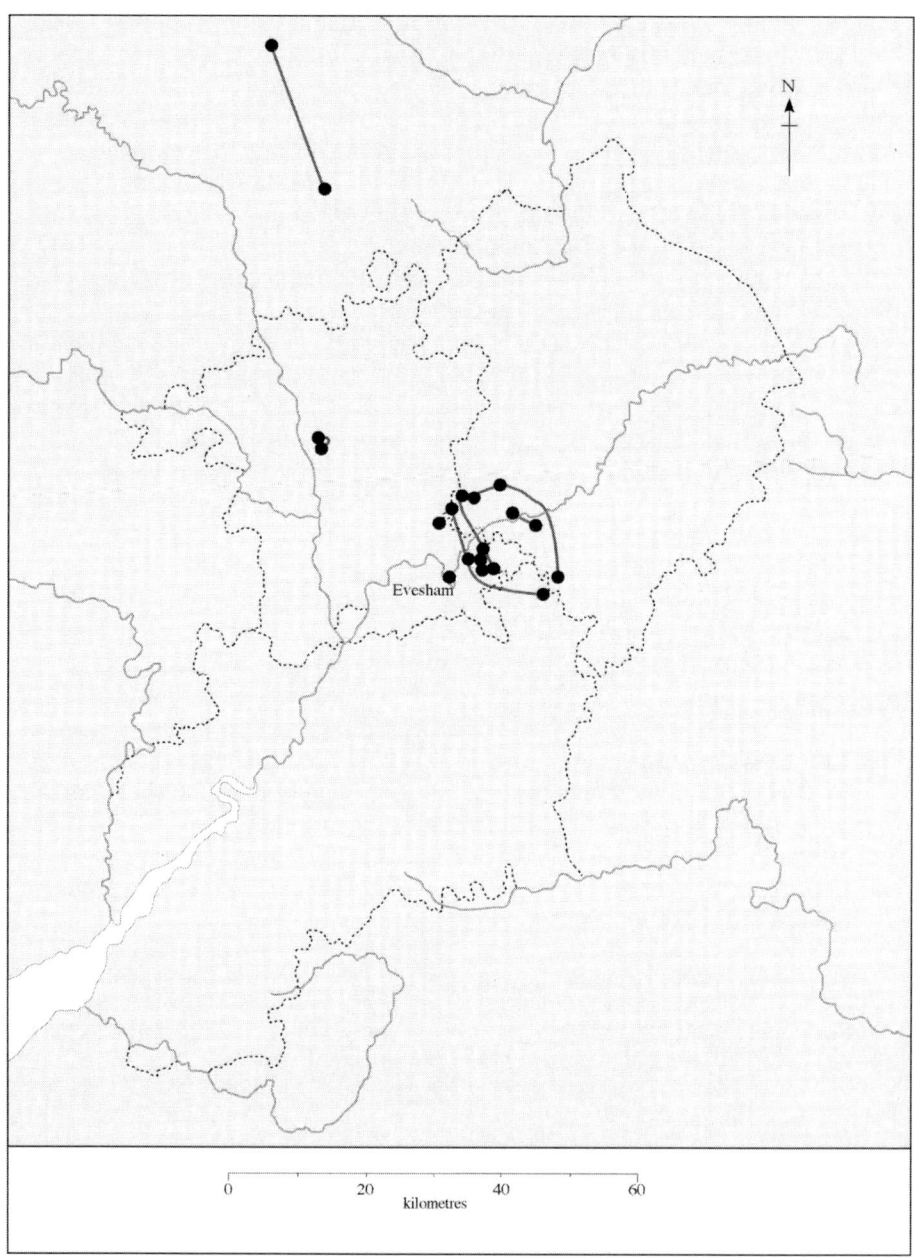

Figure 7. Knights' fees, *c.* 1192.

enfeoffments provided for five knights, the number customarily thought to have been demanded of Abbot Æthelwig in the early 1070s. A century later the knights' fees comprised mainly manors, or parts of manors, that formed a chain north-east of the monastery linking the three estates north and south of the Avon. Most of these manors had been worth relatively little in 1086. With regard to the policy of subinfeudation, the principal development since 1130 had been the inclusion of portions of more valuable manors at Bretforton and Ombersley.

Evesham G, datable to *c.* 1192, shows that several manors were completely subinfeudated by then (Figure 6). In fact, the two manors comprising the small estate in the northern Cotswolds, together with many of those in Arden–Feckenham Forest, had been held by knightly subtenants ever since the days of Abbot Walter. The pattern of subinfeudation laid down by the first Norman abbot endured a century later. The least endowed manors had been sublet in return for military and other services; the best had been retained in feudal demesne, though not necessarily intact. Parts of Badby, Bretforton, Middle and South Littleton, Newnham and Ombersley, for all of which an extent was drawn up probably in 1190, were subinfeudated to military retainers by the 1190s.[71] This is an excellent illustration of the close and logical relationship between the manorial and the seigneurial elements within feudal society. Lordship provided the essential economic, judicial, and social links between warriors and peasants, to echo a theme of Georges Duby.[72]

The opening section of Evesham G lists the subtenancies of the abbey's knights. By *c.* 1192 most knights' fees were artificial groupings of manors and portions of manors (Figure 7). Nevertheless it should be remembered that even fractions of a knight's fee were liable to 'relief, certain aids, and rights of wardship and marriage, as well as scutage'.[73] Thus the Littletons contributed to three different fees, and the components of some fees were widely scattered. With the exception of those situated in the north-eastern Cotswolds and the Northamptonshire uplands, all of the estates were being made to carry part of the military burden.[74] The distribution of subinfeudated land was probably similar to that in 1166, with the incorporation of more of Bretforton, Ombersley and South Littleton. Since 1166 another fee had been created, whilst a man called Elias of Acton may have been responsible for the service of half a knight.[75] Unlike the 1166 *carta*, Evesham G enumerates the hidage of each fee. Fees of the old enfeoffment averaged well over six hides; those of the new a little under five. Contemporary bishops of Worcester were

---

[71] Evesham G 3, 7, 8, 38.
[72] Georges Duby, *The Early Growth of the European Economy: Warriors and Peasants from the Seventh to the Twelfth Century*, trans. H.B. Clarke (London, 1974), 168–77.
[73] Reynolds, *Fiefs and Vassals*, 364.
[74] The Northamptonshire manor of Badby and Newnham was soon to be involved.
[75] Evesham G 9.

of the opinion that five hides represented the normal amount of land capable of supporting a professional warrior in this inflationary age, according to their *Red Book*.[76] An element of social differentiation can be detected in the size of these fees: the half-fee of William de Beauchamp and the full fees of Simon of Coughton and Ralph of Kinwarton were markedly larger than the rest.[77] Nevertheless it should be remembered that there was no necessary correspondence between hidage and value. Four of the knights were the same as those serving in 1166, and at least two sons had succeeded their father. The system of ensuring military service was still expanding slowly, though socially it was becoming fossilized. Evesham Abbey's low quota had enabled the abbots, however unwillingly, to grant fees of a realistic size from the knights' point of view. A distinct contrast emerges with Peterborough Abbey, for example, where military service had been a crushing burden from the start.[78] Even so, according to the monks, the knights of the Worcestershire house were discharging their obligations only half-heartedly by the late twelfth century.[79] As Reynolds observed, 'even if it [an estate] had originally been granted by a ruler or other lord, gratitude and a sense of obligation are perishable: the bond between grantor and grantee would erode as time and generations passed'.[80]

There was another tenurial dimension that is revealed systematically for the first time, that of the abbey's free tenants who were widely scattered around twenty-one different manors. Most manors without any recorded freeholding were completely subinfeudated to knights. Apart from Ralph of Oversley and the church of Stow-on-the-Wold, none of the freeholders had more than two hides of land, the size of their tenements averaging just over one hide.[81] Nearly all the hides were subject to payment of geld (the purpose of this section of Evesham G), a tax that was now seigneurial rather than royal. Only 1½ hides were deemed free, and these were held by two privileged subtenants, William the seneschal and the church of Stow-on-the-Wold.[82] The structure of the estates *c.* 1192 was essentially that developed during the

---

[76] *The Red Book of Worcester, containing Surveys of the Bishop's Manors and Other Records chiefly of the Twelfth and Thirteenth Centuries*, ed. Marjorie Hollings, Worcestershire Historical Society, 42 (4 parts, London, 1934–1950), iv, 445. On guidelines for knight service, see Sally Harvey, 'The Knight and the Knight's Fee in England', *P&P* 49 (1970), 3–43 at 38–39.

[77] Evesham G 2–4.

[78] Chew, *Ecclesiastical Tenants-in-Chief*, 84–85; King, *Peterborough Abbey*, 13–15.

[79] Similar reluctance was expressed by knights of Bury St Edmunds in 1198: Chew, *Ecclesiastical Tenants-in-Chief*, 29.

[80] Reynolds, *Fiefs and Vassals*, 58.

[81] Evesham G 32. Despite Ralph of Oversley's tenure of the whole of Wixford, a subtenancy dating back to 1121 (London, BL, MS Harley 3763, fol. 93r–v), military service had not been required. This grant may originally have been intended to secure the political support of an important lay lord. On pressures exerted by local landholders, see King, *Peterborough Abbey*, 18–23.

[82] Evesham G 19, 32.

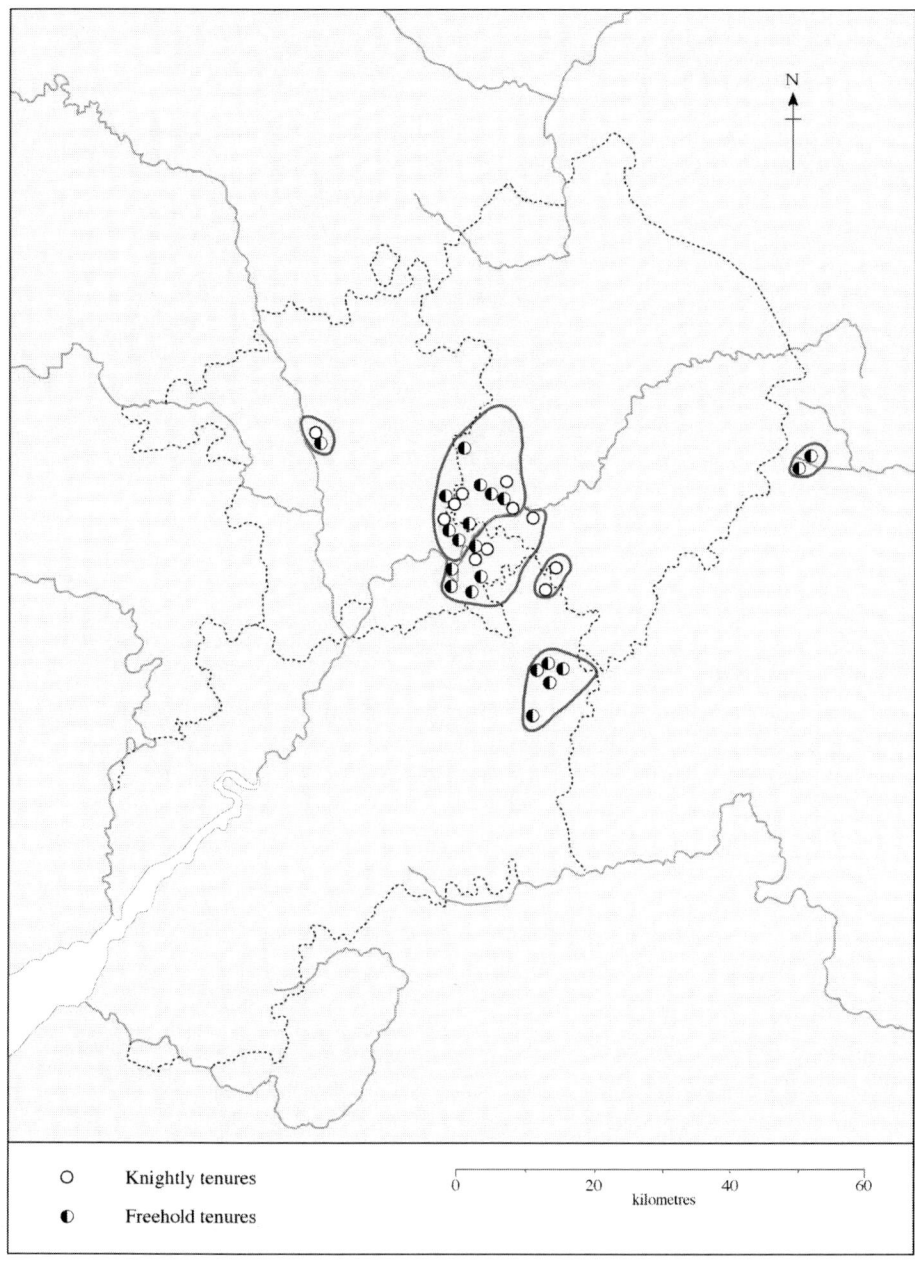

Figure 8. Knightly and freehold tenures, *c.* 1192.

O Knightly tenures

◑ Freehold tenures

Anglo-Saxon period and consolidated by Abbot Æthelwig *before* 1066. Very few permanent acquisitions had been made since that date, a feature common to many Benedictine houses.[83] The military quota imposed on the monks was not excessive, yet its subtenurial impact was complex and far-reaching. As the demand for more substantial fees grew, so did the composition of existing fees become more intricate. The fragmentary nature of some fees must have caused as much dissatisfaction among the knightly class as the small size of others. Such fees would have required ingenuity and time to exploit, and it is hardly surprising that knights were devoting their energies increasingly to farming and estate management. For some it had become a matter of necessity, as rising costs threatened their economic position. Even so, Evesham G reveals a clear distinction between knights and freeholders, not only in the arrangement of the survey in two parts, but also in the relative size of the holdings and the fact that most manors supported one social class or the other (Figure 8).[84] To judge from the available evidence, only Ralph of Oversley was economically on a par with the holders of knights' fees.

Besides the fees detailed in Evesham G, the manorial extents show that knights held additional parcels of land and that they performed other than military services.[85] For example, Richard of Ombersley, holder of half a knight's fee, had two ploughs, ten villeins (*rustici*), ten cottagers (*cottarii*), a watermill and a messuage in Evesham. He also rented a parcel of land to Henry, son of Philip, for 2*s*.[86] The messuage was held of Richard by William the seneschal, and all of this is stated to have been against the wishes of the monks. From one of the Littletons comes an instance of a man rising into the knightly class. Pain, son of Henry, held half a hide by knight service *c.* 1190, though formerly he did week work.[87] To him Evesham G attributed 2¼ hides in the newly created fee at Bretforton and South Littleton.[88] In the middle range, apparently, the class structure was both well defined and elastic. Evesham G, in effect, belongs to a substantial corpus of Evesham material relating to the period 1190–1214, a full analysis of which is beyond the scope of the present article.[89]

---

[83] For the Fenland examples of Crowland and Thorney, see S.G. Raban, 'The Property of Thorney and Crowland Abbeys: a Study in Purchase and Patronage' (PhD Thesis, University of Cambridge, 1971), 18.

[84] The exceptions are one of the Littletons and Ombersley.

[85] London, BL, MSS Cotton Vespasian B xxiv, fols. 22v–23r, 23v–24r, 26v–27r, 31v–32r, 34r–v, 35r, 36v, 49r–v, 50r–v, 50v–51r, 51v–52r, 52v–55v, 64v, 66r–v, 67r–v, 72v–73; Harley 3763, fols. 72–81v. They date from *c.* 1190, near the beginning of the abbacy of the notorious Roger Norreis.

[86] London, BL, MSS Cotton Vespasian B xxiv, fol. 26v (incomplete); Harley 3763, fol. 77v.

[87] London, BL, MS Harley 3763, fols. 74v–75.

[88] Evesham G 8.

[89] For this reason the vills have not been identified to the same level of detail in Appendix C.

Other Lists of Subtenants

Evesham E, Evesham G and Evesham O share in common the listing of tenements held of a feudal superior, on conditions that varied from person to person, from place to place, and from period to period. Such lists survive in substantial numbers from elsewhere (the 'beyond' of the subtitle) and, if treated comprehensively in conjunction with charters, could reveal a great deal about Norman and early Angevin England. They may be divided chronologically into two groups: those produced before 1135 (corresponding to the 'old enfeoffment' as far as military subtenancies are concerned) and those produced after this date.[90] What follows is merely a summary of a resource that could be utilized more fully than has hitherto been the case.

The earliest extant list was originally compiled during the abbacy of Adelelm at Abingdon (1071–1083), though some of the names belong to the first decades of the twelfth century.[91] In an instructive passage the chronicler makes it clear that the abbot gave away as fees land previously held by thegns who had been killed at Hastings.[92] Another early example is the so-called Braybrooke feodary, an account of the fees of Guy de Reinbued-curt in Cambridgeshire.[93] For each fee is recorded the name of the subtenant and sometimes a sub-subtenant, hidage and ploughland assessments, and a valuation. The facts seem to have been based on an initial stage of the Domesday inquest and thus apply to the year 1086. The knights of Archbishop Lanfrance and the 'men' (*homines*) of the abbot of Peterborough are named and their manors described in Domesday Book itself, exceptions to the general lack of any systematic treatment of military subtenants in Great Domesday.[94] A private list of archiepiscopal knights dates from a

[90] Two Benedictine monasteries preserved lists of properties alienated by their own abbots both before and after 1135: St Benet of Hulme (1101–1153) and Ramsey (1133–1177). The former survives in Oxford, Bodleian Library, Norfolk Charters, no. 608; London, BL, MSS Cotton Galba E ii, fol. 53v; Stowe 932, fol. 14v, printed in *St Benet of Holme, 1020–1210: the Eleventh- and Twelfth-Century Sections of Cotton Manuscript Galba E ii, the Register of the Abbey of St Benet of Holme*, ed. J.R. West, Norfolk Record Society, 2–3 (2 vols., Fackenham and London, 1932), i, 170–71. The latter survives in London, BL, MS Cotton Galba E x, fols. 16v–18r; TNA, E 164/28, fols. 209r–210r, printed in *Cartularium Monasterii de Rameseia*, ed. W.H. Hart and P.A. Lyons, RS 79 (3 vols., London, 1884–1893), ii, nos. 390, 392; iii, no. 635.

[91] London, BL, MS Cotton Claudius B vi, fol. 120v, printed in *Historia*, ed. Hudson, ii, 322–25, followed by a list of holders of small fragments of a knight's fee. These lists no longer exist in the earlier cartulary, of which the above manuscript is a revised copy. They are numbered 5a and 5b by Hudson.

[92] *Historia*, ed. Hudson, ii, 6–7.

[93] London, BL, MS Sloane 986, fol. 67r, printed in G.H. Fowler, 'An Early Cambridgeshire Feodary', *EHR* 46 (1931), 442–43 at 443.

[94] DB i. 4r–v; *Kent* 2 §§ 28–43; 221v–22r; *Northamptonshire* 6a §§ 1–34. These lists should be compared with the section of Exon Domesday detailing the knights of Queen Matilda in Dorset: Exeter, Dean and Chapter, MS 3500, fols. 31r–32r, printed in DB iii, 31–33.

few years later (1093 x 1096).[95] This conforms closely with the Domesday information and may comprise both feudal knights and fyrd soldiers.[96] The text formed the basis of another list datable to 1123 x 1136, which is prefaced by a thirteenth-century statement that two sulungs make one knight's fee.[97] A description of the fees of the abbey of Bury St Edmunds was put together, in its present form, possibly soon after the death of Abbot Baldwin in the winter of 1097/8.[98] For most subtenancies this text reproduces the details recorded in Little Domesday. It enables us to pinpoint a useful social distinction, for the subtenants may be divided into two groups: knights holding five or more carucates, who were lords of other free men; and small landholders with lordship over peasants.[99] What has been called 'in certain respects ... our most important source relating to the nature and extent of military service on a great Anglo-Norman honour' comes from Peterborough Abbey.[100] This is a survey of knights (*descriptio militum*) of *c.* 1105.[101] Again the fees are described in terms of hides or carucates, two of which, with an annual value of £2 10*s.*, were all that the average Peterborough knight held.[102]

An example of a list of peasant subtenants, their holdings assessed in fiscal acres, was produced by the monks of Bury St Edmunds in the first half of the reign of Henry I.[103] The peasants were probably successors of the free men (*liberi homines*) recounted in Domesday Book and, to judge from the acreages and payments due, their holdings varied a good deal in size.[104]

---

[95]   Canterbury, Dean and Chapter, MS Lit. E 28, fol. 7, printed with a facsimile in *The Domesday Monachorum of Christ Church Canterbury*, ed. D.C. Douglas (London, 1944), 105. For its date, see 63–64.

[96]   C.W. Hollister, *The Military Organization of Norman England* (Oxford, 1965), 58–60.

[97]   London, Lambeth Palace, MS 1212, fol. 177r. For the date, see Hollister, *Military Organization*, 48 note 4.

[98]   Cambridge, University Library, MS Mm iv 19, fols. 132r–34v, printed in D.C. Douglas (ed.), *Feudal Documents from the Abbey of Bury St Edmunds*, British Academy, Records of the Social and Economic History of England and Wales, 8 (London, 1932), 15–24. Another version in the same depository, MS Ee iii 60, fols. 181v–183r, is printed in *The Pinchbeck Register*, ed. Francis Hervey (2 vols., London, 1925), i, 418–421. On the date, see R.V. Lennard, *Rural England, 1086–1135: a Study of Social and Agrarian Conditions* (Oxford, 1959), 359 note 1.

[99]   D.J.A. Matthew, *The Norman Conquest* (London, 1966), 110.

[100] Hollister, *Military Organization*, 235.

[101] London, Society of Antiquaries, MS 60, fols. 19r–23r, printed in *Chronicon Petroburgense*, ed. Thomas Stapleton, Camden Society, 1st ser., 47 (London, 1849), 168–75 and in a numbered edition in Edmund King, 'The Peterborough "Descriptio Militum" (Henry I)', *EHR* 84 (1969), 84–101 at 97–101.

[102] King, 'Peterborough "Descriptio Militum"', 91, 93, 95. The same author discusses the economic and social status of these early knights in his *Peterborough Abbey*, 35–54. Peterborough documents relating to knights are listed in *Henry of Pytchley's Book of Fees*, ed. W.T. Mellows, Northamptonshire Record Society, 2 (Northampton, 1927), xxxvii–xlvi.

[103] Cambridge, University Library, MS Mm iv 19, fols. 134v–43v, printed in *Feudal Documents*, ed. Douglas, 25–44.

[104] Lennard, *Rural England*, 359–60 and 359 note 1.

A section of the Red Book of Worcester contains lists of the enfeoffments of Bishops Samson (1096–1112) and Theulf (1115–1123), contemporaries of the three Evesham abbots who feature in Evesham E and Evesham O, as well as a list of 'riding knights' (*milites equitantes*).[105] This is followed by a hidage schedule recording the names of subtenants and the rate at which their holdings were assessed for both danegeld and scutage.[106] In the text Bishop Simon (1125–1150) is referred to in the present tense and this document demonstrates the close association, at Worcester, between hidage assessments, danegeld liability and knights' fees in the second quarter of the twelfth century. The monks of Abingdon compiled a miscellaneous list of subtenants ranging from named knights to unnamed peasants.[107] Its similarity to the two Evesham lists of *c.* 1130 is emphasized by the fact that one of the most important Abingdon subtenants, William of Seacourt, in Berkshire, was also holding land of the abbot of Evesham.[108]

In the Norman period, the crown set an example to private lords with the making of Domesday Book; in the Angevin period, it did so with its demand for written returns detailing baronial knights' fees (*cartae baronum*).[109] Just as major tenants-in-chief produced surveys modelled on or copied from the inquest of 1086, so also did their descendants produce surveys modelled on or copied from that of 1166. Abingdon Abbey is a case in point. There the monks preserved both an independent list of military subtenants and a copy of the 1166 returns provided with an explanatory heading.[110] The former records the names of manors and their knightly holders. The tax assessments range from half a hide to eleven hides, the list closing with a declared total of 122½ hides. A further Abingdon list appears not to be confined to military subtenants and relates to a total of 163¼ hides.[111] The monks of Ramsey Abbey have left us two versions of their 1166 returns, one more complete than the other. The fuller version contains a statement explaining how all of the monastery's lands were hidated for the purpose of ensuring that serving

---

[105] Worcester County Record Office, St Helen's Section, 009:1/BA2636/10(ii), 243–45, printed in *Red Book of Worcester*, ed. Hollings, iv, 412–18. These lists may have been drawn up in connection with the disputed military quota.

[106] Worcester County Record Office, St Helen's Section, 009:1/BA2636/10(ii), 245, printed in *Red Book of Worcester*, ed. Hollings, iv, 418–19.

[107] London, BL, MS Cotton Claudius C ix, fols. 189v–190r, printed in D.C. Douglas, 'Some Early Surveys from the Abbey of Abingdon', *EHR* 44 (1929), 618–625 at 623–25.

[108] Evesham E 2, 10, 11; Evesham O 20, 25, 26. These items refer to 5½ hides of land at Hillborough and Weston-on-Avon and to four messuages in Evesham, all granted by Abbot Robert.

[109] Interestingly enough, during the reign of Henry I Domesday Book itself was sometimes thought of as *carta regis*: V.H. Galbraith, *The Making of Domesday Book* (Oxford, 1961), 210; *Domesday Book: its Place in Administrative History* (Oxford, 1974), 105, 110–11.

[110] London, BL, MS Cotton Claudius C ix, fols. 182r, 190r–v, of which the latter is printed in *Historia*, ed. Hudson, ii, 389–91.

[111] London, BL, MS Cotton Claudius C ix, fol. 191r.

knights were supplied to the king.[112] The shorter version introduces itself
with the words 'Hidagium militum abbatie de Ram' ...', again illustrating the
continuing practice of denoting knights' fees in terms of hides.[113] The church
of Worcester composed a list of knightly subtenants near to the time of the
cartae baronum, for the names are almost identical.[114] Another comprehensive collection of notes deals with the same church's enfeoffments down to
the time of Bishop Baldwin (1180–1184).[115] An undated list survives for St
Augustine's Abbey, Canterbury, which owed the king the service of fifteen
knights in 1166.[116] The descent of the archbishop's fees can be traced in
a list of sixty-five subtenants made five years after Henry II's inquest.[117]
This document ends with a total (*summa militum*) of just over 80½ fees, a
figure that is mathematically incorrect.[118] Most instructive of all is the list of
knights' fees drawn up, for the nuns of Shaftesbury Abbey, in the English
language.[119] On some estates and in some parts of England, tradition died
hard. Finally, dating from 1189 comes a Glastonbury list of tenants by knight
service and free tenants, whose holdings are expressed in terms of hides or
acres and whose dues and obligations varied considerably.[120] This document
is similar to Evesham G, apart from the latter's sharp separation of knights
from free tenants.

---

[112] London, BL, MSS Cotton Galba E x, fol. 16r–v, printed in *Cartularium Monasterii de
Rameseia*, ed. Hart and Lyons, iii, no. 631; Harley 5071, fol. 10v, printed in *Thomas Sprotti
Chronica*, ed. Thomas Hearne (Oxford, 1719), 215–217.

[113] London, TNA, E 164/28, fol. 234v, printed in *Cartularium Monasterii de Rameseia*, ed.
Hart and Lyons, iii, no. 548. The preceding entry in this cartulary indicates that the notional
knight's fee at Ramsey comprised four hides of land.

[114] Worcester County Record Office, St Helen's Section, 009:1/BA2636/10(ii), 243, printed
in *Red Book of Worcester*, ed. Hollings, iv, 412. It is introduced by the words 'Isti sunt feffati
ecclesie' and ends with a *summa* of thirty-six knights.

[115] Worcester County Record Office, St Helen's Section, 009:1/BA2636/10(ii), 251–257,
printed in *Red Book of Worcester*, ed. Hollings, iv, 430–442. It is entitled 'Feoda militum
episcopi Wigorn''.

[116] London, BL, MS Royal 1 B xi, fol. 145v; *Red Book of the Exchequer*, ed. Hall, i, 194.

[117] Glynde, Muniments, no. 954, printed in H.M. Colvin, 'A List of the Archbishop of
Canterbury's Tenants by Knight Service in the Reign of Henry II', in *Documents Illustrative
of Medieval Kentish Society*, ed. F.R.H. du Boulay, Kent Records, 18 (Ashford, 1964), 1–40 at
6–8, with a translation and commentary at 11–40. Since Thomas Becket was in exile in 1166,
no return was made by the archbishopric.

[118] Colvin, 'List of Tenants by Knight Service', 40.

[119] London, BL, MS Harley 61, fol. 22r–v, printed with facsimile and translation in Ann
Williams, 'The Knights of Shaftesbury Abbey', *ANS* 8 (1985), 214–237 at 233–37. A dating
range of 1135 x 1166 is proposed in *Charters and Custumals of Shaftesbury Abbey, 1089–1216*,
ed. N.E. Stacy, British Academy, Records of Social and Economic History, new ser., 39 (Oxford,
2006), 16 and note 85.

[120] Longleat, NMR 10589, fols. 1r–4r, printed in *Surveys of the Estates of Glastonbury Abbey
c. 1135–1201*, ed. N.E. Stacy, British Academy, Records of Social and Economic History, new
ser., 33 (Oxford, 2001), 79–89.

Such lists might be deemed to be good evidence of 'feudo-vassalic relations', to borrow the terminology favoured by Susan Reynolds. Here we see ecclesiastical tenants-in-chief spelling out the names of their knightly subtenants, the locations of their holdings, and the amount of service due therefrom. Are they not signs of classic feudalism in operation? Arguably they are, though they receive scant recognition in Reynolds's book, which (correctly) debunks notions of classical feudalism as a broad-based medieval, and specifically twelfth-century, phenomenon. She does admit, however, that 'England contributes much the best evidence of a connection between fiefs and military service and of the hierarchy of property rights – indeed the only evidence of either that fits the model [of classical feudalism] without heavy interpretation.'[121] Accordingly her index entry to knights' fees or fiefs relates almost exclusively to the chapter devoted to England, for 'outside England the obligation to military service, so often seen as a key feature of "feudal tenure", was generally nominal'.[122] This book is a fine example of the supreme value of the comparative approach.

The first and last entries in Evesham G imply that many of the abbey's military tenants had been enfeoffed unjustly. One of the earlier lists states that William Silvan was holding Golder in Oxfordshire at farm, but that he was withholding the rent of 10*s.* by force (*per uim*).[123] In addition there are other hints of non-cooperation on the part of rent-paying tenants.[124] These small details raise the question of how far tenants, military or otherwise, used violence or the threat of violence to their own advantage *vis-à-vis* their feudal superior. Reynolds adopts a sanguine and (dare one say?) English viewpoint, admitting to a degree of coercion but placing much greater emphasis on the efficacy of interpersonal bonds.[125] In sharp contrast a later, American work of equally astonishing breadth and sophistication mentions violence time and time again.[126] It may be possible to reconcile both points of view. England was clearly exceptional in its linkage of fiefs and military service, generally under the direction of a forceful monarchy. Apart from the years of civil war, twelfth-century England witnessed lower levels of seigneurial violence than appears to have been the norm elsewhere in Europe, including Ireland for that matter.[127] Circumstances in England were more nuanced.

---

121 Reynolds, *Fiefs and Vassals*, 480.
122 Reynolds, *Fiefs and Vassals*, 69.
123 Evesham E 17 (MS A only). The allegation does not occur in Evesham O 32.
124 Evesham E 16, 25; Evesham O 18.
125 Reynolds, *Fiefs and Vassals*, 476.
126 Bisson, *Crisis of the Twelfth Century*.
127 The twelfth century was the age of 'the trembling sod', when armies, initially native and later foreign as well, marched and counter-marched across a blood-soaked landscape, F.J. Byrne, 'The Trembling Sod: Ireland in 1169', in *A New History of Ireland; II: Medieval Ireland 1169–1534*, ed. Art Cosgrove (Oxford, 1987), 1–42.

The monks of Evesham expressed dissatisfaction *c.* 1130 mainly because post-Conquest abbots had given away so much land to tenants, often nepotistically, against the wishes of a chapter that was presumably still made up largely of Englishmen. Towards the end of the same century *c.* 1192 their chief grievance was the poor return on their 'feudal investments'. But the most traumatic shock to their contemplative lives came about in the reign of Stephen, when they experienced seigneurial violence more typical of other parts of Europe most of the time. Round about 1149, tenants of the abbey killed certain accomplices of William de Beauchamp who had demolished the cemetery wall and plundered the church.[128] By that time the Beauchamps were local seigneurs perched atop Bredon Hill at Elmley Castle, situated only four miles (6.5 km) from the abbey. The most dramatic local event of these years was the razing of an adulterine castle near Bengeworth bridge, directly across the River Avon from the monastery. This stronghold had been built probably on the hide of land retained by Urse d'Abitot, the sheriff of Worcester, following the judicial decision that Abbot Walter had proved his right to hold five hides at Bengeworth.[129] The strategic value of this site may well explain why the first Norman sheriff had been so anxious to control it. These incidents look like examples of the assertion that 'lordship as a viable way of power distinct from kingship reached its apex in much of Europe in the third quarter of the twelfth century'.[130] Yet they were hardly typical of England under its Norman and Angevin rulers.

Conclusion

When focusing on a single example, it is important to be aware of its limitations. Evesham Abbey was a Benedictine house of the old observance and of middling rank. Its quota of military service was low, thanks to Æthelwig's negotiating skills and his political usefulness to the Conqueror in those uncertain early years of the reign. In terms of the burden of military obligations to the crown Evesham ranks with Ramsey, St Albans, and Wilton, but we lack precisely comparable studies of those institutions during this relatively early period.[131] Fiefs comprised land and its natural and human resources, which varied significantly from one part of England to another. Fenland fiefs were presumably fundamentally different from Cotswold ones.[132]

---

[128] *History of the Abbey*, ed. Sayers and Watkiss, 182–85 and 184 note 1.
[129] *History of the Abbey*, ed. Sayers and Watkiss, 184–85; DB i. 175v; *Worcestershire* 10 § 12.
[130] Bisson, *Crisis of the Twelfth Century*, 322.
[131] An elaborate descent of the knights' fees of St Albans Abbey starts in 1166: Chew, *Ecclesiastical Tenants-in-Chief*, table facing 125.
[132] In 1166 the abbot of Ramsey made his return to the inquest in terms of hides rather

At the same time, the Evesham sources may well reveal a number of historical truisms. The Norman Conquest was a land-grabbing exercise not only at the level of tenants-in-chief but also at subtenurial levels.[133] Much that was done by abbots was done against the wishes of their monks. Fiefs were constructed and reconstructed on a continuing basis, with some elements of continuity. Five hides remained a notional guideline to the size of a high-status fief right to the end of the twelfth century,[134] though many fiefs were considerably smaller and the averages that I have cited are reminiscent of Sally Harvey's emphasis on the lesser sort of knight. Few of the abbey's subtenants were members of the aristocracy; most appear to have been members of an emerging gentry or local squirearchy. Knights sometimes performed services additional to their military ones, but as subtenants they were generally quite distinct socially from ordinary manorial freeholders. The feudal geography of the Evesham estates was extraordinarily complex and of course it coexisted with that of the monks' neighbours, lay and ecclesiastical. To say that the abbey's quota was 'those five knights' belies a fantastic kaleidoscope of changing subtenurial heterogeneity that lay beneath the surface.

than knights' fees, even though fees had been created: Chew, *Ecclesiastical Tenants-in-Chief*, 123–24.

[133] Compare the question of over-enfeoffment: Chew, *Ecclesiastical Tenants-in-Chief*, 119–21.

[134] As in the case of the bishopric of Salisbury and Westminster Abbey: Chew, *Ecclesiastical Tenants-in-Chief*, 121. Six hides were favoured at Shaftesbury Abbey, which like Evesham had a small quota to satisfy: Williams, 'Knights of Shaftesbury Abbey', 226–27.

Appendix A

A Numbered Edition of Evesham E

Manuscripts

A: London, BL, MS Cotton Vespasian B xxiv, fol. 11r–v (with which MS B is here collated)
B: London, BL, MS Harley 3763, fol. 71r–v
Date: *c.* 1130

[fol. 11r]
1]   § In Euesham [Evesham] dedit Rodbert*us*[a] abbas Will*elm*o camerario unam uirgatam terre de dominio sine capitulo.
2]   § In eadem uilla habet Will*elm*us de Seuecurt iiii[or] masuras[b] sine capitulo.
3]   § Item in eadem uilla habet Pagan*us* clericus v[que] masuras[b] sine capitulo.
4]   Constantinus quinque.[c]
5]   Einulfus i.
6]   § De burgo xvi mansure dono Mauritii abbatis et Rodb*er*ti[d] abbatis sine capitulo.[1]
7]   § Constantin*us* id est.[e]
8]   Rad*ulfus* dispensator iii uirgatas de villinagio[f] dono Rodb*er*ti[d] abbatis sine capitulo.
9]   § Albold*us* dimidiam hidam de villinagio[f] dono Mauritii abbatis sine capitulo.
10]   § Will*elm*us de[g] Seuecurte[h] tenet Westune[i] [Weston-on-Avon] dono Rodb*er*ti[d] abbatis sine capitulo.
11]   Idem Will*elm*us tenet Hildeburthewethe[j] [Hillborough][2] dono eiusdem abbatis sine capitulo.

---

[a] Rob*er*tus [b] mansuras [c] v [d] Rob*er*ti [e] i [f] uilenagio [g] B omits *de* [h] Seuecurt [i] Weston' [j] Hildeburewrth'

---

[1] This item, which has no equivalent in Evesham O, may have been intended to summarize Evesham E 2–5 and 7. If this hypothesis is correct, the grantor of Evesham E 7 was Abbot Maurice, since Abbot Robert was to grant all the other messuages. If Evesham E 6 is an exclusive item, the total number of messuages was thirty-three. The evidence is suggestive of a small urban nucleus focused on the monastery, perhaps with a distinct merchant quarter (*burgus*) alongside.
[2] The tenurial history of Hillborough is very difficult to resolve: Clarke, 'Early Surveys', 139 note 5.

12] § Radulfus pincerna tenet Withlakesford [Wixford] in feudi firmam pro iiii libris dono eiusdem abbatis sine capitulo.

13] § Idem Radulfus tenet Graftun^k [Ardens Grafton]^3 dono Mauritii abbatis sine capitulo.

14] § In Huniburge^l [Church Honeybourne] habet Paga*nus* clericus i hidam de uillinagio^f dono Mauricii^m abbatis sine capitulo.

15] § In Euesha*m* [Evesham] habet Rob*ertus* Smalbert unam masuram^n dono Rob*er*ti abbatis sine capitulo.^{4}

[fol. 11v]

16] Simon dispensator tenet Vlebergam^o [Oldberrow] pro xxv solidis dono Rodb*er*ti^d abbatis sine capitulo et super excommunicationem^p sancte Marje et sancti Ecgwini^q patris nostri.

17] Will*elmu*s Siluan*us* tenet j hidam apud Goldora*m* [Golder]^5 pro x solidis ad firmam per annum et detinet censum per uim^r defectu abbatum.

18] § In Acheslench^s [Atch Lench] habet Will*elmu*s Meldrope dimidiam hidam dono^t Rodberti^d abbatis contradicente capitulo.

19] § Randulfus frater abbatis Walt*er*ii habet in Withelega [Weethley] iii hidas de dominio.

20] In Kinewartuna^u [Kinwarton] iii hidas de dominio.

21] In Stoke [Lark Stoke] ij hidas^6 de dominio.

22] In Liteltona^v [Middle Littleton] ij hidas et dimidiam.

23] In Bretfertona^w [Bretforton]^7 iii hidas et i uirgatam dono Walt*er*ii^x abbatis contradicente capitulo.

24] § Will*elmu*s seneschallus^y habet apud Baddeseie^z [Badsey] v uirgatas. Ex hiis iii sunt de dominio et geld';^{8} ij sunt libere.

---

^{k} Graffeton' ^{l} Huniburne ^{m} Mauritii ^{n} j mansuram ^{o} Hulebergam ^{p} excomunicationem ^{q} Egwini ^{r} B omits *per uim* ^{s} Hacheslench ^{t} B omits *dono* ^{u} Kinewarton' ^{v} Litleton' ^{w} Bretferton' ^{x} Walt*er*i ^{y} seneschallus ^{z} Baddeseia*m*

---

^{3} Ardens Grafton was apparently one of Abbot Æthelwig's post-Conquest acquisitions that was lost by his Norman successor and in 1086 it was held of William FitzCorbucion by its pre-Conquest owners: DB i. 243r; *Warwickshire* 28 § 13. How or when Evesham Abbey recovered this manor is unknown.

^{4} Followed by Evesham F, a brief hidage schedule of an individual fief, in the lower margin.

^{5} The tradition whereby the manor of Golder (in Pyrton, Oxfordshire) was acquired by Evesham Abbey is confused, but the grantor may have been William FitzNigel, constable of the early Norman earls of Chester: *The Chartulary or Register of the Abbey of St Werburgh, Chester*, ed. James Tait, Chetham Society, new ser., 79, 82 (2 vols., Manchester, 1920–1923), i, p. xlvi; R.R. Darlington, 'Aethelwig, Abbot of Evesham', *EHR* 48 (1933), 1–22, 177–198 at 195, note 2.

^{6} Evesham O 3 records 2½ hides.

^{7} Probably Bretforton Lower End, attached to Offenham in 1086: DB i. 175v; *Worcestershire* 10 § 5. The same applies to Evesham E 27.

^{8} This statement of geldability is exceptional and may be explained by the fact that manorial demesnes were normally exempt from payment of geld.

25]   § Will*elmus* de Dunitune^aa habet in Dunitona^bb [Donnington][9] v uirgatas et dimidiam de dominio^cc et sedet in dominica mansione abbatis dono Walt*eri*i^x abbatis contradicente capitulo.

26]   § Hugo T*ra*uers habet v uirgatas (in Liteltona)^v [South Littleton] de dominio dono Walt*eri*i^x abbatis sine capitulo.

27]   § Hugo de Bretfertun'^w habet in Bretfertun'^w [Bretforton] ij hidas et dimidiam dono Walt*eri*i^x abbatis sine capitulo.

---

^aa Duninton'   ^bb Doninton'   ^cc B omits *de dominio*

[9]   Donnington is concealed in the Domesday manor of Broadwell: DB i. 166r; *Gloucestershire* 12 § 4.

Appendix B
A Numbered Edition of Evesham O

Manuscript
London, BL, MS Harley 3763, fol. 61r–v
Date: *c.* 1130

[fol. 61r]
1]   § Randulfus frater abbatis Walterii habet in Witheleia [Weethley] iij hidas de dominio.
2]   In Kinewartona [Kinwarton] iij hidas de dominio.
3]   In Stokes [Lark Stoke] ij hidas et dimidiam[1] de dominio.
4]   In Litleton' [Middle Littleton] ij hidas et dimidiam.
5]   In Bretferton' [Bretforton][2] iij hidas et j uirgatam dono Walterii abbatis contradicente capitulo.
6]   § Willelmus de Dunitona habet in Duniton' [Donnington][3] v uirgatas et[a] dimidiam de dominio dono Walterii abbatis.
7]   § In Bradewelle [Broadwell] Walterus tenet dimidiam hidam et xx^{tij} acras de cotland dono (§ Walterii).
8]   § In Tatlestroppe [Adlestrop] filius Gocelini iiij hidas dono Walterii.
9]   § In Melgarebur' [Maugersbury] Aluredus dimidiam hidam et ecclesia de Stowe j hidam[4] de dominio dono Walterii.
10]   § In Burchton' [Bourton-on-the-Water] Robertus filius Aluredi j hidam de dominio dono Walterii.
11]   § In Baddebi [Badby][5] Gosfridus frater abbatis tenet ij hidas et dimidiam dono Walterii.
12]   In eadem uilla Willelmus filius Gosfridi tenet de dominio j hidam dono Walterii.
13]   § In Lenchwic [Lenchwick] Hugo nepos abbatis tenet iij hidas et dimidiam dono Walterii.
14]   § Hugo Trauers tenet v uirgatas in Litleton' [South Littleton] dono Walterii abbatis sine capitulo.

---

a altered from *set*

1   Evesham E 21 records two hides.
2   See above, Appendix A, note 7. The same applies to Evesham O 15.
3   See above, Appendix A, note 9.
4   The hide attached to Stow-on-the-Wold church had had a separate identity since the late tenth century: DB i. 165v; *Gloucestershire* 12 § 1; Clarke, 'Early Surveys', 92.
5   *Baddeby* in the right margin in a seventeenth-century hand.

15] § Hug*o* de Bretferton' [Bretforton] tenet[b] ij hidas et dimidiam dono Walt*er*ii abbatis.[6]

16] § Alboldus dimidiam hidam de uilenagio dono Mauritii abbatis.[7]

17] § Paganus clericus tenet j hidam de uilenagio in Huniburna [Church Honeybourne] dono Mauritii abbatis et sine capitulo.

18] § In Baddebi [Badby][8] Mauriti*us* abbas dedit ecclesie (xii acras) de dominio iniuste pro omnibus decimis. Modo habet ecclesia et acras et decimas.[9]

19] § Rob*er*tus abbas dedit Will*elmo* camerario i uirgatam terre in Euesha*m* [Evesham] de dominio (§ sine capitulo).[10]

[fol. 61v]

20] In eadem uilla habet Will*elmu*s Soeuecurt [Seacourt] iiij mansuras.

21] Pagan*us* clericus v.

22] Constantinus v.

23] Einulfus j.

24] Rob*er*tus Smalberd i dono Rob*er*ti abbatis sine capitulo.

25] Will*elmu*s de Souecurt [Seacourt] tenet Weston' [Weston-on-Avon].

26] et Hildeburrewrth' [Hillborough][11] dono Rob*er*ti abbatis sine capitulo.

27] Will*elmu*s de Bellocampo tenet Chirchlench [Church Lench] dono Rob*er*ti abbatis sine capitulo.

28] Radulfus pincerna tenet Witlakesford' [Wixford] in feudi firma pro iiij libris dono Rob*er*ti abbatis sine capitulo.

29] Simon dispensator tenet Hulebarewe [Oldberrow] pro xxv solidis dono Rob*er*ti abbatis.

30] Will*elmu*s Meldrope tenet in Eccheslench [Atch Lench] dimidiam hidam dono Rob*er*ti abbatis.

31] Rad*ulfu*s dispensator tenet iij uirgatas terre dono Rob*er*ti abbatis et sine capitulo.[12]

32] § Will*elmu*s Siluan*us* tenet j hidam apud Goldora*m* [Golder][13] pro x solidis.

33] § Will*elmu*s senescallus tenet apud Badeseia*m* [Badsey] v uirgatas. Ex hiis iij sunt de dominio et geldant,[14] due sunt libere, et apud Salford' [Abbots Salford] iij uirgatas.

---

[b] after *tenet* the words *in eadem uilla* deleted

---

6 Followed by three blank lines.
7 Probably at Evesham itself.
8 *Baddeby* in the right margin in a seventeenth-century hand.
9 Followed by two blank lines.
10 *sine capitulo* in the lower margin.
11 See above, Appendix A, note 2.
12 Followed by two blank lines.
13 See above, Appendix A, note 5.
14 See above, Appendix A, note 8.

Appendix C
A Numbered Edition of Evesham G

Manuscripts
A: London, BL, MS Cotton Vespasian B xxiv, fol. 12r–v (with which MS B is here collated)
B: London, BL, MS Harley 3763, fol. 68r–v
Date: *c.* 1192

[fol. 12]
1] Hic notantur milites et liberi tenentes de abbatia de Euesham[a] [Evesham] multi iniuste fefati, pauci uero iuste. Isti nullum seruicium faciunt ecclesie nisi seruicium regis et hoc tepide.[1]
2] § Will*elmu*s de B*e*llocampo tenet in Chirchlench [Church Lench] iiii hidas pro seruitio dimidii militis.
3] § Simon filius Ranulfi[b] de Coctun[c] [Coughton] tenet in Liteltona[d] [Littleton] ii hidas et dimidiam et in Withelega[e] [Weethley] i hidam et dimidiam et in Bretfertona[f] [Bretforton] iii hidas et i uirgatam et debet i militem.
4] § Ranulfus[g] tenet in Kinewartona[h] [Kinwarton] iii hidas et[i] in Witheleia [Weethley] i hidam et dimidiam et in Stoke [Lark Stoke] ii hidas et dimidiam. Debet i militem.
5] § Rob*ertu*s de Seuecurt[j] [Seacourt] tenet iiii[k] hidas in Westona[l] [Weston-on-Avon] et Rob*ertu*s Streche v uirgatas in Hildeburwrthe [Oldberrow].[m] Ipsi debent i militem.
6] § Bertram[n] tenet in Hudicote [Hidcote Boyce] iii hidas et in Biuintona[o] [Bevington Waste][2] i hidam et Paga*nu*s Trauers v uirgatas in Liteltona [Littleton].[d] Ipsi debent i militem.

---

[a] Eouesham [b] Rannulfi [c] Cocton' [d] Litleton' [e] Witheleia [f] Bretferton' [g] Rann ulfus [h] Kinewarton' [i] B omits *et* [j] Souecurt [k] iij [l] Weston' [m] Hildeburewrthe [n] Bertram*us* [o] Biuinton'

---

[1] *et hoc tepide* added in a different hand.
[2] One hide of land at Bevington Waste ('Bvintvn'), located in Abbots Morton, Worcestershire, had been held by Evesham Abbey in 1086: DB i. 175v; *Worcestershire* 10 § 15. Amongst a number of alleged early grants in adjacent Warwickshire was Binton, the Latin spelling of which was similar: Clarke, 'Early Surveys', table 55. This is of a piece with the specious claim that Æthelwig acquired Binton ('Biuintune') when he was acting as Mannig's deputy (*prepositus*): *History of the Abbey*, ed. Sayers and Watkiss, 172–73. In 1086 a portion of Binton was held jointly with Hillborough by Osbern FitzRichard: DB i. 244r; *Warwickshire* 37 § 5. This may have been the target for an attempt by Æthelwig to obtain more land in the general area of the monks' apparently legitimate holding of Wixford after 1066: DB i. 239v; *Warwickshire* 11 § 1.

7]   § Ric*ardus* de Ambresleia[p] [Ombersley] tenet ii hidas et dimidiam et debet dimidium militem.

8]   § Pagan*us* filius Henrici tenet in Liteltona[d] [Littleton] ix uirgatas et Hugo filius Rob*er*ti tenet in Bretfortona[f] [Bretforton] ii hidas et dimidiam et debent i militem.

9]   § Elias[q] de Actona[r] [Acton] tenet ii hidas et facit seruicium regis quantum eis attinet.

10]   § Ingelram de Ambresleia[p] [Ombersley] geldat pro dimidia hida.

11]   § Ranulfus[g] Wither geldat pro dimidia hida.

12]   § Will*elmus* Guthmund[s] de Nortona[t] [Norton] geldat pro dimidia hida.

13]   § Alard*us* de Euesham[u] [Evesham] geldat pro i uirgata, quam tenet in Euesham.[u]

14]   § Radulfus de Mortona[v] [Abbots Morton] geldat pro dimidia hida.

15]   § Will*elmus* Meldrope de Hacheslench[w] [Atch Lench] geldat pro dimidia hida.

16]   § Ric*ardus* filius Augustini tenet in Liteltona[d] [Littleton] i hidam et in Saltford[x] [Abbots Salford] i hidam. Iste sunt geldabiles.

17]   § Rad*ulfus* dispensator geldat pro iii uirgatis in Litelton' [Littleton].[d]

18]   § Gaufrid*us*[y] Withelard geldat pro i uirgata in Litelton' [Littleton].[d]

19]   § Will*elmus* seneschallus[z] tenet in Baddeseia [Badsey][aa] v uirgatas. Ex hiis iii sunt geldabiles et ij libere. Idem tenet in Saltford[x] [Abbots Salford] iii uirgatas geldabiles de terra que fuit Rog*er*i Palefrei.

20]   § Ric*ardus* Franceis geldat[bb] pro dimidia hida in Baddeseia [Badsey].[aa]

21]   § Walt*erus* Frusselun[cc] geldat pro i hida in Wichwana [Wickhamford].[dd]

22]   § Joh*anne*s de Wicwana[dd] geldat pro i uirgata in Wicwana [Wickhamford].[dd]

23]   § Will*elmus* Pintel(t)hein[ee] geldat pro dimidia hida in Hamtona [Little Hampton].[ff]

24]   § Walt*erus* Grim geldat pro vi uirgatis in Salford' [Abbots Salford] et de iure debet annuatim xxxii solidos.[3]

[fol. 12v]

25]   § Rob*ertus* Gnost[gg] geldat pro una virgata in Sandburne [Sambourn].[hh]

26]   § Witlakesford[ii] [Wixford] geldat pro v hidis quas Ranulfus[g] pincerna tenet in feodi firma, et pro vna hida in Graftona[jj] [Ardens Grafton] quam idem Rad*ulfus*[kk] tenet in feodi firma.[4]

27]   § Henri[ll] geldat pro ii hidis in Rageleia [Ragley].[mm]

---

[p] Ambresl'   [q] Helias   [r] Acton'   [s] Gudmund   [t] Norton'   [u] Euesh'   [v] Morton'
[w] Accheslench   [x] Salford'   [y] Galfrid*us*   [z] senescallus   [aa] Badeseia   [bb] altered from *goldat*   [cc] Frusselu   [dd] Wicwon'   [ee] Pintelþein   [ff] Hamton'   [gg] Cnoste   [hh] Samburn'
[ii] Witlakesford'   [jj] Grefton'   [kk] Ran*ulfus*   [ll] H*en*ricus   [mm] Raggeleia

---

3   Evesham G 24 is a later addition in a different hand.
4   *et pro ... firma* added in a different hand.

28]   § Walt*erus* filius Drw[nn] geldat pro ii hidis in Bradewell' [Broadwell].

29]   § Reinald*us*[oo] filius Will*elm*i Blundel et Bernard*us* geldant[pp] pro i hida in Bradewell' [Broadwell].

30]   § Will*elmu*s de Donintona[qq] tenet v uirgatas et dimidiam in Dunitona [Donnington][qq] et sunt geldabiles. Idem tenet in Burtona [Bourton-on-the-Water][rr] i hidam geldabilem et i uirgatam pro xviii denariis.

31]   § Rob*ertus* de Slochtre [Upper Slaughter][ss] tenet i hidam geldabilem in Burtona [Bourton-on-the-Water][rr] (et)[tt] i uirgatam pro xviii denariis.

32]   § In Melgaresbyry [Maugersbury][uu] sunt ii hide geldabiles et i hida libera que pertinet ad ecclesiam de Stowe [Stow-on-the-Wold].

33]   § In Swella [Upper Swell] dimidia hida geldabilis.

34]   § Philipp*us* de Dauintr' [Daventry][vv] tenet in Neuha*m* [Newnham] i hidam geldabilem.

35]   § Will*elmu*s de Capes[ww] tenet in Baddebi [Badby] i hidam geldabilem.

36]   § Will*elmu*s West tenet dimidiam hidam geldabilem in Baddebi [Badby].

37]   § Nicholau*s* de Neuha*m* [Newnham] geldat pro i uirgata et dat annuatim ecclesie i libram piperis pro omni seruitio.

38]   § Uilla [*sic*] de Baddebi [Badby] et Neuham [Newnham] debent unum militem.[5]

39]   § Summa hidarum lxiiij hide et dimidia hida et i uirgata et dimidia et has tenent milites et francalani partim iuste, partim iniuste.[6]

[nn] Driu   [oo] Reg*inaldus*   [pp] geldat et Bernard*us*   [qq] Doniton'   [rr] Burchton'   [ss] Slout*re*
[tt] *et* above a deletion   [uu] Melgaresbur   [vv] Dauintre   [ww] Kapes

5   Evesham G 38, a later addition in a different hand, is followed by one blank line.
6   B omits Evesham G 39, which is a later addition in two different hands, with a change of hand after the second *dimidia*.

2

Voluntary Ascetic Flagellation:
From Local to Learned Traditions

John Howe

Self-flagellation in the twenty-first century seems more masochistic than religious, and spirituality today has little place for the ascetical use of a whip or other instruments of torture.[1] Yet the practice will not quite disappear. We see it in film, and not just in medieval contexts such as Ingmar Bergman's *The Seventh Seal* (1957) or *Monty Python and the Holy Grail* (1975), but also in contemporary manifestations such as Silas, the renegade Opus Dei member in Dan Brown's novel *The Da Vinci Code* (2003), or the video images of Shi'ite pilgrims flagellating themselves with chains and slashing their foreheads with swords while they commemorate 'Ashura.

Such forms of ascetic practice have long been studied in their Latin Christian context. According to the traditional narrative, which this study attempts to destabilize, self-flagellation was an ancient monastic expression of penance. How ancient has been debated, but certainly by the eleventh century it is well documented among Italian hermits. In the thirteenth century it would have entered lay society as part of the 'monasticization of the laity', the top-down process by which religious elites impose their values on the masses. In the words of André Vauchez, the preeminent authority on lay spirituality, 'The confraternities of penitents and flagellants were clearly animated by the desire to appropriate the spiritual resources of monasticism.... The most telling example of this was flagellation – a monastic practice which some lay people in the thirteenth century appropriated in order to win the rewards associated with it.'[2] The penitential confraternities of the Reformation may also be viewed as outgrowths of Franciscan and Jesuit spirituality.

---

[1] Definitions are found in Louis Gougaud, 'La discipline, instrument de penitence', in *Dévotions et pratiques ascétiques du moyen âge*, Collection 'Pax' 21 (Paris, 1925), 175–199; Jean Leclercq, 'Disciplina', *Dictionnaire de spiritualité ascétique et mystique* (17 vols., Paris, 1937–95), iii, 1291–1302 [hereafter *DSAM*]; Paul Bailly, 'Flagellants', *DSAM*, v, 392–408 (which includes a comprehensive bibliography of earlier studies); and Arnold Angenendt, 'Geißelung', *Lexikon des Mittelalters* (10 vols., Munich, 1977–99), iv, 1177.

[2] André Vauchez, *Les laïcs au moyen âge: Pratiques et expériences religieuses* (Paris, 1987),

Yet any 'most telling example' invites scrutiny, particularly if it serves to
bolster a top-down vision of medieval spirituality that may be due for revision.
Is there another way to understand the emergence of self-flagellation as an
ascetic practice in the Latin West? Could religious self-flagellation, which
was widespread in the ancient world prior to Christianity and Islam, have
lingered on in marginal popular religious contexts until it later found places
within more normative Christian and Islamic traditions? Tracing the possible
paths by which flagellation might have entered world religious systems does
not answer larger questions about how this form of self-sacrifice operates
physiologically, psychologically, or theologically, but such an investigation could help clarify the history of one asceticism and also raise further
questions about the limits of perspectives that treat Western spirituality as
an elite system.

Self-flagellation was widespread in the ancient Roman world.[3] It was
particularly associated with the East. In the Hebrew Bible, the priests of Baal,
challenged by Elijah to a sacrificial contest, slashed themselves with swords
and spears (I Kings 18:28). In the eastern Mediterranean world, flagellation
that shaded into self-mutilation and emasculation was especially associated
with priests of Cybele, Atargis, and other goddesses whose cults overlapped
and varied over millennia in a long 'process of religious assimilation and
articulation'.[4] Eastern cults such as those of Ma Bellona and Cybele, slightly

101 [Engl. trans. *The Laity in the Middle Ages: Religious Beliefs and Devotional Practices*, ed.
Daniel E. Bornstein and trans. Margery J. Schneider (Notre Dame, IN, 1993), 114 (note also
the introduction to the translated edition by Bornstein, xviii)]. Along the same lines, see André
Vauchez, *La sainteté en Occident aux derniers siècles du Moyen Âge d'après les procès de
canonisation et les documents hagiographiques*, Bibliothèque des Écoles françaises d'Athènes
et de Rome 241 (Rome, 1981), 151 [Engl. trans. *Sainthood in the Later Middle Ages*, trans.
Jean Birrell (Cambridge, 1997), 130].
3   A broad but eccentric overview can be found in Georg Friedrich Collas [Carl Felix von
Schlichtegroll], *Der Flagellantismus in Altertum* (Leipzig, 1913, repr., 1932).
4   Maarten J. Vermaseren, *Cybele and Attis: The Myth and the Cult* (London, 1977), 97–100,
115, 121, 138; H.J.W. Drijvers, 'Die Dea Syria und andere syrische Gottheiten im Imperium
Romanum', in *Die orientalische Religionen im Römerreich*, ed. Vermaseren (Leiden, 1981),
241–63; Monika Hörig, 'Dea Syria-Atargatis', in *Aufstieg und Niedergang der römischen Welt*
17 (1984), 1536–1581; Per Bilde, 'Atartagis / Dea Syria: Hellenization of Her Cult in the
Hellenistic Roman Period?', in *Religion and Religious Practice in the Seleucid Period*, ed.
P. Bilde et al. (Aarhus, 1990), 151–187; Stephen Benko, *The Virgin Goddess: Studies in the
Pagan and Christian Roots of Mariology* (Leiden, 2004), 53–82; and Hugh Bowden, *Mystery
Cults of the Ancient World* (Princeton, NJ, 2010), 96–104. The words quoted are from H.J.W.
Drijvers, *Cults and Beliefs at Edessa* (Leiden, 1980), 80.
    For inventories of major sources, see Vermaseren, *Corpus Cultus Cybelae Attidisque
(CCCA)*, Etudes préliminaires aux religions orientales dans l'Empire romain 50 (7 vols.,
Leiden, 1977–1989); and Paul-Louis van Berg, *Corpus Cultus Deae Syriae. Vol. 1 (1–2):
Les sources littéraires*, Études préliminaires aux religions orientales dans l'Empire romain 28
(Leiden, 1972).

modified to fit Roman tastes,[5] earned grudging toleration as 'organized subsystems of popular culture',[6] and received increasing imperial patronage during the second and third centuries of the Empire.[7] They still retained their exotic priesthoods, and on March 24, the Day of Blood, the priests of Cybele and Attis, the *galloi*, would flagellate themselves until they were bloody.[8] A statue representing such a *fanaticus* survives in the Capitoline Museum and features a scourge with knucklebones.[9] This is the very instrument known to Apuleius (fl. late second century CE), who disapprovingly describes how wandering eunuch priests of a Syrian goddess would bloodily and theatrically whip themselves.[10]

Religious self-flagellation also appeared outside of the more exotic cults of Eastern deities, although in contexts still removed from more respectable Olympian religion. It was part of the rites of Bona Dea.[11] Lucian of Samosata associated it with the Cynics, whose ascetical traditions also fell outside of normal civic religion.[12] A marginal aspect of the Lupercalian rites, which existed as public spectacle in some form at least until Pope Gelasius attempted

---

[5] Kirk Summers, 'Lucretius' Roman Cybele', in *Cybele, Attis and Related Cults: Essays in Memory of M.J. Vermaseren*, ed. Eugene N. Lane, Religions in the Graeco-Roman World 131 (Leiden, 1996), 337–65.

[6] For the evidence indicating that in the Latin world the adherents of the cult of Dea Syria were 'primarily in the lower social group', see Richard Gordon, 'Religion in the Roman Empire: The Civic Compromise and Its Limits', in *Pagan Priests: Religion and Power in the Ancient World*, ed. Mary Beard and John North (Ithaca, NY, 1990), 245–248; and Appendix III in *Apuleius Madaurensis Metamorphoses, Book VIII: Text, Introduction, Commentary*, ed. B.L. Hijmans Jr. et al., Groningen Commentaries on Apuleius (Groningen, 1985), 286.

[7] Gabriel Sanders, 'Kybele und Attis', in *Die orientalische Religionen im Römerreich*, 264–97, esp. 279–83; A.T. Fear, 'Cybele and Christ', in *Cybele, Attis and Related Cults*, 37–50.

[8] Vermaseren, *Cybele and Attis*, 97–100, 115, 121, 38; Benko, *Studies in the Pagan and Christian Roots*, 72–79. Regarding the name 'Galloi', see Lane, 'The Name of Cybele's Priests the "*Galloi*"', in *Cybele, Attis and Related Cults*, 117–33.

[9] Vermaseren, *CCCA*, iii, 466; reproduced as fig. V(1), in Gabriel Sanders, 'Kybele und Attis', in *Die orientalische Religionen im Römerreich*, 296. For another image of such a whip, incorporated into a funerary portrait from the neighborhood of Rome, see Bowden, *Mystery Cults*, 99.

[10] Apuleius, *Metamorphoses*, VIII xxvi–xxxi and IX i–iv and viii–x, ed. and trans. by J. Arthur Hanson (2 vols., Cambridge, MA, 1989), ii, 112–119. Word by word commentary on these passages can be found in *Apuleius, Book VIII*, ed. Hijmans Jr. et al., 223–77; and *Book IX*, 33–105.

[11] H.H.J. Brouwer, *Bona Dea: The Sources and Description of a Cult* (Leiden, 1989), 336–7; H.S. Versnel, 'The Festival for Bona Dea and the Thesmophoria', *Greece and Rome* 39 (1992), 31–55, esp. 35.

[12] Lucian, *The Death of Peregrinus*, chapters xvii and xxviii, ed. M.D. Macleod, *Luciani Opera* (4 vols., Oxford 1972–1987), iii, 194 and 198. A translation is found in Lionel Casson, *Selected Satires of Lucian* (Chicago, IL, 1962), 370 and 375. Peregrinus is placed into both philosophical and Freudian contexts in E.R. Dodds, *Pagan and Christian in an Age of Anxiety: Some Aspects of Religious Experience from Marcus Aurelius to Constantine* (Cambridge, 1965), 60–63.

to suppress them in 496, involved the naked lupercal runners whipping women who were seeking fertility.[13]

Did religious flagellation exist outside of urban centers? We know very little about the '*superstitiones*' of Rome's rural populations.[14] Apuleius claimed that exotic flagellant priests of Eastern goddesses could attract crowds and donations wherever they went.[15] Although he observed this in the course of a novel set in Greece, he may also have had other places in mind, including his North African homeland where Augustine would later deplore the presence of such priests.[16] And one account from northern Italy demonstrates that self-flagellating holy men remained part of late antique rural piety. Bishop Maximus of Turin (d. between 408 and 423), in a sermon written soon after 405, warns estate owners of northern Italy about the 'devotees of Diana' who frequent the rural countryside:

Such a priest prepares himself with wine for his goddess' wounds, and since he is drunk the wretch does not feel his own pain. But they do this according to plan, so that they may be less troubled by their wounds on succumbing to the drunkenness of wine. Vain indeed is the soothsayer who thinks to add to piety with cruelty. And how merciful is such a god to others when he is so bloodthirsty to his own priests?

Let us briefly describe the appearance of a soothsayer of this kind. His head is unkempt, with long hair, his breast is bare, his legs are half hidden by a mantle, and, like a gladiator, he carries a sword in his hands and is prepared to fight. Indeed, he is worse than a gladiator because, while the one is obliged to struggle with someone else, he is compelled to fight with himself; the one seeks out another's vitals, but he tears his own members to pieces; and, if it may be said, the gladiator's trainer urges the one to cruelty but the demon urges the other. Judge whether this man, wearing this garb and bloodied with this carnage, is a gladiator or a priest.[17]

---

[13] William M. Green, 'The Lupercalia in the Fifth Century', *Classical Philology* 26 (1931), 60–69. Some iconographic evidence for Lupercalian flagellation is presented in Henning Wrede, 'Der Venus Felix Peinvolles Schicksal im Lupercal', *Mitteilungen des Deutschen Archaeologischen Instituts, Römische Abteilung* 102 (1995), 345–348 and plates 82–83.

[14] On the city-centered nature of our sources, see Jacques Fontaine, 'Valeurs antiques et valeurs chrétiennes dans la spiritualité des grands propriétaires terriens à la fin du IVe siècle occidental', in *Epektasis: Mélanges patristiques offerts au Cardinal Jean Daniélou*, ed. J. Fontaine and Charles Kannengiesser (Paris, 1972), 571–95.

[15] See note 10 above.

[16] Augustine, *City of God* II. iv and VII. xxvi. Augustine comments on these priests in the context of Carthage where they had a major temple: see J.B. Rives, *Religion and Authority in Roman Carthage from Augustus to Constantine* (Oxford, 1995), 74–5.

[17] Maximus of Turin, *Sermo* cvii, ed. Almut Mutzenbecher, *CCSL* 23 (Turnhout, 1962), 420–421 [Engl. trans. Boniface Ramsey, *The Sermons of St. Maximus of Turin*, Ancient Christian Writers 50 (New York, 1989), 237]. The exact details of this bloody asceticism are lost in colorful rhetoric: 'caput nuda habens pectora pallio crura semicincta, et more gladiatorum paratus ad pugnam ferrum gestat in manibus, nisi quod gladiatore peior est, quia ille adversus alterum dimicare cogitur, iste contra se pugnare conpellitur; ille aliena petit viscera, iste propria membra dilaniat; et si dici potest, ad crudelitatem illum lanista istum numen hortatur.' J.N. Hillgarth,

Because Maximus assumes that his audience of land owners will know what he is talking about when he exhorts them to banish religious 'gladiators' from their properties, such infamous holy men must have been a recognizable part of the northern Italian religious scene.[18] The reference to Diana, however, should not necessarily be taken literally inasmuch as such language can be used for pre-Roman or marginal cults in general.[19] Rural paganism was particularly intractable in northern Italy.[20] Here, even at the end of the Middle Ages, barely Christianized 'pagan survivals' could still be found, as Carlo Ginzburg demonstrated in his accounts of the 'good walkers' (*Benandanti*) and of surviving fragments of pre-Christian cosmologies.[21]

In the post-Roman world, self-flagellation and mutilation may have continued in the same geographical areas, in both East and West. In the fifth century, the bishop of Edessa had to forbid his clerics from emasculating themselves,[22] and there are hints that castrated Syrian initiates of goddess cults could still be found in the eighth century.[23] Continuity of at least some

---

Christianity and Paganism, 350–750: The Conversion of Western Europe (Philadelphia, PA, 1986), 56, interpreting '*ferrum*' in the more general sense of 'weapon', reads the passage as a direct description of self-flagellation: 'he brandishes a weapon in his hand … as his trainer works on the gladiator, so his god urges this man to self-flagellation'. Ramsey's translation, the one quoted in the text, takes 'ferrum' as a literal sword and reads the passage as a description of self-mutilation. Maximus himself apparently did not see any need for greater specificity, perhaps because, like Apuleius and some other authors, he associated religious zealots of this sort with both self-mutilation and flagellation.

[18] On Maximus and his fight for Christianization, see Mark Humphries, *Communities of the Blessed: Social Environment and Religious Change in Northern Italy, AD 200–400* (Oxford, 1999), 175–77. For archaeological evidence relating to his elite Christian audience, see Gisella Cantino Wataghin, 'Christianisation et organization ecclésiastique des campagnes: L'Italie du nord aux IVe–VIIIe siècles', in *Towns and Their Territories between Late Antiquity and the Early Middle Ages*, ed. Gian Pietro Brogiolo, Nancy Gautier, and Neil Christie, The Transformation of the Roman World 9 (Leiden, 2000), 209–34.

[19] J. Dölger, 'Christliche Grundbesitzer und heidnische Landarbeiter. Ein Ausschnitt aus der religiösen Auseinandersetzung des vierten und fünften Jahrhunderts', *Antike und Christentum* 6 (1950), 313–19.

[20] Rita Lizzi, 'Ambrose's Contemporaries and the Christianization of Northern Italy', *Journal of Roman Studies* 80 (1990), 156–173; Humphries, *Communities of the Blessed*, 17, 186, 214–15.

[21] Carlo Ginzburg, *The Night Battles: Witchcraft and Agrarian Cults in the Sixteenth and Seventeenth Centuries*, trans. John and Anne Tedeschi (Baltimore, MD, 1992); *The Cheese and the Worms: The Cosmos of a Sixteenth-Century Miller*, trans. John and Anne Tedeschi (Baltimore, MD, 1982), esp. 20–21 and 58–61; *Ecstasies: Deciphering the Witches' Sabbath*, trans. Raymond Rosenthal (Chicago, IL, 2004), esp. 13–14 and 296–97.

[22] Hans Drijvers, 'The Persistence of Pagan Cults and Practices in Christian Syria', in *East of Byzantium: Syria and Armenia in the Formative Period*, ed. Nina G. Garsoïan et al. (Washington, DC, 1982), 33–43, esp. 38.

[23] Frank R. Trombley, *Hellenic Religion and Christianization, c. 370–529*, Religions in the Graeco-Roman World 115 (2 vols., Leiden, 1993–94), i, 43, 171, and 314.

aspects of goddess lore is suggested by how much tenth and eleventh-century Islamic authors still knew about the cultic honors goddesses traditionally received.[24] In greater Syria, self-chastisement and self-mutilation became part of Shi'ite ideology of martyrdom and redemption. Today public processions commemorating the murder in 680 at Karbala of Husayn ibn Ali (Mohammed's grandson) feature pilgrims who bloody themselves with chains and swords in a ceremony of grief. The aim is to move people to tears, salvific tears in that those who weep for Husayn are believed to gain pardon for their own sins. Shi'ite historical theology and the prompt construction of a pilgrimage shrine at Karbala document early commemoration of Husayn's martyrdom, but because the Ummayids and Abbasids frequently suppressed the public rituals, and because the first Shi'ites left few historical records, it is unclear exactly when this mourning began to incorporate flagellant rites: face slapping and rhythmic chest beating are attested as ancient practices in the earliest extant sources, from around the millennium, but the bloodiest use of chains and swords in the current rituals is described with a vocabulary not found in Arabic sources prior to the nineteenth century.[25]

When and where does ascetical self-flagellation first appear in Christianity? Although the 'black legend' of early monastic culture cavalierly assumes that this practice must have been early,[26] it has not actually been found in paleo-monastic or early Byzantine monastic literature. The *terminus ante quem* is its presence in eleventh-century Italian eremitical circles, where, as will be seen below, Peter Damian (d. 1073)[27] presents it as an ancient tradition, one 'by no means recently invented by modern ingenuity',[28] and

---

[24] Tamara Green, 'The Presence of the Goddess in Harran', in *Cybele, Attis and Related Cults*, 87–100, esp. 97–100.

[25] Mahmoud Ayoub, *Redemptive Suffering in Islam: A Study of the Devotional Aspects of 'Ashura' in Twelver Shi'ism* (The Hague, 1978), 141–59 and 181–91; Yitzhak Nakash, 'An Attempt to Trace the Origin of the Rituals of "Āshūrā"', *Die Welt des Islams* 33 (1993), 161–181 (suggests that Shi'ite flagellation might have been influenced by late medieval Latin Christianity!); James A. Bill and John Alden Williams, *Roman Catholics and Shi'i Muslims: Prayer, Passion, and Politics* (Chapel Hill, NC, 2002), 72–73; Yitzhak Nakash, *The Shi'is of Iraq* (Princeton, NJ, 2nd edn, 2003), 141–62; Heinz Halm, *Shi'ism*, trans. Janet Watson and Marian Hill (New York, NY, 2nd edn, 2004), 48 and 138–41; Ali J. Hussain, 'The Mourning of History and the History of Mourning: The Evolution of Ritual Commemoration of the Battle of Karbala', *Comparative Studies of South Asia, Africa, and the Near East* 25 (2005), 78–88.

[26] For example, Stephen Tomkins, *A Short History of Christianity* (Grand Rapids, MI, 2005), 54: 'There were now hundreds of thousands of monks and nuns throughout the deserts and countryside of Christendom.... They tied weights to their necks and groins, lived in trees or tombs and whipped themselves and each other.'

[27] For a revision of the traditional obit of 1072, see John Howe, 'Did St. Peter Damian Die in 1073? A New Perspective on His Final Days', *Analecta Bollandiana* 128 (2010), 67–86.

[28] Peter Damian, *Epist. 56, Die Briefe des Petrus Damiani*, ed. Kurt Reindel, MGH Briefe der deutschen Kaiserzeit 4(1–4) (4 vols., Munich, 1983–93), ii, 155 [trans. Owen J. Blum, with the

discusses or mentions it in sixteen different works.[29] Peter was responding to shocked contemporaries who considered it a novelty,[30] a line of argument that would be taken up again by Reformation and early modern critics who assert that it did not antedate Peter Damian.[31] Defenders of the practice's ancient orthodoxy, however, have identified its antecedents in the Bible,[32] in the spirituality of martyrdom,[33] in Irish penitential discipline,[34] in other

assistance of Irven M. Resnick on vols. 5 and 6), *The Letters of Peter Damian*, The Fathers of the Church Medieval Continuation 1–3 and 5–7 (6 vols., Washington, DC, 1989–2005), ii, 362 [volume references refer to series volume number].

[29] The total of sixteen works is a figure taken from Leclercq, *Saint Pierre Damien ermite et homme d'Église* (Rome, 1960), 100.

[30] These critics are known through Peter's letters of rebuttal, especially *Epist*. 44, 45, 56, and 161, *Die Briefe des Petrus Damiani*, ii, 7–33; ii, 34–39, ii, 153–61, and iv, 135–44 [trans. Blum, ii, 221–43, 2:244–49, ii, 361–68, and vi, 131–41].

[31] Patrick Vandermeersch, *La chair de la passion: Une histoire de foi: La flagellation* (Paris, 2002), 137–86, esp. 178 and 186; 'Self Flagellation in the Early Modern Era', in *The Sense of Suffering: Constructions of Physical Pain in Early Modern Culture*, ed. Jan Frans van Dijkhuizen and Karl A.E. Enenkel (Leiden, 2009), 253–265, esp. 254.

[32] Theologians of asceticism from the High Middle Ages onward ingeniously argued that Jesus Christ is the supreme example of voluntary flagellation since, as God, He controlled his own fate and yet chose to allow Himself to be scourged. Moreover, in the Vulgate, Paul, when speaking of 'chastising his body' (I Cor. 9:27), employs the same word, 'castigare', that Benedict and others would use to designate whipping. For early versions of such arguments, see Peter Damian, *Epist*. 44 and 56, ed. Reindel, ii, 22–23 and 155–157 [trans. Blum, ii, 233 and ii, 362–64].

[33] Peter Damian, *Epist*. 56, *Die Briefe des Petrus Damiani*, ii,157 [trans. Blum, ii, 364]. This emphasis on martyrdom is contextualized in Kennerly Merritt Woody, 'Damiani and the Radicals', PhD dissertation (Columbia University, 1966), 49–50.

[34] The Irish tradition is complex. Irish penitential and canonical sources that were written in Latin do not mention any form of ascetical flagellation: see Ludwig Bieler, *The Irish Penitentials*, Scriptores Latini Hiberniae 5 (Dublin, 1963), *passim*, where the beating of a monastic exploiter provides the only possible exception (85). 'Blows' do appear in the sources written in Old Irish, whose language appears to be early but whose textual witnesses date from the end of the Middle Ages. On this, see D.A. Binchy, 'The Old Irish Penitential' and 'The Old Irish Table of Commutations', translations published as appendices to Bieler, *The Irish Penitentials*, 258–283. These Old Irish sources do specify beating, whipping, and other disciplinary actions – sometimes required and sometimes optional – but they are not self-inflicted. John T. McNeill and Helena M. Gamer, *Medieval Handbooks of Penance: A Translation of the Principal Libri Poenitentiales and Selections from Related Documents* (New York, NY, 1938), 33 and 423, argue, not too convincingly, for a possible exception in the 'Customs of Tallaght' because of the requirement that a penitent wash his hands afterwards. Arguments based on linguistic details can be tricky to pursue; Rob Meens, 'The Historiography of Early Medieval Penance', in *A New History of Penance*, ed. Abigail Firey (Leiden, 2008), 73–95, esp. 94–5, warns that the editions in this field are still far from definitive.

penitential disciplines,[35] and in ecclesiastical legal discipline.[36] The case for a long mainstream tradition of voluntary ascetical flagellation has been most influentially argued by Louis Gougaud and Jean Leclercq, who attempted to document it in the lives of early medieval saints.[37]

Yet a more critical analysis of their dossier – ten examples in all – reveals major problems. Eight instances involve early saints attested in late sources, in hagiographies written only after the practice had already become widespread in Italy.[38] Only two of the examples cited by Gougaud and

---

[35] Some penitentials require flogging as a penance. See, for example, the early medieval Spanish penitentials in *Paenitentialia Hispaniae*, ed. Francis Bezler, *CCSL* 156A (Turnhout, 1998), 11, 35–36, 42(2x), 54, 64, 65, and 66(2x); or the Old Irish sources utilizing blows signaled in note 34 above. A possible bridge between legal penalty and ascetical practice could be the substitution of flagellation for canonical penances, as discussed in Hermann Josef Schmitz, *Die Bußbücher und die Bußdisciplin der Kirche* and *Die Bußbücher und das kanonische Bußverfahren* (2 vols., Mainz, 1883 and Düsseldorf, 1898), i, 150–2, but Schmitz sees substitutionary flagellation as a development of the tenth century or later, citing Peter Damian as his earliest example. One could push back this chronology. For example, 'blows' might be an optional penance in some Old Irish cases (see note 34 above) and are a possible 'redemption' for canonical penance in the *De Ecclesiasticis Disciplinis* composed by Regino of Prüm *c.* 906: *Reginonis Abbatis Prumiensis Libri Duo de Synodalibus Causis*, ed. F.G.A. Wasserschleben (Leipzig, 1849; repr. Graz, 1964), 389–92. These passages that would be reiterated *c.* 1015 by Burchard of Worms in his *Decretum* (references in *PL* 132, cols. 369–70).
     Yet this sort of substitutionary flagellation was so unusual that Cyrille Vogel passes over it quickly in his 'Composition légale et commutations dans le système de la pénitence tarifiée', *Revue du droit canonique* 8 and 9 (1958 and 1959), 289–318 and 1–38, esp. at 9–14 [repr. with same pagination in *En rémission des péchés: Recherches sur les systèmes pénitentiels dans l'Eglise latine*, ed. Alexandre Faivre, Variorum Collected Studies Series 450 (Aldershot, 1994)], and omits it entirely in the sections on commutations in *Les 'Libri Paenitentiales'*, Typologie des sources du moyen âge occidental 27 (Turnhout, 1978). Ludger Körntgen, *Studien zu den Quellen der frühmittelalterlichen Bußbücher*, Quellen und Forschungen zum Recht im Mittelalter 7 (Sigmaringen, 1993), 57–59, 157–62, and 167, offers a good discussion of substitutionary penance but finds little connection between institutional disciplinary penalties and penitential discipline.
[36] Traditional Western legal systems, following more ancient practices, include whipping as a possible penalty for certain criminals in certain cases. This is true in ecclesiastical as well as secular law. In Western rules for religious, including the *Regula Benedicti*, whipping is sometimes the recommended punishment for recalcitrant monks and canons. For examples, see Vogel, *La discipline pénitentielle en Gaule des origines à la fin du VIIe siècle* (Paris, 1952), 143; and Michael S. Driscoll, *Alcuin et la pénitence à l'époque carolingienne*, Liturgiewissenschaftliche Quellen und Forschungen 81 (Münster, 1999), 76–77.
[37] Gougaud, 'Discipline', 184–5; and Leclercq, 'La flagellazione volontaria nella tradizione spirituale dell'Occidente', in *Il Movimento dei Disciplinati*, 73–83 [repr. as 'Saint Pierre Damien et la flagellation volontaire', in his *Témoins de la spiritualité occidental*, Tradition et spiritualité 5 (Paris, 1965), 112–25]. Their conclusions are accepted, for example, in Giles Constable, *Attitudes toward Self-Inflicted Suffering in the Middle Ages*, Stephen J. Brademas Sr. Lecture 9 (Brookline, MA, 1982), 16 [repr.with same pagination in *Culture and Spirituality in Medieval Europe*, Collected Studies Series 541 (Aldershot, 1996)].
[38] The asceticisms of Kentigern (d. *c.* 603) and William of Gellone (d. *c.* 812) are known from legendary materials written in the twelfth century or later. The reference for Kentigern

Leclercq are drawn from actual early medieval hagiographical texts. One is from the early ninth-century life of Bavo (fl. seventh century), but its statement that Bavo would 'chastise himself with laceration of the body' is imprecise about the form of asceticism involved and may be nothing more than general ascetical color (compare I Cor 9.27).[39] The other is from the life

comes from the life by John Capgrave (d. 1464), the end product of a complicated literary tradition analyzed in Alan MacQuarrie, 'The Career of Saint Kentigern of Glasgow: *Vitae, Lectiones*, and Glimpses of Fact', *Innes Review* 37 (1986), 3–24; that for William of Gellone (d. 812), from 1120–1130, as seen in Rombaut Van Doren, 'Guiglielmo, monaco a Gellone', *Bibliotheca Sanctorum* (14 vols., Rome, 1961–70 and 1988), vii, 467–470. The example from the *miracles* of Virgil of Salzburg (d. 784) postdates 1181: see *Miracula Virgilii* (*BHL* 8682) xiii, ed. Wilhelm Wattenbach, *MGH SS* 11, 92. The *vitae* of Guido of Pomposa (d. 1046) and Theobaldus of Provence (d. 1066) were written by Italians in the later eleventh century and witness flagellation's new eleventh-century vogue, not any earlier mainstream tradition. Guido of Pomposa (d. 1046) is described as a flagellant in the *Vita Guidonis Abbatis* (*BHL* 8876) ii. In *AASS*, Martii iii, 914, a text which alludes to eyewitnesses but has a number of strange lacunae; the *Vita Mathildis* by Donizo (fl. 1115) [ed. Ludwig Bethmann, *MGH SS* 12, 348–409 at 373–74] says Guido threatened to flagellate his nude body in front of the Marian altar unless Mathilda's father Boniface reformed his conduct and undertook penance. On these sources, see Pio Laghi, 'S. Guido, abbate di Pomposa', *Analecta Pomposiana* 3 (1967), 9–25. Theobaldus of Provence (d. 1066) practiced voluntary flagellation according to the *Vita Theobaldi* (*BHL* 8031 and 8032), probably originally written in northern Italy by Abbot Peter of Vangadizza between 1066 and 1068 [*AASS*, Junii v, 594]; and Luc d'Achery and Jean Mabillon, *Acta Sanctorum Ordinis Sancti Benedicti* [hereafter ASOSB] (6 vols. in 9, Paris, 1668–1701), vi. 2, 163–75 (which contains additional Pauline justifications). On the dating, see John Howe, 'Greek Influence on the Eleventh-Century Western Revival of Hermitism', 2 vols., PhD dissertation (University of California at Los Angeles, 1979), i, 345 and ii, 573–4. Poppo of Stavelot (d. 1048) is perhaps an early example, but, given that his biography may have been written as late as 1064, its claim that Poppo flagellated himself to counteract temptations of the flesh, found in a laundry list of alleged secret ascetical practices, might represent either Poppo's actual practice or the new popularity of self-flagellation in the 1060s. See Abbot Everhelmus of Hautmont (d. 1069) and Onulfus of Saint-Pierre of Ghent, *Vita Popponis* (*BHL* 6898), c.28, ed. Wilhelm Wattenbach, *MGH SS* 11, 291–319 at 312. Everhelmus was Poppo's nephew who commissioned and contributed to the work; Onulfus was the actual author. On Poppo's connections with Italy, see Reindel, *Briefe*, ii, 35.

Even later is the case of Walter of Pontoise (d. 1093), who, according to a posthumous *vita* and *gesta* from Marmoutier, is said to have had himself scourged by his monks in chapter. See *Vita Galterii* (*BHL* 8796) c. iii.13 and 15, *AASS* Aprilis i, 762; *De Rebus Gestis in Majori Monasterio Saeculo XI*, ASOSB, vi.2, 392.

[39] *Vita Bavonis* (*BHL* 1049) c. 5, ed. B. Krusch, *MGH SS Rerum Merovingicarum* iv, 538: 'Ardebat autem nimium animo ... ut semet ipsum magna laceratione corporis cum alacritate castigaret mentis.' This language could refer to voluntary flagellation, but, since the same chapter goes on to describe Bavo as 'multis tribulationibus se ipsum macerans', it appears to refer to extreme asceticism in general. Note that whereas other ascetical practices such as tears, fasts, and vigils are specifically itemized, flagellation is not. The particular penitential context at issue here is described in Anne-Marie Helvétius, 'Les modèles de sainteté dans les monastères de l'espace belge du VIIIe au Xe siècle', *RB* 103 (1993), 51–67 at 61. On the cult of Bavo, see Adriaan Verhulst, 'Saint Bavon et les origines de Gand', in *Saint Géry et la christianisation dans la nord de la Gaule, Ve–IXe siècles: Actes du colloque de Cambrai, 5–7 octobre 1984*, ed. Michel Rouche [= *Revue du Nord* 269 (1986), 455–70].

of Pardulfus (d. 737?), written *c.* 750, describing a ritual where the saint was beaten by a whip-wielding disciple, a practice perhaps closer to the floggings prescribed for transgressions in Benedict's *Rule* than to an on-going tradition of self-inflicted ascetical penance.[40] Thus, although Gougaud and Leclercq argued that voluntary self-flagellation gradually developed out of early medieval penitential spirituality, these learned scholars never successfully documented that transition, nor have more recent researchers, despite the multitude of studies on Late Antiquity, the body, and asceticism stimulated by the work of Peter Brown,[41] No new examples are produced by searching for variations of *flagell** and *disciplin** in the electronic version of Migne's *Patrologia Latina*.[42]

Self-flagellation as an orthodox ascetical tradition in the Latin West certainly does appear in eleventh-century northern Italy. Here, as noted above, it was practiced and promoted by Peter Damian, the influential dean of the emerging college of cardinals.[43] Why mid eleventh-century Italy? Some

---

[40] *Vita Pardulfi* (*BHL* 6459/6460), c. 7, ed. Bruno Krusch and Wilhelm Levison, *MGH SS Rerum Merovingicarum* 7, 28. The apparently unprecedented nature of this anomalous example is also noted in Arnold Angenendt, 'Sühne durch Blut', *Frühmittelalterliche Studien* 18 (1984), 437–476 at 462. However, a similar later practice, not cited by Gougaud and Leclercq, is ascribed to Benedict of Aniane (d. 821) by his disciple Ardo, in his *vita* (*BHL* 1096), c. 6, *AASS*, Februarii ii, 616.

[41] For an overview, see the bibliography cited in Teresa M. Shaw, *The Burden of the Flesh: Fasting and Sexuality in Early Christianity* (Minneapolis, MN, 1998), 255–84. A thorough analysis of Italian Christian asceticism, which does not identify instances of self-flagellation, is offered in Georg Jenal, *Italia Ascetica atque Monastica: Das Asketen- und Mönchtum in Italien von den Anfängen bis zur Zeit der Langobarden (ca. 150/250–604),* Monographien zur Geschichte des Mittelalters 39 (Stuttgart, 1995).

[42] The *Patrologia Latina Database*, produced by Chadwick-Healey Inc., offers hundreds of occurrences of the words, especially of versions of the Vulgate's phrase '*flagella Dei*', but virtually nothing that pertains to this ascetical practice prior to the eleventh century. The one apparent exception is Augustine's *De Magnificentiis B. Hieronymi* (*BHL* 3867), in versions from *PL* 22 and 33, which claims that Jerome 'Ter in die continue carnem diris verberibus flagellavit, ita ut ex ejus corpore rivuli sanguinis effluebant.' However, patrologists today do not accept this work as an authentic part of Augustine's canon: see *Clavis Patrum Latinorum*, ed. Eligius Dekkers and Aemilius Gaar, CCSL (3rd edn, Turnhout, 1995), 136 (#367). In fact, the manuscript tradition does not appear to antedate the thirteenth century: see, for example, Manfried Oberleitner, *Die handschriftliche Überlieferung der Werke des hl. Augustinus. I: Italien: Werkverzeichnis*, Österreichische Akademie der Wissenschaften phil.-hist. Klasse, Sitzungsberichte 263 (Vienna, 1969), 355–57; and Rainer Kurz, *Die handschriftliche Überlieferung der Werke des hl. Augustinus, V: Bundesrepublik Deutschlands und West Berlin: Werkverzeichnis*, Österreichische Akademie der Wissenschaften phil.-hist. Klasse, Sitzungsberichte 306 (Vienna, 1976), 357–61.

[43] Peter Damian received a relatively contemporary *vita* from his junior colleague John of Lodi, the *Vita Petri Damiani* (*BHL* 6706), ed. Stefan Freund, *Studien zur literarischen Wirksamkeit des Petrus Damiani*, MGH Studien und Texte 13 (Hannover, 1995). Peter's major writings on voluntary flagellation are cited below. The standard biographies of Peter Damian are Owen J. Blum, *St. Peter Damian: His Teaching on the Spiritual Life*, Catholic University of America Studies in Mediaeval History n.s. 10 (Washington, DC, 1947), 1–36;

scholars have linked the origins of the practice to Peter's own personal psychological idiosyncrasies that allegedly resulted from an unhappy childhood and from a guilt-ridden rejection of the whole physical world.[44] Others have situated it in a wider context, considering it a symptom of a more general ascetical and mystical enthusiasm that characterized eleventh-century reformers.[45] Others see it even more broadly as the product of an increasingly influential legal mentality which not only would have extended the use of scourging, a traditional penalty, but also would have allowed for its use as substitutiary penance.[46] All of these hypotheses assume that voluntary religious flagellation originated out of Western Christianity's elite social, religious, and intellectual traditions. But does a close reading of the sources support this?

Perhaps scholars should pay more attention to the non-elite holy men who surrounded Peter Damian. Peter never claimed to have invented voluntary self-flagellation, which he assumed was an ancient tradition. So when did he first encounter it? Peter's *vita*, written between 1076 and 1084 by his disciple John of Lodi (d. 1106), does not include self-imposed flagellation in the long list of private ascetic practices it attributes to Peter before he became a hermit, and it gives an ambiguous possible reference in a list of the ascetic practices of the young hermit. It offers a clear description of ascetical flagellation only in a final inventory of spiritual practices presented in conjunction with events that occurred after 1060.[47] The practice is also not emphasized in Peter

Fridolin Dressler, *Petrus Damiani: Leben und Werk*, Studia Anselmiana 34 (Rome, 1954); and Leclercq, *Saint Pierre Damien*. Materials for a more precise narrative are systematically assembled in Giovanni Lucchesi, *Per una Vita di San Pier Damiani: Componenti cronologiche e topografiche* (Cesena, 1972) [rpt. with the same pagination from *San Pier Damiano nel IX Centenario della morte (1072–1972)* (4 vols., Cesena, 1972–78), i, 13–179 and ii, 13–160. See also Stefan Freund, 'Forschungen zu Petrus Damiani, 1983–95', *Revue Mabillon*, n.s. 7 (1996), 289–9; Ugo Facchini, *Pier Damiani, un padre del secondo millennio: Bibliografia 1007–2007* (Rome, 2007), esp. 388–89; and William D. McCready, *Odiosa Sanctitas: St. Peter Damian. Simony, and Reform*, Studies and Texts 177 (Toronto, 2012).

[44] Henry Osborn Taylor, *The Mediaeval Mind: A History of the Development of Thought and Emotion in the Middle Ages* (2 vols., 4th edn, Cambridge, MA, 1938), i, 263–70. The fragmentary surviving data on Peter's childhood is assembled in Lester K. Little, 'The Personal Development of Peter Damian', in *Order and Innovation in the Middle Ages: Essays in Honor of Joseph R. Strayer*, ed. William C. Jordan, Bruce McNab, and Teofilo F. Ruiz (Princeton, 1976), 317–341 and 523–528, esp. at 336–40.

[45] Albert Dresdner, *Kultur- und Sittengeschichte der italienischen Geistlichkeit im 10. und 11. Jahrhundert* (Breslau, 1890), 291–300; Woody, 'Damiani and the Radicals', 49–50.

[46] A gradual development of self-imposed flagellation out of canonical punishments that included scourging is postulated by Gougaud, 'La discipline', 175–80, and Leclercq, 'La flagellazione', 74–75.

[47] John of Lodi, *Vita* cc. 2, 5, and 18, ed. Freund, 209–12, 218–23, and 251–53. The second list of Peter Damian's spiritual exercises has him excel in 'disciplinae videlicet metanoeis', but, given the ambiguity of the term 'disciplina' and the qualifier linking it specifically to 'prostrations', the meaning is more likely ascetical discipline in general. The final list, which

Damian's most important early writing, begun around 1042, his hagiographical life of Romuald (d. *c.* 1027), a nobleman from Ravenna who came to be
honored as the founder of the Camaldolese order. Peter wrote the *Vita Romualdi*
at the urging of Romuald's well-informed followers at San Vincenzo di Petra
Pertusa (near Furlo, in the province of Pesaro in the Marches). He turned
this biography into a virtual encyclopedia of early Camaldolese ascetical
practices, adding for good measure many parallels from the lives of the desert
fathers. If voluntary flagellation had been part of Romuald's spirituality, Peter
ought to have described it. But he only mentions self-imposed flagellation
in a somewhat ambiguous passage at the very end, and only in a marginally
monastic context: 'But why do I speak of monks', asks Peter, 'when even
their humble servants [*famuli*], those who are the guardians of their flocks,
fast, keep silence, and perform acts of discipline in turn among themselves
[*disciplinas inter se invicem facerent*] and for any idle words whatsoever
require penance [*penitentiam flagitarent*]'. While one might speculate that
the practices of the swineherds reflect those of their masters, Peter does not
state this. Thus the first people reported as 'doing the discipline' are not the
aristocratic Romuald and his friends but their servants.[48]

Voluntary flagellation makes its first prominent appearance in a letter Peter
Damian wrote *c.* 1055 x 1057 to a Florentine hermit named Teuzo. Peter
disapproved of Teuzo's urban life and celebrity status. To instill humility,
he wrote to him about the heroic deeds of real hermits in real deserts. In his
letter, he offers as examples of asceticism his colleagues at the priory of Fonte
Avellana, discussing in great detail one Dominic Loricatus (d. 1060) and
itemizing his extensive self-scourging. He preemptively defends the practice,
apparently concerned that Teuzo would not recognize self-flagellation as
standard spirituality.[49] Here Peter was right. He soon had to send another
justification to scandalized monks of Florence,[50] and then an additional one
to an otherwise unidentified 'Petrus Cerebrosus' ('Peter the Hothead').[51]

Since Peter Damian approvingly cites voluntary self-flagellation in this
Florentine correspondence, some scholars have assumed that he introduced it
into his monastery of Fonte Avellana.[52] Yet a reverse scenario is more likely.
Fonte Avellana, a foundation located on the border between Umbria and the

includes clear detailed descriptions of the practice, concerns Peter's life after he had returned
from his mission to Milan, i.e. after 1059–60. On the date of the *vita*, see Freund, *Studien zur
literarischen Wirksamkeit des Petrus Damiani*, 180–82.

[48] *Vita Romualdi* (*BHL* 7324) c. 64, ed. Giovanni Tabacco, FSI 94 (Rome, 1957), 105. That
Peter Damian failed to associate voluntary flagellation with Romuald was noted by Dressler,
Petrus Damiani, 25, but not by subsequent scholars.
[49] *Epist.* 44, *Die Briefe des Petrus Damiani*, ii, 7–33 [trans. Blum, ii, 221–43].
[50] *Epist.* 45, *Die Briefe des Petrus Damiani*, ii, 34–39 [trans. Blum, ii, 244–9].
[51] *Epist.* 56, *Die Briefe des Petrus Damiani*, ii, 153–61 [trans. Blum, ii, 361–8].
[52] For example, Bailly, 'Flagellants', *DSAM*, v, 392. See also note 31 above.

Marches, already existed at the end of the tenth century.[53] Its traditions were established long before Peter Damian arrived there around 1035. Since there is little evidence for the practice of self-administered flagellation in his early career and writings, it is more likely he learned about it from Fonte Avellana's hermits than vice versa. Perhaps he learned it from Dominic Loricatus specifically;[54] certainly he found Dominic its preeminent practitioner, since he observes that 'by the example of this old man in taking the discipline, the custom spread in our area, so that not only men but even noble women eagerly took up this form of purgatory'.[55]

Who was Dominic Loricatus? According to Peter Damian's letters, which include a revision of a *vita Dominici* he had written right after Dominic's death, he was a priest who had renounced his ministry because his ordination had been procured through simony. The cured goatskin that was his parents' bribe indicates their poverty. Dominic became a hermit at Luceoli, on the Umbrian border north of Fonte Avellana, where for many years he was associated with a group of strict hermits who lived in eighteen cells under the direction of an otherwise unknown 'John of Montefeltro'. He became

[53] Pietro Palazzini, 'Fonte Avellana e Pier Damiani', in *Le Abbazie delle Marche: Storia e arte. Atti del Convegno internazionale, Macerate, 3–5 aprile 1990*, ed. Emma Simi Varanelli, Pubblicazioni della Facoltà di Lettere e Filosofia dell'Università di Macerata 66, Sezione 'Atti di Convegni' 20 (Cesena, 1992), 127–158, esp. 129–31.

[54] The only detailed reference by Peter Damian to voluntary flagellation which the scholarly tradition suggests might antedate his friendship with Dominic is in a hard-to-date description of the spirituality of Fonte Avellana, found in *Epist.* 18, *Die Briefe des Petrus Damiani*, i, 168–79, esp. 173 and 175 [trans. Blum, 1:159–170, esp. 164 and 166]. Although Reindel dates this letter to the years 1045 x *c.* 1050, Woody, 'Damiani and the Radicals', 197, claims that there is no basis for the traditional *c.* 1050 *terminus ante quem*. He redates the letter to *c.* 1058 because it refers to Peter's ill-health and contains an inventory of possessions which Fonte Avellana acquired while Peter was prior, a listing suggesting that the audience might have included the priors left behind when he became cardinal. These circumstantial arguments fit both with the long sequence of monastic developments described and with the presence in this letter of passages that parallel others in letters that Peter certainly wrote in the later 1050s. For example, the material on the discipline is paralleled in *Epist.* 50 (from 1057), *Die Briefe des Petrus Damiani*, ii, 77–131, esp. 94 and 98 [trans. Blum, 289–334, esp. 301 and 304]. In *Epist.* 50, a section on Dominic does appear and the optional character of the discipline in hermit life is emphasized (ed. *Die Briefe des Petrus Damiani*, ii, 100–3 and 109 [trans. Blum, ii, 307–08 and 312]). Yet even Reindel's early dating for *Epist.* 18 would not necessarily destroy the case for Dominic as Peter Damian's original model for flagellation, since even in this letter Peter does not claim to have created the customs described but only to 'rejoice if I am able to keep up with the footsteps of my brethren' (*Die Briefe des Petrus Damiani*, i, 170 [trans. Blum, i, 161]).

[55] *Epist.* 66 and 109, *Die Briefe des Petrus Damiani*, ii, 247–79, esp. 275–76 and iii, 200–23, esp. 215 [trans. Blum, iii, 40–69, esp. 64–66 and iv, 207–26, esp. 219]. This use of 'purgatory' as a noun, in a letter written 1059–1060, fits poorly with the theory that 'purgatory' crystalized as a substantive notion only in the late twelfth century, as argued in Jacques Le Goff, *The Birth of Purgatory*, trans. Arthur Goldhammer (Chicago, IL, 1984), 54–76.

famous for his extensive practice of 'the discipline', using a new type of whip made of leather thongs rather than bundles of twigs. He acquired his epithet 'Loricatus' by wearing a penitential cuirass (a *lorica*). Peter claims that Dominic, with the permission of his prior, had asked to be received at Fonte Avellana in order to be guided by Peter, who would accept him only as 'a true philosopher and teacher', 'my father and master', 'my lord and teacher'.[56]

But Dominic was not unique. Holy men of non-elite backgrounds and limited literacy abounded in Umbria, Romagna, and the Marches. Among them was Romuald's original master, Marinus, a simple untaught wandering holy man whose spirituality involved singing different psalms under different trees.[57] There was also the extraordinarily dirty Brother Martin Storacus who joined Peter Damian's congregation at Fonte Avellana; he was so illiterate that he scarcely knew fifty psalms, but his distinctions included not only a notable lack of hygiene but also his ankle-length hair and two pet snakes.[58] Iron-clad hermits, quite untaught, wandered around.[59] When Peter Damian abandoned his original career as a teacher in the secular schools, he was convinced that God had chosen to convert the world not with 'philosophers and orators' but with 'fishermen ... simple and unlettered [*idiotas*]'.[60]

Peter considered Dominic to be one of these: a holy man 'whose speech, to be sure, is the vernacular, but whose life is truly accomplished and elegant'.[61] His distinction lay in the intensity and frequency of his ascetic practice.

For many years he wore an iron corselet next to his flesh and engaged in implacable combat with the evil spirits. This eager fighter was always ready for battle, armed not only in spirit, but also bodily went forth against the enemy lines. He was so accustomed to this way of life that hardly a day passed without chanting two psalters, beating his naked body with both hands armed with scourges ...[62]

Dominic's ultimate record was thirteen psalters.[63] As long as he and the other hermits were not too self-destructive, Peter Damian accepted and, indeed,

---

[56] *Epist.* 109 final section (= *BHL* 2239), *Die Briefe des Petrus Damiani*, iii, 207–23, esp. 207–10 and 216 [trans. Blum, 4:211–26, esp. 214 and 216].

[57] *Vita Romualdi* c.4, ed. Tabacco, 20–21.

[58] *Epist.* 44, *Die Briefe des Petrus Damiani*, ii, 15–17 [trans. Blum, ii, 226–28].

[59] *Epist.* 56 and 109, *Die Briefe des Petrus Damiani*, ii, 159–60 and iii, 218–19 [trans. Blum, ii, 366–7 and iv, 222–23].

[60] *Epist.* 117, *Die Briefe des Petrus Damiani*, iii, 316–29, esp. 319 [trans. Blum, iv, 318–31, esp. 321]. Peter Damian's contrasts between foolish wisdom and holy fools are treated in Irven M. Resnick, 'Attitudes towards Philosophy and Dialectic during the Gregorian Reform', *The Journal of Religious History* 16 (1990), 115–125 at 116–17.

[61] *Epist* 109, *Die Briefe des Petrus Damiani*, iii, 210 [trans. Blum, 4, 214]. See also *Epist.* 44, *Die Briefe des Petrus Damiani*, ii, 21 [trans. Blum, ii, 231].

[62] *Epist.* 44, and 109, *Die Briefe des Petrus Damiani*, ii, 21 and iii, 211 [trans. Blum, ii, 232 and iv, 215].

[63] The highest of several record totals that Peter Damian lists in various letters over the years –

admired their ascetic practices.[64] Although the use of the discipline at Fonte Avellana was officially 'voluntary', it became institutionalized to a considerable extent.[65] It shows up in descriptions of some other exemplary monks. Leo of Preggio, an '*indoctus*' who knew only the psalms, took up the practice at an advanced age after he had become a hermit there.[66] The future Bishop Rudolph of Gubbio (d. 1064), who entered around 1057 and acquired the practice, was a different case, a man whose family had controlled a *castello* and had given him the education proper to a bishop.[67] Rudolph, like Peter Damian and Peter's other upper-class spiritual disciples, demonstrates the spread of the practice among people of higher social rank.

For self-flagellation to become accepted it needed an impeccably orthodox justification. When Peter Damian described Dominic to his elite correspondents, he framed Dominic's penitential practices with the exalted purpose of imitation of Christ: 'Our Dominic ... bore in his body the stigmata of Jesus, and fixed the sign of the cross not only on his forehead, but printed it on every part of his body.'[68]

The aftermath of Peter Damian's initiative is suggestive. Although he promoted flagellation among pious laymen and laywomen,[69] the surviving

---

twelve psalters and a start on a thirteenth – appears in *Epist.* 66, *Die Briefe des Petrus Damiani* ii, 275–76 [trans. Blum, iii, 64–66].

[64] References in Blum, *St. Peter Damian*, 118–19. Penances which Peter Damian would not recommend were still tolerated so long as they did not cause too much harm: see, for example, *Epist.* 44, *Die Briefe des Petrus Damiani*, ii, 15 [trans. Blum, ii, 227], where Peter disapproves of Martin Storacus' long hair.

[65] *Epist.* 133, *Die Briefe des Petrus Damiani*, iii, 452–54, esp. 454 [trans. Blum v, 73–5, esp. 74] emphasizes the voluntary nature of flagellant devotion, but on its place in the monastic routine, both as an individual practice and in chapter, see *Epist.* 18, 50, and 168, *Die Briefe des Petrus Damiani*, i, 173 and 175, ii, 94 and 98, and iv, 238–39 [trans. Blum, i, 164 and 166; ii, 301 and 304; and vi, 236–37].

[66] *Epist.* 44, 117, and 153, *Die Briefe des Petrus Damiani*, ii, 20–21, iii, 325–26, and iv, 63–65 [trans. Blum, ii, 230–31, iv, 327–28, and vi, 67–68].

[67] *Epist.* 109 (*BHL* 7282), *Die Briefe des Petrus Damiani*, iii, 202–7 [trans. Blum, iv, 207–11]. On Rudolf's social context, see Elisabetta Archetti Giampaolini, *Aristocrazia e Chiese nella Marca del Centro-Nord tra IX e XI secolo*, Università degli Studi di Macerata Pubblicazioni della Facoltà di Lettere e Filosofia 38 (Rome, 1987), 233–35, 250, and 272.

[68] *Epist.* 109, *Die Briefe des Petrus Damiani*, iii, 222 [trans. Blum v, 226]. The christomimetic reference is also invoked in *Epist.* 161, *Die Briefe des Petrus Damiani*, iv, 137 and 140–44 [trans. Blum vi, 131–41, esp. 134 and 137–41]. The word 'stigmata' here refers to 'marks' in general without its later technical meaning. Peter Damian's more general emphasis on Christ is described in Giandomenico Gordini, 'La santità nelle biografie e nei sermoni damianei', in *Fonte Avellana nella Società dei secoli XI e XII: Atti del II Convegno del Centro di Studi Avellaniti* (Urbino, 1978), 366–394, esp. 377–82. However, in the course of his many writings justifying ascetical flagellation, Peter Damian invokes many more holy precedents, described in Blum, *St. Peter Damian*, 114–20; Leclercq, *Saint Pierre Damien*, 100–5; and Vandermeersch, *La chair de la passion*, 48–52.

[69] *Epist.* 66 and 109, *Die Briefe des Petrus Damiani*, ii, 276 and iii, 215 [trans. Blum iii, 66 and iv, 219].

documentation appears to suggest that he advanced it most successfully in the context of monastic chapter meetings at which monks confessed their faults and received lashes as public penance. At Montecassino, despite resistance to this practice, he won the field at least temporarily;[70] the canons at Velletri also adopted a similar practice.[71] Other communities ultimately followed, including the Carthusians, the Praemonstratensians, and even the Cluniacs.[72]

In a recent work, Patrick Vandermeersch argues that this form of flagellation, undertaken in a community setting and generally administered by another monk rather than by oneself, constitutes a penitential form of the discipline that differs in its psychological dynamics from self-flagellation. He goes on to claim that individual ascetic self-flagellation would not be accepted in orthodox circles until the Reformation period, when it would be popularized by Jesuits.[73] But Vandermeersch's attempt to treat individual monastic self-flagellation as a Reformation innovation fails when confronted with hagiographical testimonies concerning earlier ascetic saints from Dominic Loricatus forward.[74] Indeed, Peter Damian himself tended quite explicitly to distinguish public flagellation in chapter from private self-flagellation.[75]

In northern Italy, this form of ascetic spirituality made another dramatic advance two centuries later when lay flagellant confraternities began to whip themselves in public processions. Although Peter Damian had promoted ascetic self-flagellation among monks and canons and in pious prayer circles, it was still a relatively private affair. It is noteworthy that the first public ceremonies occurred right in Peter Damian's old neighborhood, so strikingly that it became a commonplace that 'Umbria gave birth … to the flagellants'.[76] Around the beginning of the thirteenth century, the 'order of

---

[70] *Epist.* 161, *Die Briefe des Petrus Damiani*, iv, 135–44 [trans. Blum, vii, 131–41]; Leo Marsicanus, *Chronica Monasterii Cassinensis* III.20, ed. Hartmut Hoffmann, in *MGH SS* 34, 386–387. Although the relevant section of the chronicle is not found in the surviving autograph of Leo's first recension, Hoffmann attributes it to him ('Einleitung', in MGH *SS* 34, xxi and xxvii).

[71] *Epist.* 168, *Die Briefe des Petrus Damiani*, iv, 238–74, esp. 239 [trans. Blum, vii, 236–43, esp. 236].

[72] Henri De Lubac, *Exégèse médiévale: Les quatres sens de l'Écriture* (4 vols., Paris, 1959–64), i, 53–54 [Engl. trans. Mark Sebanc and E.M. Macierowski, *Medieval Exegesis* (3 vols., Grand Rapids, MI, 1998–2009), I, 22; Bailly, 'Flagellants', *DSAM*, v, 393–95].

[73] Vandermeersch, *La chair de la passion*, 111–14 and 16–65; Vandermeersch, 'Self Flagellation', 257–59.

[74] For some examples of the practice, see Vauchez, *La sainteté en occident*, 406, 422, and 433 [trans. Birrell, 351, 365, and 374]; Michael Goodich, *Vita Perfecta: The Ideal of Sainthood in the Thirteenth Century*, Monographien zur Geschichte des Mittelalters 25 (Stuttgart, 1982), 114 and 132.

[75] An example is Peter Damian extolling the practices of Bishop Rudolph of Gubbio to Pope Alexander II in *Epist.* 109, *Die Briefe des Petrus Damiani*, iii, 205 [trans. Blum iv, 210].

[76] George Holmes, *Florence, Rome and the Origins of the Renaissance* (Oxford, 1988), 69.

penitents' at Perugia included voluntary flagellation among its practices.[77] Then in Lent of 1260, a penitent visionary, Ranieri Fasani (d. before March 1282), warned the Perugians to take 'the discipline' in public procession or face divine retribution.[78] Soon flagellant penitent groups were appearing in many parts of Italy and came in several prominent waves: one in 1260 associated with Ranieri; another around 1300 associated with processions of white clad 'Bianchi'; and a third associated with the penitential activities in response to the Black Death.[79] Although penitential processions in which self-flagellation played a prominent role spread throughout Italy, and then into the regions of modern France, Austria, Germany, and even Poland, the vast majority of flagellant confraternities until the end of the Middle Ages were still found in northern Italy.[80]

What inspired Ranieri and his first followers? The Camaldolese had houses in the Perugian area, but nothing connects them to the new enthusiasm.[81] Nor is there any obvious direct link to Franciscan devotions.[82] Flagellant processions

---

[77] Gilles Gérard Meersseman, *Dossier de l'Ordre de la Pénitence au XIIIe siècle*, Spicilegium Friburgense 7 (Freiburg, 1961), 49. For the ultimate institutionalization of the Perugian penitents, see Anna Belardinelli, 'L' "Ordo Poenitentium" à Perugia', in *I Frati penitenti di San Francesco nella Società del due e trecento: Atti del 2° Convegno di Studi Francescani, Roma, 12–13–14 ottobre 1976*, ed. Mariano d'Alatri (Rome, 1977), 309–324.

[78] 'Lezenda de fra Rainero Faxano' (*BHL* 7082d), ed. Emilio Ardu, 'Frater Raynerius Faxanus de Perusio', in *Il movimento dei disciplinati nel settimo centenario dal suo inizio (Perugia 1260): Convegno internazionale: Perugia 25–28 Settembre 1960*, Appendice al Bollettino 9 (Perugia, 1962), 93–98. This fourteenth-century *vita* emphasizes that the novelty was not the discipline itself but its public practice ('Dominus Jhesus ... vult quod disciplina, quam occulte diu fecisti, publice fiat in populis', 96). Ranieri Fasani is now known not only by his relatively late *life*, but also by contemporary Perugian documents discussed in Ardu, 'Frater Raynerius Faxanus de Perusio', 87–89. Research is summarized in G. Cecchini, 'Flagellanti', in *Dizionario degli Istituti di Perfezione* (10 vols., Rome, 1974–1980), iv, 60–72. For the date of origin of the devotion, see Ardu, 'Frater Raynerius Faxanus de Perusio', 368–70.

[79] Étienne Delaruelle, 'Les grandes processions de pénitents de 1349 et 1399', in *Il movimento dei disciplinati*, 109–45; Daniel E. Bornstein, *The Bianchi of 1399: Popular Devotion in Medieval Italy* (Ithaca, NY, 1993); Catherine Vincent, 'Discipline du corps et de l'esprit chez les flagellants au Moyen Age', *Revue Historique* 615 (2000), 593–614; Andreas Dehmer, '*Passio* und *Compassio*: Geissellungsrituale italienischer Bussbruderschaften im späten Mittelalter', in *The Sense of Suffering*, ed. van Dijkhuizen and Enenkel, 221–251.

[80] Pier Lorenzo Meloni, 'Topografia, diffusione e aspetti delle confraternite dei disciplinati', in *Risultati e prospettive della ricerca sul movimento dei disciplinati: Convegno Internazionale di Studio, Perugia, 5–7 dicembre 1969* (Perugia, 1972), 15–98 at 20 and 40[A]. The pervasiveness of ascetical self-flagellation at the end of the Middle Ages is illuminated in G. Alberigo, 'Contributi alla storia delle confraternite dei disciplinati e della spiritualità laicale nei secc. XV e XVI', in *Movimento dei disciplinati*, 156–252.

[81] Gary Dickson, 'The Flagellants of 1260 and the Crusades', *JMH* 15 (1989), 229–30 [repr. with same pagination in his *Religious Enthusiasm in the Medieval West: Revivals, Crusades, Saints*, Collected Studies Series 695 (Aldershot, 2000)].

[82] Roots in itinerant Franciscan traditions are often presumed: see for examples, Cyrilla Barr, 'The *Laude Francescane* and the Disciplinati of Thirteenth-Century Umbria and Tuscany: A Critical Study of the Cortona Codex 91', 2 vols., PhD dissertation (The Catholic University

do not seem to have evolved directly out of any existing clerically organized confraternities or penitential groups,[83] and they appear to have been popular rather than learned in origin. Although the evidence for the practices found in northern Italian chronicles tells us more about the devotion's spread than about its beginnings, the two which do discuss its roots suggest an eremitical, rather than clerical or monastic, milieu. The *Annals of Genoa*, which were continuously updated during this period, offer two conflicting origin stories that were circulating at the time:

it is said that the flagellation [which started in Perugia] had its beginning from a certain boy who was still in his earliest years [a conflation of flagellant enthusiasm with the children's crusade stories current at this time]; others say it was started by a certain hermit who was living a strict life in these regions in a certain cave, who is said to have claimed that he heard through an angelic message that if the men of Perugia would not do penance their city would be destroyed [a version congruent with the legend of Ranieri, but with more elaborate eremitical background].[84]

A chronicler from Asti, Guglielmo Ventura, claims that 'in the year 1260 … hermits going out from their "tombs", came to the cities, preaching the Gospel, just as Jonas the Prophet had preached in Nineveh, and they were saying: "Do penance since the Kingdom of Heaven will be at hand." Then I saw men, from the greatest to the least, hitting their shoulders vigorously with whips …'[85]

If Ranieri the Penitent had lived as a hermit or had eremitical contacts,

---

of America, 1965), esp. i, 5–7; also Réginald Grégoire, 'Movimenti di spiritualitá in Umbria nei secoli XIII e XIV', in *La Spiritualitá di S. Chiara da Montefalco; Atti del I Convegno di studio, Montefalco, 8–10 agosto 1985*, ed. Silvestro Nessi (Montefalco, 1986), 37–68, esp. 43–48. However, the early emergence of penitential groups in the area suggests a preexisting movement ultimately absorbed by rather than created by Franciscan spirituality: see Belardinelli, 'L'"*Ordo Poenitentium*" à Perugia', esp. 309–14. Moreover, when the Franciscans did arrive in Perugia, they do not seem to have immediately taken the lead in organizing flagellant groups: Meersseman, 'Disciplinati e penitenti nel duecento,' in *Movimento dei Disciplinati*, 43–72 at 60–61, has demonstrated that the Perugian flagellant confraternity dedicated to Francis and connected to the Franciscan church appears only shortly before 1280, even later than its Dominican counterpart.

[83] Raffaello Morghen, 'Ranieri Fasani e il movimento dei disciplinati del 1260', in *Movimento dei Disciplinati*, 29–42 at 32, separates the 'moto spontaneo di popolo' from the confraternities that were part of contemporary lay spirituality; Meersseman, 'Disciplinati e penitenti nel duecento', *Movimento dei Disciplinati*, 49–50, contrasts them with organized groups of penitents. Barr, 'The *Laude Francescane*', demonstrates that the songs associated with flagellant processions are simple vernacular hymns very different from the learned musical traditions of the era.

[84] *Annali Genovesi di Caffaro e de'suoi continuatori*, new ed. Luigi Tommaso Belgrano and Cesare Imperiale di Sant'Angelo, FSI 11–14 (4 vols., Rome, 1890–1926), iv, 39–40.

[85] *Memoriale Guilielmi Venturae Civis Astiensis*, ed. Ludovico Antonio Muratori, *RIS* (28 vols., Milan 1723–38, 1751), xi, 153. For additional chronicle references concerning the spread of the devotion, see Arsenio Frugoni, 'Sui flagellanti del 1260', *Bullettino dell'Istituto Storico Italiano per il Medio Evo e Archivio Muratori*, 75 (1963), 211–37.

it would not be too surprising. Around this time, sixty-eight hermits and recluses in the neighborhood of Perugia were listed as receiving public stipends.[86] Others may have been off the dole or outside the *contado*. Indeed, back in Peter Damian's day, Rodulfus Glaber had observed with regard to a hermit in monastic dress that 'Italy abounds with such men'.[87] It does not seem unreasonable to think that the same substratum of popular religiosity that was influential in the mid-eleventh century remained a dynamic force in the mid-thirteenth.

Exotic forms of ascetic practice needed orthodox justifications, and the lay flagellant processions unsurprisingly promoted their practice as a form of christomimesis. To emphasize this connection, some pilgrimages lasted thirty-three days, inspired by the number of years Christ lived on earth.[88] The phrase 'in memory of the Passion of Christ' appears in the statutes of virtually all flagellant companies, and many met on both Fridays and Sundays, emphasizing respectively the Passion and the Resurrection.[89] The art and ritual of flagellant confraternities consciously and consistently invoked the suffering of Christ.[90]

This present study is not concerned with the later history of religious flagellation, upon which much has already been written.[91] Suffice it note that in Spain, Counter-Reformation flagellant confraternities developed out of those established by the Genoese in Valencia in the late fifteenth century,

---

[86] Mario Sensi, 'Incarcerate e recluse in Umbria nei secoli XIII e XIV: Un bizzocaggio centro-italiano', in *Il movimento religioso femminile in Umbria nei secoli XIII–XIV: Atti del Convegno Internazionale di Studio nell'ambito delle celebrazioni per l'VIII centenario della nascita di S. Francesco d'Assisi, Città di Castello, 27–28–29 ottobre 1982*, ed. Roberto Rusconi, Quaderni del 'Centro per il Collegamento degli Studi Medievali e Umanistici nell'Università di Perugia' 12 (Florence, 1984), 105–6.

[87] Rodulfus Glaber, *Historiarum Libri Quinque* III iv, ed. John France, OMT (Oxford, 1989), 102–3.

[88] Franz-Reiner Erkens, 'Busse in Zeiten des Scharzen Todes: Die Züge der Geissler,' *Zeitschrift für Historische Forschung* 26 (1999), 485–513, esp. 495.

[89] John Henderson, 'The Flagellant Movement and Flagellant Confraternities in Central Italy, 1260–1400', *Studies in Church History* 15 (1978), 147–160 at 157.

[90] See, for example, Kathleen Giles Arthur, 'Cult Objects and Artistic Patronage of the Fourteenth-Century Flagellant Confraternity of Gesù Pellegrino', in *Christianity and the Renaissance: Image and Religious Imagination in the Quattrocento*, ed. Timothy Verdon and John Henderson (Syracuse, NY, 1990), 336–359; E.K. Lee, 'Art and Ritual Drama of the Flagellant Confraternities in 13th–15th Century Italy', *Arte medievale* 4 (2005), 69–82.

[91] On the Early Modern period, see Cyrille Vogel, 'Le pélerinage pénitentiel', in *Pellegrinaggi e culto dei santi in Europa fino alla Iᵃ crociata, 8–11 ottobre 1961*, Convegni del Centro di Studi sulla Spiritualità Medievale 4 (Todi, 1963), 113–53, esp. 151 [repr. with same pagination in *En rémission des péchés*]; Robert A. Schneider, 'Mortification on Parade: Penitential Processions in Sixteenth- and Seventeenth-Century France', *Renaissance and Reformation,* n.s. 10 (1986), 123–146; and Ann W. Ramsey, 'Flagellation and the French Counter-Reformation: Asceticism, Social Discipline, and the Evolution of a Penitential Culture', in *Asceticism*, ed. Vincent L. Wimbush and Richard Valantasis (New York, 1995), 576–87.

while in France the pioneers are associated with another Genoese confraternity headquartered in Marseille.[92] First the Franciscans and then the Jesuits promoted the practice, both as a form of private devotion and as part of the spirituality of public confraternities. In Spain Easter week processions continued to be central, with the emphasis on christomimesis sometimes enhanced by additional rites connected to the feasts of the Discovery of the True Cross and the Exaltation of the True Cross.[93] The passion of Christ remains at the core of related devotions in the New World such as the shrine cult of El Señor de Wank'a near Cusco and the much-discussed 'Penitentes' of New Mexico.[94]

What can be concluded from this survey of the history of ascetic self-flagellation in the greater Roman and post-Roman world? Its ancient geography, insofar as this is known, centers on Syria and Italy, closely paralleling the core geography of analogous traditions in the medieval world. Is this a coincidence? Connections are difficult to document because there were no incentives for sophisticated monotheistic religions to acknowledge any borrowings from their polytheistic predecessors, and any cultural transmissions would naturally have been reinterpreted as traditional orthodox practices. Thus, in the Syrian Near East, self-flagellation emerges in Shi'ite Islam linked to mourning for Mohammed's grandson Husayn; in the Latin West, it reappears as a way to imitate Christ, first among Italian hermits, and later among lay flagellant companies.

Grass-roots origins for ascetic customs were actually quite common. Ancient religious practices involving sacred places, healing shrines, votive offerings, sacrifices, vigils, pilgrimages, penitential processions, and other rituals all found niches in later world religions. Perhaps self-flagellation should be added to this list. That possibility has broader consequences for the study of the medieval Latin Church. Scholars have traditionally interpreted medieval spirituality using a top-down model that envisions active clergy molding a more passive laity. The practice of self-flagellation, according to André Vauchez, was the 'most telling example' of this dynamic. In more recent decades, however, there has been much more emphasis on 'circularity', which, as Carlo Ginzberg describes it, postulates that 'between the culture of the dominant classes and that of the subordinate classes, there existed, in preindustrial Europe, a circular relationship composed of

---

[92] Vandermeersch, *La chair de la passion*, 116 and 225; Vandermeersch, 'Self Flagellation', 256.
[93] Vandermeersch, *La chair de la passion*, 17–19 and 218; Vandermeersch, 'Self Flagellation', 257–61.
[94] Michael J. Sallnow, 'Pilgrimage and Cultural Fracture in the Andes', in *Contesting the Sacred: The Anthropology of Christian Pilgrimage*, ed. John Eade and Michael J. Sallnow (London, 1991), 137–153, esp. 144–45; J. Manuel Espinosa, 'The Origin of the Penitentes of New Mexico: Separating Fact from Fiction', *The Catholic Historical Review* 79 (1993), 454–77, esp. 456–59.

reciprocal influences which traveled from low to high as well as from high to low.'[95] This perspective is being increasingly, and productively, applied to penitential practices in general.[96] If popular traditions and humble hermits did, in fact, play a role in the acceptance of self-flagellation as an approved ascetic practice, as the available evidence seems to suggest, then the model of religious development that emphasizes 'circularity' between high and low classes and cultures in the flow of practices and sensibilities receives further support.

[95] Ginzburg, 'Preface to the English Edition', in *The Cheese and the Worms*, xii.
[96] See Abigail Firey, 'Introduction', and Rob Meens, 'Historiography of Early Medieval Penance', in *New History of Penance*, ed. Firey, 1–18, esp. at 4, and 73–95, esp. at 88 and 92–93.

3

The Material and the Visual: Objects and Memories in the *Historia ecclesiastica* of Orderic Vitalis*

Daniel Roach

A string of recent publications has sought to emphasize the relationship between the memorial and the material in the medieval period.[1] Drawing

* This is a revised version of the paper presented at the Haskins Society conference in November 2011. I would like to thank the organizers for the opportunity to present and discuss my research and the participants of the conference for their warm and encouraging comments and questions. I am also extremely grateful to Simon Barton, Julia Crick, Leonie Hicks, Simon John and Amy Remensnyder, for kindly providing feedback on subsequent revised drafts of this paper, and to Laura Gathagan and Bill North for their careful editorial work. Earlier versions were presented at the conference of the Society for the Medieval Mediterranean in Southampton, and at the Medieval Studies Seminar at the University of Exeter, both held in 2011. This research was made possible by the generous financial assistance of the Arts and Humanities Research Council.

[1] See, for example, Amy G. Remensnyder, *Remembering Kings Past: Monastic Foundation Legends in Medieval Southern France* (Ithaca, NY, and London, 1995); Amy G. Remensnyder, 'Legendary Treasure at Conques: Reliquaries and Imaginative Memory', *Speculum* 71:4 (1996), 884–906; Philippe Buc, 'Conversion of Objects: Suger of Saint-Denis and Meinwerk of Paderborn', *Viator* 28 (1997), 99–143; Elisabeth van Houts, *Memory and Gender in Medieval Europe, 900–1200* (Basingstoke, 1999), 93–120; Chris Wickham, 'Topographies of Power: Introduction', in *Topographies of Power*, 1–8; Matthew Innes, 'Keeping it in the Family: Women and Aristocratic Memory, 700–1200', in *Medieval Memories: Men, Women and the Past, 700–1300*, ed. Elisabeth van Houts (Harlow, 2001), 17–35; Megan Cassidy-Welch, *Monastic Spaces and their Meanings: Thirteenth-Century English Cistercian Monasteries* (Turnhout, 2001); Mary Carruthers, *The Book of Memory. A Study of Memory in Medieval Culture* (Cambridge, 2nd edn, 2008); Nicholas Orme, 'The Commemoration of Places in Medieval England', in *Memory and Commemoration in Medieval England: Proceedings of the 2008 Harlaxton Symposium*, ed. Caroline M. Barron and Clive Burgess (Donington, 2010), 271–91; Caroline Walker Bynum, *Christian Materiality: An Essay on Religion in Late Medieval Europe* (New York, 2011). On relics, Patrick J. Geary, *Furta Sacra: Thefts of Relics in the Central Middle Ages* (Princeton, 1978), and Peter Brown, *The Cult of the Saints: Its Rise and Function in Latin Christianity* (London, 1981), remain seminal. More generally, see Alexandra Walsham, 'Introduction: Relics and Remains', in *Relics and Remains*, ed. Alexandra Walsham, Past and Present supplement 5 (Oxford, 2010), 9–36. For a recent and stimulating treatment of the relationship between the memorial and the material, see Andrew Jones, *Memory and Material Culture* (Cambridge, 2007).

on this body of work, this essay explores the dynamic relationship between physical objects and the memories associated with them in the *Historia ecclesiastica* of Orderic Vitalis. Written between *c.*1114 and 1141 at the abbey of St Evroul, located in the pays d'Ouche on the southern frontier of Normandy, the massive thirteen-book *Historia* is widely recognized by scholars as being one of the most important sources for the history of the Anglo-Norman world and beyond, and it has been the subject of much study since the 1950s.[2] Whilst it is a well known fact that Orderic drew on a large number of written and oral sources in the writing of the *Historia*,[3] the exact role played by the material and the visual in this process has remained largely unexplored. The focus of this article is thus on the way in which these objects are described in Orderic's narrative and the implications of this for our understanding of the *Historia* as a whole.

Leonie Hicks has recently highlighted 'the visibility of the past' as an important theme in historical writing, observing that for the Anglo-Norman chroniclers, 'monuments and places ... were much more than just illustra-

---

[2] *The Ecclesiastical History of Orderic Vitalis*, ed. and trans. Marjorie Chibnall (6 vols., Oxford, 1968–80) [cited hereafter as OV with volume and page]. There is a vast literature on Orderic, but the best starting point remains Marjorie Chibnall, *The World of Orderic Vitalis* (Woodbridge, 1984). Many of Chibnall's essays on Orderic can also be found in Marjorie Chibnall, *Piety, Power and History in Medieval England and Normandy* (Aldershot, 2000). Four other major studies of Orderic exist: Hans Wolter, *Ordericus Vitalis: Ein Beitrag zur Kluniazensischen Geschichtsschreibung* (Wiesbaden, 1955); Roger Ray, 'The Monastic Historiography of Ordericus Vitalis', PhD dissertation (Duke University, 1967); James Bickford Smith, 'Orderic Vitalis and Norman Society: *c.*1035–1087', DPhil thesis (University of Oxford, 2006); Amanda Jane Hingst, *The Written World: Past and Place in the Work of Orderic Vitalis* (Notre Dame, IN, 2009). To these should be added the lengthy article by Leopold Delisle, 'Notice sur Orderic Vital', in *Orderici Vitalis ecclesiasticae historiae libri tredecim*, ed. August Le Prévost, (5 vols., Paris, 1838–55), v, i–cvi. For further assessments of Orderic in the wider context of Norman historiography, see Antonia Gransden, *Historical Writing in England c.550–c.1307* (London, 1974), 136–65; Jean Blacker, *The Faces of Time: Portrayal of the Past in Old French and Latin Historical Narrative of the Anglo-Norman Regnum* (Austin, TX, 1994), 10–17, 66–77, 153–60; Leah Shopkow, *History and Community: Norman Historical Writing in the Eleventh and Twelfth Centuries* (Washington, D.C., 1997), 46–47, 96–105, 160–63, 201–6, 231–34; Emily Albu, *The Normans in their Histories: Propaganda, Myth and Subversion* (Woodbridge, 2001), 180–213; Elisabeth van Houts, 'Historical Writing', in *A Companion to the Anglo-Norman World* ed. Christopher Harper-Bill and Elisabeth van Houts (Woodbridge, 2003), 103–21. On the scope of the *Historia*, see Lucien Musset, 'L'horizon géographique, moral et intellectuel d'Orderic Vital, historien Anglo-normand', in *La Chronique et l'histoire au moyen âge. Colloque des 24 et 25 Mai 1982*, ed. Daniel Poirion (Paris, 1984), 101–22.

[3] On Orderic's sources, see Chibnall's introductory notes, OV i, 48–100. For more on his oral sources, see Elisabeth van Houts' stimulating recent article on the subject, 'Conversations Amongst Monks and Nuns, 1000–1200', in *Understanding Monastic Practices of Oral Communication: Western Europe, Tenth–Thirteenth Centuries*, ed. Steven Vanderputten (Turnhout, 2011), 267–91. I am extremely grateful to the author for providing me with a copy of this piece of her work.

tions to or diversions from the main narrative: they were in fact integral to the message they were trying to convey'.[4] Thus, while such descriptive passages are interesting in and of themselves, the purpose of examining this largely unexplored aspect of Orderic's *magnum opus* here is to highlight the textual richness of the *Historia* and to demonstrate what these passages reveal about the purpose of its narrative. For the more one studies Orderic, the more one notices passages concerning objects that he claimed were still in existence at the time of his writing, such as a memorial roll, a Psalter, and a stone arch.[5] Although these written references are all that now survives of this material world, such passages reveal that numerous stories in the *Historia* were derived from the memories associated with it. They were not an incidental part of the narrative but were integral to it, for they brought the past into the present, deliberately reminding the monks of Orderic's monastery of St Evroul about their illustrious history. Indeed, their incorporation into the narrative reveals an author who was extremely conscious of these physical reminders of the past. It is the specific nature of their contribution to the *Historia*'s narrative which is of primary interest here, for when compared with the histories of two of his most prominent contemporaries, William of Malmesbury and Henry of Huntingdon, it can be seen that Orderic used such passages in a way that was very different from theirs.[6]

The presence of physical objects in the *Historia* has not been wholly overlooked in the scholarship. Indeed, some tantalizing observations have been made on the subject. Thus, in commenting on Orderic's information for the history of the monastery of St Evroul during the Merovingian period, Marjorie Chibnall observed that it was, in part, made up of 'the stories that gathered around ruined buildings, healing springs and place-names, to explain their origins', and later in the same article she commented on the information collected by Orderic 'from the traditions of old men and the surviving remains of the earlier church'.[7] More recently, Elisabeth van Houts has examined two passages in the *Historia*: the first being Orderic's comment that the bones of those who had died at the Battle of Stamford Bridge in September 1066 were still there for all to see, and the second, his description of the great Psalter at St Evroul.[8] In his doctoral study of Orderic, James Bickford Smith noted the passing down of communal memory at St

---

4   Leonie V. Hicks, 'Coming and Going: The Use of Outdoor Space in Norman and Anglo-Norman Chronicles', *ANS* 32 (2009), 40–56 at 49. See also Leonie V. Hicks, 'Magnificent Entrances and Undignified Exits: Chronicling the Symbolism of Castle Space in Normandy', *JMH* 35 (2009), 52–69.
5   See below, pp. xxx–xxx, xxx–xxx.
6   For these, see below pp. xxx–xxx.
7   Marjorie Chibnall, 'The Merovingian Monastery of St. Evroul in the Light of Conflicting Traditions', *Studies in Church History* 8 (1971), 31–40 at 31, 37.
8   van Houts, *Memory and Gender*, 100, 114–15. On the bones at Stamford Bridge and the Psalter, see OV ii, 42, 168.

Evroul from the older monks to the novices of Orderic's own day, something which ensured that '"past" affairs remained current'. Significantly, he also observed 'the casual shifting between past and present in Orderic's narrative' in his description of Abbot Osbern's memorial roll.[9] Finally, the relationship between the concepts of past and place in Orderic's work, particularly as they concerned the monastery of St Evroul, has been emphasized by Amanda Jane Hingst.[10]

We begin our study with Orderic's treatment of the memorial roll at St Evroul. This is an important passage that repays careful attention and it will be quoted in full here. For in relating how Osbern, the third abbot of St Evroul (1061–66),[11] governed the abbey, Orderic wrote the following in Book III of the *Historia*:[12]

He instituted a general anniversary to be held thus each year on 26 June for the fathers and mothers, brothers and sisters of all the monks of the monastery of Ouche. On a very long roll indeed the names of all the brothers are written, when they enter into the order at God's summons; then, the names of their fathers and mothers and brothers and sisters are written down. This roll is kept upon the altar all year, and the diligent remembrance of those inscribed on it is carried out in sight of God … The anniversary about which we speak is thus celebrated on 26 June. Both evening and morning, all the bells ring for a long time for the office of the dead; the roll of the dead is untied and laid out on the altar, and prayer is faithfully offered to God, first for the dead, and then for living relatives and benefactors and for all the faithful … The church of Ouche has assiduously observed this anniversary just as abbot Osbern instituted it up to the present day, and has eagerly passed it on to the monks of Noyon-sur-Andelle and St Georges-de-Boscherville, and its other followers.

The move from past to present tense here is striking, as Bickford Smith noted. But so, too, is the description of the memorial roll itself. Orderic speaks of it in the present tense as though it was still in existence at the time of writing,

---

[9]   Bickford Smith, 'Orderic Vitalis', 43–44. I am extremely grateful to the author for providing me with a copy of his work. For the passage on the memorial roll see OV ii, 116.

[10] Hingst, *The Written World*, see especially Ch.1, entitled 'Ouche: The History of a Place', 1–18.

[11] For more on Osbern and the other abbots of St Evroul, see Véronique Gazeau, *Normannia Monastica* (2 vols., Caen, 2007), ii, 273–91.

[12] 'Hic constituit generale anniuersarium fieri singulis annis vi° kal. Iulii sic pro patribus et matribus, pro fratribus et sororibus omnium monachorum Uticensis coenobii. In rotulo quidem longissimo omnium fratrum dum uocante Deo ad ordinem ueniunt nomina scribuntur; deinde patrum et matrum eorum fratrumque ac sororum uocabula subscribuntur. Qui rotulus penes aram toto anno seruatur, et sedula commemoratio inscriptorum in conspectu Domini agitur … Anniuersarium uero de quo loquimur; vi° kal. Iulii sic agitur. Omnia signa sero et mane ad officium defunctorum diu pulsantur, uolumen mortuorum super altare dissolutum palam expanditur; et deprecatio prius pro defunctis postea pro uiuis parentibus et benefactoribus cunctisque fidelibus Deo fideliter offertur.… Hoc sicut Osbernus abbas constituit, Uticensis aecclesia usque in hodiernum diem uigilanter custodit; et Nogionensibus atque Balcherensibus aliisque sequacibus suis ardenter tradidit.' OV ii, 114–16.

and that the liturgy was still current. The phrase 'usque in hodiernum diem' stresses the enduring nature of this anniversary, indicating that the names of those who had died in the first fifty years or so of St Evroul's history in the second half of the eleventh century continued to be remembered at the time of Orderic's writing in the first half of the twelfth century. Finally, the reference to Noyon-sur-Andelle and St Georges-de-Boscherville, monasteries closely connected to St Evroul, shows the close relationship that the monks of Ouche enjoyed with the houses with which they were connected in prayer.[13] The former was a dependent priory of St Evroul, while the latter was inhabited by monks from St Evroul; both are mentioned a number of times in the *Historia*.[14]

This account of Abbot Osbern's memorial roll raises a number of important questions concerning the ways in which Orderic wrote about material objects elsewhere in the *Historia*: how do they compare with this story? Are there any similarities in the textual construction of such passages? Most importantly of all, why were such stories included within the narrative? In order to begin answering these questions, this discussion will now turn to an examination of another passage in the *Historia*, again taken from Book III. Here Orderic relates how Robert II of Grandmesnil, one of the founders of St Evroul (who later became its second abbot),[15] having abandoned the world and taken the

---

[13] By 1130, the *liber memorialis* of St Evroul contained in all the names of about eighty houses of monks and nuns with which it was joined in prayer unions. This manuscript survives and is contained within the composite volume known as the chapter-book of St. Evroul (Paris, Bibliothèque Nationale, MS latin 10062). For an edited version of the text, see Jean Laporte, 'Tableau des services obituaires assurés par les abbayes de Saint-Evroul et de Jumièges', *Revue Mabillon* 46 (1956), 141–88. For more on the significance and extent of this network, see also OV i, 85–87. Much work has been done on *libri memoriales*; a good place to start is Véronique Gazeau, 'La mort des moines: sources textuelles et méthodologie (XIe-XIIe siècles), in *Inhumations et édifices religieux au Moyen Age entre Loire et Seine*, ed. Armelle Alduc-Le Bagousse (Caen, 2004), 13–21. See also *The Durham Liber Vitae and its Context*, ed. David Rollason et al. (Woodbridge, 2004). On the relationship between monks and their benefactors more generally, see *Religious and Laity in Western Europe, 1000–1400: Interaction, Negotiation, and Power*, ed. Emilia Jamroziak and Janet Burton (Turnhout, 2006).

[14] For further references to Noyon-sur-Andelle and St Georges-de-Boscherville see OV iv, 256; vi, 146–52, 234–36. A useful list of selected surviving sources and secondary literature on both of these houses can be found in Leonie V. Hicks, *Religious Life in Normandy, 1050–1300: Space, Gender and Social Pressure* (Woodbridge, 2007), 180, 184–85.

[15] As co-founders and benefactors of St Evroul, the Grandmesnil family appear throughout the *Historia ecclesiastica*. On Robert of Grandmesnil, see Gazeau, *Normannia Monastica*, ii, 275–76; for the Grandmesnil family more generally, see Barbara MacDonald Walker, 'The Grandmesnils: A Study in Norman Baronial Enterprise', PhD thesis (University of California Santa Barbara, 1968); Joseph Decaëns, 'Le patrimoine des Grentemesnil en Normandie, en Italie et en Angleterre aux XIe et XIIe siècles', in *Les Normands en Méditerranée: dans le sillage des Tancrède*, ed. Pierre Bouet and François Neveux (Caen, 1994), 123–40; Mark Hagger, 'Kinship and Identity in Eleventh-Century Normandy: The Case of Hugh de Grandmesnil, c.1040–1098', *JMH* 32 (2006), 212–30.

monastic habit at his foundation in 1050, managed to acquire the dowry lands of his mother, Hawise, for the monks of St Evroul.[16] And this was not all that he obtained for the monastery:[17]

By his mother's gift at that time he also acquired a great Psalter for the monks of Ouche, illuminated with an array of pictures, which, to this day, is regularly used when the choir of monks chant psalms to the praise of God. This is the book that Emma, the wife of the English king Æthelred, had given to her brother Robert, archbishop of Rouen; and William, the prelate's son, took it from his father's chamber, as happens in families, and gave it to his beloved wife Hawise, whom he sought to please in all things. The aforesaid man also acquired many other goods for his church and was pleasing to the brothers in procuring many ecclesiastical ornaments as well as necessary support.

A number of the features encountered in Orderic's description of Abbot Osbern's memorial roll are repeated here. The shift from past to present tense is particularly prominent, as Orderic notes what had been acquired and then moves on to a description of the Psalter itself. This time it is achieved by using the phrase 'usque hodie', a simpler version of that used to describe the usage of the memorial roll. Here, though, Orderic interestingly spends a great deal of time relating the illustrious history of the book and the circumstances surrounding its acquisition by the monks of St Evroul.[18] In order to do so he delves into the distant past, this time moving from the present into the pluperfect. Notably, the object in question is again described in the present tense, implying its continued existence at the time of Orderic's writing in the twelfth century. It is also significant that in the narrative the past memories associated with the Psalter follow immediately on from the description of the book itself. Indeed, it is tempting to suggest that there may have been a dynamic relationship between the memories and the object, that the memories of Robert II of Grandmesnil's faithful labours in the service of the monastery, as well as some details about the past owners of the Psalter were in a sense 'attached' to the book,[19] and were freshly recalled by the monks of St Evroul each time they opened it and chanted the psalms. In this way, the book provided them with a snapshot from the early history of St Evroul and

---

[16] OV ii, 40–42.

[17] 'Tunc etiam magnum psalterium uariis picturis decoratum dono matris suae Uticensibus contulit, quod usque hodie monachorum concio psalmodiis intenta frequenter ad laudem Dei reuoluit. Hoc uolumen Emma coniunx Edelredi regis Anglorum Rodberto Rotomagensium archiepiscopo fratri suo praesentauerat; et Willelmus eiusdem praesulis filius de camera patris sui familiariter sustulerat, dilectaeque suae coniugi Haduisae omnimodis placere uolens detulerat. Alia quoque multa bona praefatus uir aecclesiae suae adquisiuit; et tam in ornamentis aecclesiasticis quam in necessariis subsidiis procurandis fratribus acceptabilis fuit.' OV ii, 42.

[18] van Houts, *Memory and Gender*, 114–15; see also Buc, 'Conversion of Objects', 101.

[19] Geary, *Furta Sacra*, 5–9; Buc, 'Conversion of Objects', 100–1; van Houts, *Memory and Gender*, 93.

enabled Orderic to relate a story about one of the key characters from that period. It may even have been of extra significance to the monks given that Robert, having been forced into exile in 1061, remained in southern Italy for the rest of his life and never returned to St Evroul.[20] The Psalter may thus have stood in as a memorial to him, given the absence of a tomb in his honour within the church itself.[21]

The more one studies the *Historia*, the more one sees that such stories are actually woven into the very fabric of the narrative, appearing throughout all of its thirteen books. A word search conducted using the *Patrologia Latina* database[22] reveals that the phrase *usque hodie* is used fifty-two times in this *Historia*, with thirty-one of these instances appearing in books III to VI (seventeen in book III alone) where the narrative focusses heavily on the early history of St Evroul. Similarly, the phrase *usque in hodiernum diem* appears twenty-eight times, and *usque in hodiernam* once. A similar search of Henry of Huntingdon's *Historia Anglorum* reveals fifteen instances of the phrase *usque hodie* and one of *usque in hodiernum diem*. Henry mostly uses the phrase to refer to the physical mark left on the landscape of England by the Britons, Romans, and other peoples.[23] Only twice is it used in relation to the Normans, once in reference to the continued existence of the castle which William the Conqueror built at Ely when he besieged the island in 1071,[24] and a second time with regard to the preservation of the Domesday records in the treasury.[25] Similarly, William of Malmesbury's *Gesta Regum Anglorum* contains only two instances of *usque hodie*, both of which refer to the Saracen possession of much of Spain.[26] Besides these, there are a number of other references to the Roman and Saxon past,[27] including one to King Æthelred's grave, which, William informed his readers, survived 'up

---

[20] OV ii, 90–102; iv, 22–24.

[21] Interestingly, Walter Daniel's account of Ailred of Rievaulx's death described Ailred surrounded by his favourite objects, including a glossed Psalter among other things. For more on this see Cassidy-Welch, *Monastic Spaces*, 220–21.

[22] http://pld.chadwyck.co.uk

[23] Henry of Huntingdon, *Historia Anglorum*, ed. and trans. Diana Greenway (Oxford, 1996), 26, 30, 34, 58, 70 (twice), 162, 176, 192, 194, 328.

[24] Henry of Huntingdon, *Historia*, 396.

[25] Henry of Huntingdon, *Historia*, 400. For more on Henry of Huntingdon, see John Gillingham, 'Henry of Huntingdon and the Twelfth-Century Revival of the English Nation', in *Concepts of National Identity in the Middle Ages*, ed. Simon Forde, Lesley Johnson, and Alan V. Murray (Leeds, 1995), 75–101; and Diana Greenway, 'Authority, Convention and Observation in Henry of Huntingdon's *Historia Anglorum*', *ANS* 18 (1996), 105–15.

[26] William of Malmesbury, *GR*, i, 281, 645. For more on William of Malmesbury, see Rodney M. Thomson, *William of Malmesbury* (2nd edn, Woodbridge, 2003), and, most recently, Paul Antony Hayward, 'The Importance of Being Ambiguous: Innuendo and Legerdemain in William of Malmesbury's *Gesta Regum* and *Gesta Pontificum Anglorum*', *ANS* 33 (2011), 75–102.

[27] William of Malmesbury, *GR* i, 18, 26, 40.

to the present day' (*usque diem hodiernum*).[28] Orderic's two most prominent contemporaries thus used this phrase to refer to the visibility of the past in general and to those people who had conquered and settled in England in the centuries before they wrote. In stark contrast to these, Orderic almost always employed the phrase to serve a much more specific purpose in the narrative of the *Historia ecclesiastica*, namely to point back to the monastic past of his own house, St Evroul. Much more similar in form is Symeon of Durham's *Libellus de Exordio atque Procursu istius hoc est Dunhelmensis Ecclesie*, where the phrase *usque hodie* and its cognates are repeatedly and, indeed, exclusively used to refer to objects which underline the significance of the church of Durham and the illustrious nature of its history.[29] These include the undecayed right arm of King Oswald, the stone cross built at Lindisfarne (which, though damaged when the Vikings sacked Lindisfarne, was later repaired and moved to the cemetery of the church of Durham), and, perhaps most spectacularly of all, the Lindisfarne Gospels.[30] This comparison thus indicates that Orderic's *Historia* is much closer in form to monastic chronicles such as Symeon's *Libellus* and suggests that it should, in future, be studied alongside such texts as these rather than in relation to the other, more general, works of Anglo-Norman history written in the first half of the twelfth century, from which it differs so dramatically.[31]

In Orderic's *Historia ecclesiastica* the phrase *usque hodie* is used to describe the continued existence of numerous churches that were connected to St Evroul. These include the abbeys of Bec and St Martin of Troarn;[32] the church of St Peter in Neufmarché which was granted to the monks of St Evroul by Hugh of Grandmesnil and continued to be occupied by the monks of St Evroul up to the present;[33] the chapel of St Nicholas in Heundicourt in the Vexin which was built there by a monk of St Evroul at the request of its fourth abbot, Mainer (1066–89);[34] and the church of St Mary at Maule

---

[28] William of Malmesbury, *GR* i, 75.

[29] There also seem to be similarities between Orderic's *Historia* and the Fenland chronicles, a subject which I hope to explore more in future. For more on the Fenland chronicles, see Jennifer Paxton, 'Textual Communities in the English Fenlands: A Lay Audience for Monastic Chronicles?', *ANS* 26 (2004), 123–37.

[30] Symeon of Durham, *Libellus de Exordio atque Procursu istius hoc est Dunhelmensis Ecclesie*, ed. and trans. David Rollason (Oxford, 2000), 22, 60, 68, 104, 108, 118–20, 126–28, 134–36, 206. For more on Symeon of Durham, see David Rollason, *Symeon of Durham: Historian of Durham and the North* (Stamford, 1998); on Anglo-Norman Durham more generally see *Anglo-Norman Durham, 1093–1193*, ed. David Rollason, Margaret Harvey and Michael Prestwich (Woodbridge, 1994).

[31] This misreading of the *Historia ecclesiastica* goes some way towards explaining why it has for so long been compared unfavourably with William of Malmesbury's *Gesta Regum Anglorum* in particular, for which see Gransden, *Historical Writing*, 136, 151–65.

[32] OV ii, 12, 22.

[33] OV ii, 130.

[34] OV ii, 150–52 (twice).

which was a dependent priory of St Evroul, donated to it by Peter of Maule.[35] Sometimes the phrase *usque hodie* simply refers to the presence of monks in these houses, namely that they still possessed active communities. In other instances, only a part of the building remained, and so it was these ruins that Orderic highlighted in order to connect the past with the present in the narrative. Thus, in recounting the life of St Evroul, he related how the saint took refuge in a monastery in a place that the locals called 'Deux Jumeaux' even in Orderic's own day, after a miracle that had once occurred there in which two twins were raised from the dead. What remained of the monastery itself was just as important: 'the old name for the village, taken from this event, still persists, and a great mass of stones from the foundations of the buildings and the ruined walls gives clear witness that there a house of men of great esteem once brought lustre to the region of Bayeux'.[36]

Similarly, in a much later part of the *Historia*, Orderic told how William of Évreux, who had previously established the chapel of St Martin at Noyon and populated it with monks from St Evroul, began in 1108 to build a great church there in honour of St Mary. But he died long before its completion and left no heir to continue the building project. Furthermore, in the years that followed, the region of Évreux became something of a war-zone as Henry I sought to assert his control over the area. As a result, Orderic related, the monastery at Noyon 'has remained unfinished to this day'.[37] Thus, in these two final instances it was the ruined or incomplete nature of the buildings themselves that acted as a continual reminder of their past history. Their inclusion in the *Historia* allowed the memories associated with them to live on in the text.[38]

The phrase also appears in passages that are unconnected with physical objects that record the on-going nature of memories of individuals. These include the story of Giroie's heroic stand against Herbert of Maine,[39] and a description of the prayers of the monks of St Evroul for another of the monastery's co-founders, Giroie's son, William Giroie; both of these kinds of remembrance are said to have continued up to the present.[40] Likewise,

---

[35] OV iii, 178.

[36] 'Antiquum ab euentu eidem uico nomen usque hodie perseuerat, et ingens congeries lapidum in fundamentis edificiorum et ruinis maceriarum euidens testimonium dat; quod magnae dignitatis hominum habitacio Baiocensum pagum illustrauerat.' OV iii, 268. See also Chibnall, 'The Merovingian Monastery of St. Evroul', 37.

[37] 'usque hodie imperfectum consistit', OV vi, 148.

[38] For more on the textual representation of monasteries see Julia M.H. Smith, '*Aedificatio sancti loci:* The Making of a Ninth-Century Holy Place', in *Topographies of Power*, 361–96.

[39] OV ii, 22.

[40] OV ii, 62. Like their kinsmen the Grandmesnil family, the Giroie appear throughout the *Historia ecclesiastica*. Two studies exist on the family: Jean-Marie Maillefer, 'Une famille aristocratique aux confins de la Normandie: Les Géré au XIe siècle', in *Autour du pouvoir ducal Normand Xe–XIIe siècles*, ed. Lucien Musset, Jean-Michel Bouvris, and Jean-Marie Maillefer,

the death of the first abbot of the monastery, Thierry (1050–57), was observed by the monks on 1 August each year, and his customs and teachings similarly continued to be preserved by them 'to this day'.[41] Interestingly, *usque hodie* is also twice used by Orderic to emphasize the loss of objects and prestige. Thus, Orderic describes the long-running power struggle between Abbot Osbern and Robert II of Grandmesnil over the abbacy of St Evroul in the early 1060s as an extremely difficult time for the monastery, during which some of the lands, churches, and tithes of its original endowment were stolen by knights connected to the Giroie family who were angered by what they perceived to be the unfair treatment of their kinsman, Robert. 'So, at that time, the church of Ouche lost many possessions which, to this day, it has by no means been able to regain', Orderic lamented.[42] Similarly, after Arnold of Échauffour, William Giroie's son, had been fatally poisoned by Mabel of Bellême sometime in the 1060s,[43] he used the phrase *usque hodie* to refer to the resultant decline of the Giroic family: 'With Arnold's death', he wrote, 'the noble family of Giroie was completely ruined; and to this day not one of their descendants has been quite able to regain the fortunes of his ancestors.'[44]

A number of examples suggest that memories concerning the history of St Evroul itself were also associated with buildings and other monuments on the grounds of the abbey and various features of the landscape, as well as with the smaller objects described at the outset of this paper. Two of the clearest instances of this association between memory and place appear in quick succession in Book VI of the *Historia*. The first comes as Orderic relates a further story from the life of the monastery's original founder, St Evroul. After having been provided with bread by the generous saint, a certain travelling beggar dug his staff into the ground and pulled it out with miraculous results:[45]

Les Cahiers des Annales de Normandie 17 (Caen, 1985), 175–206; Pierre Bauduin, 'Une famille châtelaine sur les confins normanno-manceaux: les Géré (Xe–XIIIe s.)', *Archéologie Médiévale* 22 (1992), 309–56.

41 OV ii, 74.

42 'Unde multa Uticensis aecclesia tunc perdidit; quae usque hodie recuperare nullatenus potuit.' OV ii, 98.

43 For the background to this long-lasting enmity between the Giroie and Bellême families see Walker, *Grandmesnils*, 26–39; Eleanor Searle, *Predatory Kinship and the Creation of Norman Power, 840–1066* (Berkeley and Los Angeles, CA, 1988), 179–82; Gérard Louise, *La seigneurie de Bellême (Xe-XIIe siècles): Dévolution des pouvoirs territoriaux et construction d'une seigneurie de frontière aux confins de la Normandie et du Maine à la charnière de l'an mil* (2 vols., Le Pays Bas-Normand, 1990–1991), ii, 288–89, 316–17, 347–49. For a more recent interpretation, see Matthew Bennett, 'Violence in Eleventh-Century Normandy: Feud, Warfare and Politics', in *Violence and Society in the Early Medieval West*, ed. Guy Halsall (Woodbridge, 1998), 126–40 at 130–34.

44 'Defuncto itaque Ernaldo tota Geroianorum nobilitas pene corruit; nec ullus posterorum stemma priorum ex integro usque hodie adipisci potuit.' OV ii, 124.

45 'nec adhuc elemosinae portitor de loco recessisset, subito fons magnus cuspidem baculi

The bearer of alms had not yet left the place when, suddenly, there gushed forth from where the point of his stick had been a great spring of water, which bubbles up and flows there up to the present day. The healing of many sick people has been worked in that place, and the fever-ridden from distant regions are brought there because of their desire to be cured. Indeed, many have been commanded through a vision to seek out the forest of Ouche to recover their health and to drink from the fountain of St Evroul which flows there.

The continued bubbling of the spring thus acted as a permanent reminder of the healings worked there in centuries past.[46] Similar in nature is the second such comment in which Orderic connected the built environment of St Evroul with distant memories of buildings that had previously existed on the same site. Here again, the story appears during his narration of the life of the monastery's founder, St Evroul. Orderic relates how the wife of Childebert, king of the Franks, had a church built there in honour of the Virgin Mary 'on the hill between the River Charentonne and the wood'. He concludes with a summary of what little he knew about the usage of this church at that time:[47]

It is said that there was a monastery of nuns there as well as a cemetery full of monks and great men, whose corpses were taken there for burial because the ground in the valley was marshy.... This is why many signs of a noble presence are visible there in the aforesaid church of the Virgin Mother, and fine tombs are preserved there to the present day, which are without a doubt believed to be those of notable persons.

Tombs played an important role in the retention and retrieval of communal memory in the medieval period. For Orderic, they constituted a highly visual and long-lasting reminder of those who had gone before him and his contemporaries at the monastery of St Evroul, and they are repeatedly the focus of his attention.[48] Thus, he recounts elsewhere how St Evroul himself died and was

---

secutus erupit, qui usque in hodiernum diem ebulliens ibidem fluit. In quo loco multae infirmorum sanitates patratae sunt; et de longinquis regionibus febricitantes pro desiderio curationis illuc asciti sunt. Per uisum etiam pluribus iussum est; ut pro salute nanciscenda Uticensem saltum quaererent, et de Sancti Ebrulfi fonte qui manat illic biberent.' OV iii, 276.

[46] A further example relating to the monastic landscape is the story Orderic relates in book XIII concerning the name of the village of Le Sap, which, he claims, was derived from the silver fir tree which stood near the church of St Peter there, OV vi, 470. The sixth abbot of St Evroul, Roger Le Sap (1091–1122), came from here and this likely explains Orderic's inclusion of this detail at this point in the narrative.

[47] 'Fertur quod ibi cenobium fuerit sanctimonialium, necnon cimiterium monachorum et sullimium uirorum, quorum illuc cadauera baiulabantur ad sepeliendum, quia in ualle palustris humus erat ... Unde in predicta aede uirginis matris plurima insignis habitationis indicia panduntur, et usque in hodiernum diem honorabiles ibidem sarcofagi seruantur, qui spectabilium fuisse personarum sine scrupulo creduntur.' OV iii, 286; Chibnall, 'The Merovingian Monastery of St. Evroul', 37.

[48] For comparison, see Paxton, 'Textual Communities', 132–37; Cassidy-Welch, *Monastic Spaces*, 115–16, 217–41.

buried in a marble tomb in the church of St Peter, where healings continued
up to the present;[49] and how after the tomb of St Guthlac, at the abbey of
Crowland in Lincolnshire,[50] was opened, it was discovered that, miraculously,
the body had not yet decomposed and the coffin was therefore left there on
the ground as a monument to him, 'where it has been honourably kept to
this day'.[51] Whilst Orderic's account of the tomb of William the Conqueror
should also be noted,[52] the vast majority of these tomb-centred passages focus
on the history of St Evroul itself.

Perhaps the most poignant of these stories comes early in book VIII of
the *Historia*. Here, in a passage the length of which conveys the significance
of the subject to him, Orderic presented a summary of the life and death
of Robert of Rhuddlan. Robert's father, Humphrey of Tilleul, had fought
alongside Hugh of Grandmesnil, one of the four founders of St Evroul, in
the Norman conquest of England,[53] but he had also married Hugh's sister
Adeliza. Given these close connections to the Grandmesnil family, and the
proximity of Tilleul to St Evroul,[54] it is not surprising that two of Robert's
brothers were monks at St Evroul, and that having made generous donations
to the monastery throughout his life, Robert was himself buried there after his
death in battle against the Welsh in 1093, just like his parents before him.[55]
The Tilleul family was therefore of great importance to Orderic, and they
are repeatedly portrayed in the *Historia* as faithfully serving their monastery.
What interests us most here, though, is the possible connection between the
vignettes that Orderic related about Robert of Rhuddlan's life and death, and
the lasting reminder of these memories in the form of his tomb located within
the cloister of St Evroul. For some years after Robert's death, his brother, the
monk Arnold of Tilleul, travelled to England and obtained permission for the
bones of his brother to be taken back to St Evroul. Arnold was a long-serving

[49] OV iii, 302.
[50] Crowland was another house closely connected to St Evroul; Orderic visited the abbey for
five weeks (probably at some point in the second half of the 1110s) and incorporated an account
of its early history into Book IV of the *Historia*, OV iv, xxiv–xxix and 322–50. The monks of
Crowland may also have been Orderic's source of information for affairs elsewhere, on which
see Stephen Marritt, 'Crowland Abbey and the Provenance of Orderic Vitalis's Scandinavian
and Scottish Material', *Notes and Queries* 53 (2006), 290–92.
[51] 'ubi usque hodie honorabiliter requiescit', OV ii, 336.
[52] OV iv, 110. Orderic famously reported that William's body, squeezed into a coffin that was
far too small for it, burst open, causing a great stench to overwhelm the crowd of bystanders
at his funeral (OV iv, 106–8).
[53] J.F.A. Mason, 'The Companions of the Conqueror: An Additional Name', *EHR* 71 (1956),
61–69.
[54] Lewis Loyd identified the Tilleul family as being from Tilleul-en-Auge, which is located
approximately 10 km north-east of Grandmesnil and 47 km north-west of St Evroul: Lewis C.
Loyd, *The Origins of Some Anglo-Norman Families* (Leeds, 1951), 85 under 'Rhuddlan'.
[55] OV iv, 134–46. For more on Robert of Rhuddlan, see R.R. Davies, *The Age of Conquest:
Wales, 1063–1415* (Oxford, 1991), 30–31, 82–83.

contemporary of Orderic's at the monastery, and his vital role in the growth of the house is repeatedly noted in the *Historia*.[56] Orderic therefore took this opportune moment of describing Robert's tomb to honour Arnold's memory in his narrative:[57]

> He was truly devoted to the needs of his church, for which he often crossed the English Channel, and he travelled to Apulia and Calabria and Sicily in order that he might provide support for his church from the loot of his kinsmen ... and by gentle force he took away from them as much as he could in order that he might confer it on his monastery. In this way, he procured ornaments and other valuables for his church from the property of his kinsmen.... In these and other efforts of this sort the aforesaid man strived quite boldly and founded upon his zealous effort, a stone arch stands to this day over the tomb of his brother [Robert of Rhuddlan].

What is most immediately striking about this passage is the reported continued existence of the stone arch over Robert of Rhuddlan's tomb. Erected some years after his death, the context in which this arch appears in the narrative – at the end of Orderic's tribute to Arnold – suggests that this addition to the tomb may have added a further layer of meaning to the memories already cultivated at Robert's burial site.[58] For not only did Orderic note that it was located in the cloister against the south side of the church, but he also tells us that it was he himself who composed the epitaph inscribed on the tombstone.[59] It is thus extremely plausible to imagine that the stone arch acted as a visible reminder not only of Robert of Rhuddlan's military exploits in Wales but also of his brother Arnold's faithful labours in the service of the monastery of St Evroul. Still in existence at the time of Orderic's writing, its location within the monastery provided him with these small, yet significant, fragments of the history of the Tilleul family.

---

[56] OV iii, 118–20; iv, 336; V. 170; vi, 320–22, 340.

[57] 'Hic nimirum aecclesiae suae utilitatibus satis inhiauit, pro quibus Britannicum pelagus multotiens transfretauit, atque Apuliam et Calabriam Siciliamque ut de spoliis parentum suorum aecclesiae suae subsidium suppeditaret penetrauit ... ipsisque benigna ui quantam potuit ut monasterio suo conferret abstulit. Sic de rebus parentum suorum ornatus et alia commoda aecclesiae suae procurauit, ipsosque consanguineos utilitatibus monasterii subiugauit ... Predictus uir his et huiusmodi nisibus sat procaciter studuit, eiusque studio conditus super tumulum fratris sui lapideus arcus usque hodie consistit.' OV iv, 142.

[58] For more on the way in which monuments embody and reflect change, see Jones, *Memory and Material Culture*, 21–22.

[59] OV iv, 142–46. Orderic also wrote the elegies for Walter of Auffay and his wife Avice, and a stone vault was built over her tomb. However, the phrase *usque hodie* is conspicuous here by its absence (OV III. 256–58). A further point of interest is the specific mention of the location of the tombs and other objects. We are told that Robert of Rhuddlan was buried on the south side of the church, Avice was buried by the door, and, in a further example, the relics of St Neot were placed on the north side of the church, next to the altar dedicated to the Virgin Mary (OV ii, 342). Orderic's residence at St Evroul and his visit to Crowland almost certainly provide the explanation for his inclusion of these details.

Thus far it has been argued that the landscape, built environment, and memorial objects associated with the monastery of St Evroul and its affiliate houses aided the recollection of memories associated with them and also, by extension, the writing of the *Historia*. But how exactly might this process have worked? Though a portion of the community's memories were deliberately stored in material objects such as the memorial roll and psalter, and inscribed upon the tombs of dead monks and benefactors, oral transmission was also necessary, in order to ensure that future generations of novices and benefactors correctly understood their full significance.

Orderic's narrative offers some clues here about this process of remembrance, as has already been shown. There is, however, one further passage in the *Historia* that offers an even clearer glimpse of this collaborative relationship, in which material objects and oral memories can be seen working side by side. In discussing the growth of St Evroul and the continued benefactions to the monastery towards the end of Book III, Orderic related how the church of St Martin of Parnes was also granted to his house at some point during the late 1060s. The mention of St Evroul's acquisition of this church led him, in turn, to write an account of the life of St Judoc, whose relics were preserved at Parnes, and to include a series of posthumous miracle stories associated with the bones.[60] What interests us most here, though, are some of Orderic's final comments about the relics of St Judoc, in which he relates how the bones were returned to the church of St Martin after having been lost and then recovered in the tenth century. The relics also endured an unsuccessful attempt at theft when the bundle in which they had been hidden was intercepted before it had been taken far from the church.[61] What follows comes at the end of Orderic's account of this story:[62]

[the bundle] was carefully placed by the priest and parishioners in the church of St Martin, where it has now been reverently preserved for over seventy years. Innumerable miracles have been worked on the sick in that place, and they happen frequently to

---

[60] OV ii, 152–68. Two pieces of internal evidence suggest that the date for the donation of the church of St Martin of Parnes may have been 1066. First, Abbot Mainer – to whom, Orderic tells us, the church was granted—began his abbacy at St Evroul in that year. Second, after completing his account of the life of Judoc, Orderic moves on immediately to relate the battle of Stamford Bridge and the Norman conquest of England that followed.

[61] For more on the theft of relics during this period, see Lucien Musset, 'L'exode des reliques du diocèse de Sées au temps des invasions normandes', *Société historique et archéologique de l'Orne* 88 (1970), 3–22; Felice Lifshitz, 'The Migration of Neustrian Relics in the Viking Age: The Myth of Voluntary Exodus, the Reality of Coercion and Theft', *EME* 4 (1995), 175–92.

[62] 'in aecclesia Sancti Martini a presbitero et parrochianis studiose collocatum est, iamque ibidem plusquam septuaginta annis uenerabiliter seruatum est. Innumera inibi super infirmos miracula facta sunt; et usque hodie promerente petencium fide ut tota uicinitas adtestatur frequenter fiunt ... Praeterea meritis sancti Iudoci multa Parnis miracula facta sunt cotidieque fiunt, quorum nonnulla scripta sunt; et plura per incuriam scientium seu per imperitiam uidentium uel expertorum silentio occultata sunt.' OV ii, 166.

this day, when the faith of those who ask merits it, as the whole neighbourhood attests.... By the merits of St Judoc many miracles happened thereafter at Parnes and still happen daily. Some of them have been written down, but many, through the negligence of those who knew them or through the ignorance of those who saw or experienced them, have been hidden by silence.

As with the other examples cited in this paper, this passage centres on a material object, in this case the relics of St Judoc, and describes the on-going nature of their significance from the past into the present moment, when Orderic was writing the *Historia*. Yet it also develops the relationship between object and narrative, past and present, more fully and explicitly in two instances. The first of these, as noted above, is Orderic's explicit reference to the relationship between the relics and the oral tradition that surrounded them.[63] Orderic's inclusion of the phrase 'as the whole neighbourhood attests' is particularly instructive in this regard. For it indicates that the strong communal memories at Parnes, going back for perhaps a period of seventy years, if Orderic is to be believed, were themselves sustained by the continued presence of the relics of St Judoc in the church of St Martin and the miracles that were associated with them. Just as the memory of the saint and past miracles inspired present pilgrims, so present miracles and visitations renewed memory.

Whilst this passage in the *Historia* makes clear the relationship between the material (the object) and the oral (the memories relating to the object), it also reveals Orderic's belief that important memories needed to be written down in order to survive. For though the oral tradition could buttress the miracle tradition surrounding the relics as long as it remained strong, Orderic was also keenly aware that with the fading of these memories, the rich and miraculous history of the relics would also be forgotten. The neglect or ignorance of oral witnesses meant that these memories would not be written down and so would eventually be concealed or hidden (*occultata sunt*) by silence and forever inaccessible thereafter.[64] But once written down, the oral tradition associated with these and other objects lived on in the text, available for subsequent generations of monks at St Evroul to read aloud together and then spread orally once more.[65] Through its inclusion of narratives of place and object, the *Historia* thus came by implication to incorporate the memories of St Evroul's wider community of the living and the dead: the monks, founders, benefactors, and associated houses, many of whom have been encountered in this discussion.

---

[63] For a further example of this relationship, see Julia M.H. Smith, 'Oral and Written: Saints, Miracles, and Relics in Brittany, *c.*850–1250', *Speculum* 65 (1990), 309–43.
[64] For more on the subject of forgetting, see Patrick J. Geary, *Phantoms of Remembrance: Memory and Oblivion at the End of the First Millennium* (Princeton, 1994).
[65] The writing down of such stories may even have 'increased the value of the relic'; see Geary, *Furta Sacra*, xi.

The presence of such stories in the *Historia*'s narrative was designed to serve the purposes of the monastic community. It thus chimed well with Orderic's intention that the *Historia* provide the novices at St Evroul with the history of their house, of which they would otherwise have been unaware.[66] For while material objects interested Orderic a great deal in their own right, what mattered most was that they were in some way related to the history of his monastery, St Evroul. References to them appear with great regularity throughout the *Historia* in passages that move repeatedly between past and present tense. The widespread use of such passages reveals that the information related in the work was, in many places, derived from and underpinned by physical objects in the possession of the monks of St Evroul and its related houses, or by monuments and other features of the monastic landscape. They enabled Orderic to write a history that stretched back into the past, whilst at the same time remaining firmly rooted in the monastic landscape of the present. For he was writing not a general history of the kings of England or of the Norman people, but rather a monastic history the aim of which was realized in his monastic readers by, among other things, the presence of numerous finely crafted passages that anchored key elements and people from the monastery's past in the physical objects, structures, and places of the monks' present.

---

[66] See for example, OV iii, 122, 150; vi, 8.

4

Anonymus Vaticanus: Another Source for the Normans in the South?[1]

Charles D. Stanton

Contained in two manuscripts preserved in the Biblioteca Apostolica Vaticana is a little-known chronicle by an anonymous writer of the mid-twelfth century which may shed more light on an epoch-making event on the eve of the Crusades: the Norman conquest of Sicily. This source, collated into a single transcription by Giambattista Caruso in 1723[2] and reproduced in the *Rerum Italicarum Scriptores* by Ludovico Muratori in 1726,[3] is called the *Historia Sicula a Normannis ad Petrum Aragonensem* by Anonymus Vaticanus. Despite the fact that it is one of a very few sources to describe a seminal episode in Mediterranean history, the *Historia Sicula* has not been discussed in any depth for over a century. This essay seeks to correct that oversight.

In his formative work, *Mohammed and Charlemagne*, the great Belgian historian Henri Pirenne contended that 'the rapid and unexpected advance of Islam' had precipitated 'the end of Mediterranean unity' by vanquishing the *mare nostrum* of ancient Rome.[4] The resultant loss of Sicily to the Aghlabids of North Africa in the ninth century established what maritime historian A.R. Lewis termed 'the Islamic Imperium'[5] and inspired the fourteenth-century Arab scholar Ibn Khaldūn to claim that 'the Muslims had gained control

---

[1]   This study was enabled by the American Academy in Rome which graciously provided the use of its incomparable facilities on the Janiculum; by the Biblioteca Apostolica Vaticana which allowed sustained access to the subject manuscripts; and by Dr Marie-Agnes Lucas-Avenel of the Université de Caen Basse-Normandie who generously provided an advance copy of her forthcoming paper in *Anglo-Norman Studies* entitled 'Le récit de Geoffroi Malaterra ou la légitimation de Roger, Grand Compte de Sicile'.

[2]   *Anonymi Historia Sicula a Normannis ad Petrum Aragonensem*, ed. G.B. Caruso, in *Bibliotheca Historica Regni Siciliae* (2 vols., Palermo, 1723), ii, 829–59.

[3]   *Anonymi Historia Sicula a Normannis ad Petrum Aragonensem*, in *RIS*, ed. L. Muratori (28 vols., Milan, 1726), viii, cols. 745–80.

[4]   H. Pirenne, *Mohammed and Charlemagne*, trans. B. Miall (New York, NY, repr. 1992), 284.

[5]   A. Lewis, *Naval Power and Trade in the Mediterranean A.D. 500 to 1100* (Princeton, NJ, 1951), 132.

over the whole of the Mediterranean'.[6] At the beginning of the eleventh century, the Mediterranean was, in effect, a Muslim lake with most of its major islands, including Sicily, firmly ensconced in *Dar al-Islam* (the 'House of Islam'). By the end of the eleventh century, however, Sicily was back in Christian hands, the Crusades had begun, and western Italian fleets were funneling through the Strait of Messina to compete with those of Venice for dominance of East-West trade on the sea. Western naval power was in the ascendant, and Islam was in full retreat. Recent scholarship has determined that the primary cause for this rather remarkable reversal of fortune was the Norman conquest of Sicily,[7] and the Norman knight chiefly responsible for that feat was Roger de Hauteville who, with some initial help from his more famous brother, Robert Guiscard, managed to subdue the island after a dogged thirty-year campaign.[8]

Yet, despite the importance of this event, there is only one conventionally accepted source that describes both the conquest and its principal conqueror in any detail: the chronicle of Geoffrey Malaterra.[9] The other chief chroniclers of the Normans in the south – Amatus of Montecassino[10] and William of Apulia[11] – barely mention Roger and note nearly nothing of the subjugation of Sicily after the pacification of Palermo in January 1072,[12] despite the fact that the island was not fully subdued until 1091.[13] This selectivity is not entirely surprising. Amatus, a monk of Montecassino, wrote his *Historia Normannorum* essentially to glorify the exploits of the abbey's two main benefactors, Robert Guiscard and Richard of Capua, and stopped upon the death of the latter in 1078, well before the conquest of Sicily was complete.[14] William of Apulia composed the *Gesta Roberti Wiscardi* at the

---

6   Ibn Khaldūn, *The Muqaddimah. An Introduction to History*, trans. F. Rosenthal (Princeton, NJ, 1967), 210.
7   C. Stanton, *Norman Naval Operations in the Mediterranean* (Woodbridge, 2011); 'The Use of Naval Power in the Norman Conquest of Southern Italy and Sicily', *HSJ* 19 (2007), 120–36.
8   G.A. Loud, *The Age of Robert Guiscard. Southern Italy and the Norman Conquest* (Harlow, 2000), 153–54.
9   Geoffrey Malaterra, *The Deeds of Count Roger of Calabria and Sicily and of his brother Duke Robert Guiscard*, trans. K. Wolf (Ann Arbor, MI, 2005); *De rebus gestis Rogerii Calabriae et Siciliae comitis et Roberti Guiscardi ducis fratris eius,* ed. E. Pontieri, *RIS*, new ser. 5 (Bologna, 1927–1928).
10   *The History of the Normans by Amatus of Montecassino*, trans. P. Dunbar, ed. G. Loud (Woodbridge, 2004); *Storia de' Normanni*, ed. V. de Bartholomaeis, Fonti per la storia d'Italia 76 (Rome, 1935).
11   William of Apulia, *La Geste de Robert Guiscard*, trans. M. Mathieu (Palermo, 1961).
12   *History of the Normans by Amatus of Montecassino*, Bk. VI, ch. 13–19, 155–58 (=*Storia de' Normanni*, Bk. VI, ch. XIII–XIX, 275–82); Malaterra, *Deeds of Count Roger*, Bk. 2, ch. 45, 124–25 (=*De rebus gestis Rogerii*, Bk. II, ch. XLV, 52–53); William of Apulia, *La Geste de Robert Guiscard*, Bk. III, lines 187–337, 174–83.
13   Malaterra, *Deeds of Count Roger*, Bk. 4, ch. 15, 190 (=*De rebus gestis Rogerii*, Bk. IV, ch. XV, 93).
14   E. Albu, *The Normans in their Histories* (Woodbridge, 2001), 108–9; Loud, 'Introduction',

behest of Guiscard's son Roger Borsa, the duke of Apulia; thus, he took little interest in events in Sicily and even less in Guiscard's younger brother, Roger. He also concluded his chronicle before the seizure of Sicily was accomplished, essentially ending his narrative with the death of Robert in 1085.[15]

Only Geoffrey Malaterra, a Benedictine monk in the abbey of Saint Agata of Catania whose primary patron was Roger de Hauteville, had a vested interest in covering the conquest to its conclusion and portraying the Norman knight who completed it.[16] Accordingly, it is his account alone of the major Latin sources that includes details of the subjugation of Sicily following the fall of Palermo in 1072. Malaterra is the sole source, among the three primary Latin chroniclers of the Normans in the South, for the violent altercations between Robert Guiscard and Roger that occurred in the aftermath of the island's initial invasion. He even gives a detailed description of a bitter battle, replete with siege and counter-siege, which ensued between the two brothers in 1062 over the apportionment of their Calabrian conquests.[17] In contrast, neither Amatus nor William of Apulia touched upon the breakdown in relations between the Hauteville siblings, despite the fact that it could well have derailed the conquest and cost them their lives in the process. As a result, Malaterra's version of the events suffers from a lack of corroboration. The *Historia Sicula* of Anonymus Vaticanus may be able to provide that corroboration and possibly even fill in some factual gaps in Malaterra's narrative. It is the only other extant Latin source that describes the Norman experience in the south from the appearance of the first sons of Tancred de Hauteville to the completion of the conquest.

Modern scholars have largely been dismissive of the *Historia Sicula* as a source for the Normans in the south. Indeed, most hardly reference it at all. Graham Loud, a leading authority on medieval Italy, makes no mention of it in his *The Age of Robert Guiscard: Southern Italy and the Norman Conquest*[18] and Julia Becker does not even include it in her extensive listing of primary sources for *Graf Roger I. von Sizilien*.[19] Nor does Paul Oldfield use the source in his comprehensive *City and Community in Norman Italy*.[20]

History of the Normans by Amatus of Montecassino, 1–3; K. Wolf, *Making History: The Normans and their Historians in Eleventh-Century Italy* (Philadelphia, PA, 1995), 88.

[15] Albu, *Normans in their Histories*, 110; Mathieu, 'Introduction', in *La Geste de Robert Guiscard*, 11; Wolf, *Making History*, 123–24.

[16] Albu, *Normans in their Histories*, 111; Wolf, 'Introduction', *Deeds of Count Roger*, 6–10; *Making History*, 143–46.

[17] Malaterra, *Deeds of Count Roger*, Bk. 2, ch. 21–28, 96–102; *De rebus gestis Rogerii*, Bk. II, ch. XXI–XXVIII, 35–39.

[18] Loud, *Age of Robert Guiscard*.

[19] J. Becker, *Graf Roger I. von Sizilien, Wegbereiter des normannischen Königreichs* (Tübingen, 2008).

[20] P. Oldfield, *City and Community in Norman Italy* (Cambridge, 2009).

Others, like the popular historian John Julius Norwich[21] and Huguette
Taviani-Carozzi,[22] list it in their bibliographies, but do not discuss it within
their respective narratives on the Italo-Normans. Even those researchers who
have concentrated on the Norman historiography of the era have, by chance
or intention, omitted the *Historia Sicula*. Emily Albu produced an excellent
volume which covered the Norman chroniclers, both north and south, but
reserved no space for Anonymus Vaticanus.[23] Kenneth Baxter Wolf, who
prepared the only existing English translation of Malaterra, makes not even
the slightest allusion to Anonymus Vaticanus in his monographic study
*Making History: The Normans and their Historians in Eleventh-Century
Italy.*[24]

The principal reason for this omission is that earlier historians of the
Norman South, predominantly those from the eighteenth and nineteenth
centuries, regarded the *Historia Sicula* as just a crude summary of Malaterra.
Giambattista Caruso, the first transcriber of the chronicle, dismissed it as an
'opusculum' ('a minor work').[25] Muratori did not argue with this assessment
but allowed that it at least passably presented the events of the conquest up
until the death of Roger I.[26] In 1835, M. Champollion-Figeac printed an Old
French version of the *Historia* from the early fourteenth century entitled the
Chronique de Robert Viscart et de ses freres and attributed it to Amatus.[27]
This ascription was subsequently contested in 1849 by Roger Wilmans
who designated the *Historia Sicula* as 'nothing more than a paltry excerpt
from Geoffrey Malaterra', written in 'barbarous Latin'.[28] Odon Delarc, who
published his own version of the Old French translation of Amatus in 1892,
concurred.[29]

A lone voice in opposition was the Sicilian orientalist, Michele Amari,
who instead characterized it as 'a good compendium' of Norman tradition
in southern Italy and Sicily. He surmised that it was perhaps 'palatine' in
nature, suggesting it may have been commissioned by a feudal lord.[30] More
importantly, Amari found enough discrepancies between Malaterra's chronicle

---

[21] J.J. Norwich, *The Normans in the South, 1016–1130* (London, 1967).

[22] H. Taviani-Carozzi, *La Terreur du Monde. Robert Guiscard et la conquête normande en
Italie* (Paris, 1996).

[23] Albu, *Normans in their Histories*.

[24] Wolf, *Making History*.

[25] Caruso, 'Monitum', *Anonymi Historia Sicula*, ii, 828.

[26] Muratori, 'Monitum', *Anonymi Historia Sicula*, viii, col. 743.

[27] *Chronique de Robert Viscart et de ses frères*, ed. M. Champollion-Figeac, *L'Ystoire de li
Normant et la Chronique de Robert Viscart* (Paris, 1835), 261–313; 'Prolégomènes', *L'Ystoire
de li Normant*, pp. lxxii–lxxxi.

[28] R. Wilmans, 'Ist Amatus von Monte Cassino der Verfasser der Chronica Roberti Biscardi?',
Archiv der Gesellschaft für Ältere Deutsche Geschichtskunde, 10 (1851), 122–30, especially
126–28.

[29] O. Delarc, 'Introduction', *Ystoire de li Normant* (Rouen, 1892), xxxvii–xl.

[30] M. Amari, *Storia dei Musulmani di Sicilia* (3 vols, Florence, 1868) iii, 24 note 1.

and that of Anonymus Vaticanus to be convinced that, while Anonymus certainly had access to Malaterra, he must have had at his disposal other sources as well, possibly even Arab sources.[31] Accordingly, Amari referenced the *Historia Sicula* of Anonymus Vaticanus in his account of the conquest of Sicily in *Storia dei Musulmani di Sicilia* more than fifty times.[32]

Even more convinced of the validity of the *Historia Sicula* as a source was Alex Heskel, a German scholar from Kiel. In his 1891 inaugural doctoral dissertation, Heskel contended that Anonymus composed his chronicle independent of Malaterra's work but that the two chroniclers shared some common sources, now lost.[33] According to Heskel, one of the sources would have covered the early years of Norman immigration to southern Italy, while another would have detailed 'the deeds of Robert and Roger until the end of the struggle in Sicily'. He also theorized that at least 'one of these sources, which came to Malaterra's attention, had been in poetic form', and insisted that Anonymus shows the same affinity to verse in his work as well.[34] Ferdinand Chalandon found Heskel's arguments compelling: 'The thesis of Heskel, very ingeniously established, appears quite right to me and I adopt his conclusions.'[35] But Ernesto Pontieri, who published the most recent transcription of Malaterra, remained unconvinced since there is no proof of any lost source which either Malaterra or Anonymous Vaticanus may have used.[36] Rather, he was inclined to take Malaterra at his word when, in his dedicatory letter to Bishop Angerius of Catania, the monk attributed his information 'to those who have reported the events to [him]'.[37] In other words, Malaterra claimed to have relied on oral tradition rather than written narratives. Accordingly, Pontieri as well as the latest editor of Amatus, Vincenzo de Bartolomeis, have adopted Amari's hypothesis: Malaterra's chronicle was one of several sources used by Anonymus to fashion the *Historia Sicula*.[38]

The *Historia Sicula* of Anonymus Vaticanus does, in fact, track Malaterra's narrative for the most part. Like Malaterra, it begins in the Cotentin region of Normandy with Tancred, the patriarch of the Hauteville clan, and recounts, in general terms, the exploits of the older sons in southern Italy up to the appearance around 1046 of Robert, later given the sobriquet 'Guiscard'

---

31 Amari, *Storia dei Musulmani di Sicilia*, iii, 100–101, note 2.

32 Amari, *Storia dei Musulmani di Sicilia*, iii, 24–200.

33 A. Heskel, *Die Historia Sicula des Anonymus Vaticanus und des Gaufredus Malaterra. Ein Beitrag zur Quellenkund für die Geschichte Unteritaliens und Siziliens im 11. Jahrhundert.* Inaugural Dissertation (Kiel, 1891), 53, 62–63 and following, and 71, 79–81.

34 Heskel, *Die Historia Sicula des Anonymus Vaticanus*, 83–86.

35 Chalandon, *Histoire de la Domination Normande en Italie et en Sicile* (2 vols., Paris, 1907), i, xxxvii–xxxviii.

36 E. Pontieri, 'Prefazione', in *De rebus gestis Rogerii Calabriae et Siciliae comitis*, xx–xxi.

37 Malaterra, *Deeds of Count Roger*, 'Letter to Bishop Angerius', 41 (=*De rebus gestis Rogerii*, 'Epistola ad Cathanensem Episcopum', 3).

38 Bartholomaies, 'Prefazione', in *Storia de' Normanni di Amato di Montecassino*, xix–xx.

(meaning 'cunning' in Old French). The narrative of Anonymus Vaticanus proceeds in much greater detail from that point until the death of the youngest son, Roger, in 1101. A brief, sketchy accounting of the Hohenstaufen era follows, culminating with the coronation of Peter III of Aragon as king of Sicily. Thirty-three of the thirty-six columns which comprise Muratori's transcription concern the careers of Robert and Roger de Hauteville. Only the final three columns cover the 181 years between Roger's death and the arrival of the Aragonese in 1282.[39]

This uneven accounting has led modern scholars unanimously to conclude that at least two authors contributed to the work: Anonymus Vaticanus and a continuator. The consensus is that Anonymus himself ceased writing around 1147 because, in reference to the untimely death of the great count's son and heir, Simon, the chronicler declares, 'He was succeeded by that greatest of men ... Roger ... King of Sicily [and] the most powerful [ruler] of Tripoli in Africa ...', whose praises Anonymus declines to sing 'since even the eloquence of Cicero would have been insufficient ...'.[40] The allusion to Tripoli, which was taken in 1146, without mentioning the seizure of strategi- cally more vital Mahdiyah in 1148, reliably pinpoints the date of the author's last words to between 1146 and 1148.[41] The continuation of the chronicle clearly commences at the beginning of the following paragraph with the phrase: 'After the death of Count Roger, just as is contained in the chronicle, Roger, his own son, succeeded ...'.[42]

The foregoing references to King Roger are probably why Michele Amari concluded that the *Historia Sicula* was 'palatine'.[43] The timing of the composition strongly suggests that this 'palatine' patron was in all likelihood King Roger II himself. Not only did Anonymus compose the work at the height of Roger's reign, the evidence also implies that he was almost certainly Sicilian. He mistakenly identifies the town where Robert Guiscard was briefly held captive in 1062 as Geraci in Sicily[44] (about 14 miles southeast of Cefalù) instead of Gerace in Calabria, as Malaterra contends.[45] The

[39] *Anonymi Historia Sicula*, ed. Muratori, viii, cols. 745–80; Champollion-Figeac, 'Prolégomènes', in *L'Ystoire de li Normant et la Chronique de Robert Viscart*, lxxi.

[40] *Anonymi Historia Sicula*, ed. Muratori, viii, col. 777. 'Huic successit ille hominum maximus ... Rogerius ... Rex Siciliae, Tripolis Africae potentissimus ...', '... quoniam Ciceronis eloquentiam insufficientem fuisse ...' Moreover, there is a reference in col. 754 to the kings of Sicily ('Regibus exceptis') whose line did not begin until the coronation of Roger II in December 1130.

[41] Amari, *Storia dei Musulmani di Sicilia*, iii, 24 note 1.

[42] *Anonymi Historia Sicula*, ed. Muratori, viii, cols. 777–78: 'Prout mortem Comitis Rogerii, prout continentur in Chronica, successit Rogerius sibi filius suus ...'

[43] Amari, *Storia dei Musulmani di Sicilia*, iii, 24.

[44] *Anonymi Historia Sicula*, ed. Muratori, viii, cols. 757–58.

[45] Malaterra, *Deeds of Count Roger*, Bk. 2, ch. 24, 98 (=*De rebus gestis Rogerii*, Bk. II, ch. XXIV, 37).

grandiose language used to extol the actions of the Hauteville brothers also bespeaks a commissioned work. It therefore seems reasonable to assume that Anonymus had at his disposal another 'palatine' work: Malaterra's chronicle, commissioned by the king's father, Count Roger. As such, it would assuredly have formed the template for the twelfth-century chronicler's composition.

Writing half a century later, Anonymus should, however, have had the benefit of material not available to Malaterra. This would explain why the chronicles are similar but not the same. In point of fact, there are many differences between the two narratives; some are substantial. For instance, many of the names of the principal personalities differ. Malaterra calls Roger's son-in-law whom he appointed as governor of Catania 'Hugoni de Gircaea' (Hugh of Gircé),[46] while Anonymus referred to him as 'Hugo de Brachia'.[47] The Breton who saved the count from assassination at the siege of Taormina in 1079 was 'Eviscardus' to Malaterra,[48] but was 'Casaldus' in *Historia Sicula*.[49] At times the appellations adopted by Anonymus actually seem more accurate, as if he had the benefit of updated information. For example, Malaterra calls the emir of Castrogiovanni in 1086 'Chamutum',[50] but Anonymus gives the more correct name of 'Hamus',[51] referring to 'Hamûd', probably of the Banu-Hamûd of the Hammudid Dynasty of Al-Andulus in the early eleventh century.[52] There are dozens of other examples.

Moreover, the descriptions of several major events contain noticeable disparities in detail. For instance, Malaterra relates that, during the battle for Syracuse in 1084, Ibn El-Werd, the city's Arab emir, was wounded with a javelin thrown by a certain Lupino,[53] but Anonymus insists that Roger did the deed himself using a lance,[54] reinforcing the notion that the work was 'palatine' in nature. Anonymus' claim that Roger had Ibn El-Werd's cadaver salvaged from the bottom of Syracuse harbor and sent to Tamin of Mahdiyah was probably also done to glorify the Great Count, for it is certainly a fiction,[55] given Roger's amicable relations with the Zirid emir of Ifriqiyah since 1079, six years before the siege of Syracuse.[56]

---

[46] Malaterra, *Deeds of Count Roger*, Bk. 3, ch. 10, 139 (=*De rebus gestis Rogerii*, Bk. III, ch. X, 61).

[47] *Anonymi Historia Sicula*, ed. Muratori, viii, col. 767.

[48] Malaterra, *Deeds of Count Roger*, Bk. 3, ch. 15, 146 (=*De rebus gestis Rogerii*, Bk. III, ch. XV, 66).

[49] *Anonymi Historia Sicula*, ed. Muratori, viii, col. 773.

[50] Malaterra, *Deeds of Count Roger*, Bk. 4, ch. 5, 180–81 (=*De rebus gestis Rogerii*, Bk. IV, ch. V, 87).

[51] *Anonymi Historia Sicula*, ed. Muratori, viii, col. 773.

[52] Amari, *Storia dei Musulmani di Sicilia*, iii, 173.

[53] Malaterra, *Deeds of Count Roger*, Bk. 4, ch. 2, 178 (=*De rebus gestis Rogerii*, Bk. IV, ch. II, 86).

[54] *Anonymi Historia Sicula*, ed. Muratori, viii, col. 775.

[55] *Anonymi Historia Sicula*, ed. Muratori, viii, col. 776.

[56] Malaterra, *Deeds of Count Roger*, Bk. 3, ch. 17, 147 (=*De rebus gestis Rogerii*, Bk. III, ch.

Occasionally, an episode appears in one narrative but not the other. Anonymus, for instance, relays the fanciful tale of an unidentified member of the Hauteville clan who, during the Norman siege of Palermo in 1072, pursued a particularly formidable Muslim horseman into one of the city's gates, slew him and galloped out again under a hail of arrows by way of another gate.[57] Malaterra makes no mention of any such incident. Conversely, Anonymus does not even allude to the abortive siege of Palermo in 1064, whereas Malaterra described it in full, even noting that the Normans had the misfortune of bivouacking on a tarantula-infested hill.[58] In other cases, Anonymus simply seems to be better informed. Malaterra does not say specifically how Robert Guiscard amassed his army for the protracted siege of Bari in 1068, but Anonymus Vaticanus specifies that the duke issued a public edict.[59] He claims Guiscard declared another 'general edict' in 1084 in order to raise the force needed to evict the German monarch Henry IV from Rome; Malaterra, in contrast, is silent on the means of recruitment.[60] Anonymus even observes that the ship-mounted ballistae and arbalests of the Normans were superior to those of the Saracens during the battle for Syracuse.[61] Malaterra makes no such comparisons.

Perhaps the most telling indication that Anonymus enjoyed the benefit of hindsight and possibly even some supplemental information is his description of how the Hautevilles fortified Palermo after its capture in 1072. Whereas Malaterra merely mentions a 'castle was strengthened',[62] the twelfth-century historian attests that 'they constructed in a short time two very strong fortresses, one near the sea, the other in a place which is called Galga'.[63] The 'one near the sea' is almost certainly the Castellammare on La Cala, the old port of Palermo. Michele Amari believed that 'Galga', the name of the other site, is derived from the Arabic *El-Halka*, meaning 'high place'.[64] Accordingly, he was confident that the other fortress was built on the very spot where the Palazzo dei Normanni of Palermo sits today.

XVII, 66–67). Malaterra relates how, during the siege of Taormina in 1079, ships sent by Tamin of Mahdiyah offered assistance to Roger, apparently based upon some prior pact between the two.

[57] *Anonymi Historia Sicula*, ed. Muratori, viii, col. 765.

[58] Malaterra, *Deeds of Count Roger*, Bk. 2, ch. 36, 114 (=*De rebus gestis Rogerii*, Bk. II, ch. XXXVI, 46–47).

[59] *Anonymi Historia Sicula*, ed. Muratori, viii, col. 763: 'publico edicto'; R. Bünemann, *Robert Guiskard 1015–1085, Eine Normanne erobert Süditalien* (Köln, 1997), 58 note 17.

[60] *Anonymi Historia Sicula*, ed. Muratori, viii, col. 771: 'generale edictum'; Bünemann, *Robert Guiskard*, 136 note 240 .

[61] *Anonymi Historia Sicula*, ed. Muratori, viii, col. 775.

[62] Malaterra, *Deeds of Count Roger*, Bk. 2, ch. 45, 124 (=*De rebus gestis Rogerii*, Bk. II, ch. XLV, 53): 'castello firmato'.

[63] *Anonymi Historia Sicula*, ed. Muratori, viii, col. 765: '… duo fortissima Castra, alterum juxta mare, alterum in loco, qui dicitur Galea [Galga], brevi tempore constituerunt'.

[64] Amari, *Storia dei Musulmani di Sicilia*, iii, 139 note 1.

Even more significantly, it would appear that Anonymus may have had access to Muslim sources inaccessible to Malaterra. There were so many discrepancies in the details of the Battle of Cerami between the two chronicles, for instance, that Amari was led to speculate that Anonymus drew on an Arab account, no longer available.[65] For example, Malaterra records that Roger sent his nephew Serlo ahead to Cerami with thirty-six knights on the same day of the battle,[66] while Anonymus insists that Serlo was dispatched two days prior with only thirty knights.[67] Both authors exaggerate the slaughter, but Anonymus contends that 20,000 Muslims were killed versus Malaterra's 15,000.[68] Muslim historians apparently did document the clash, thus allowing for the possibility that Anonymus could have used their accounts. For example, Al-Suyuti, a fifteenth-century Egyptian scholar, noted the Christian conquest of Sicily in the year 455 of the Hegira (1063), the same year as the pivotal encounter at Cerami that foreshadowed the final fall of 'Saracen' Sicily, a notation that suggests that Al-Suyuti's earlier sources had records of events in eleventh-century Italy.[69] While far from conclusive, such clues are at least intriguing. It is well-documented that King Roger had a number of Muslim scholars like the great Moroccan geographer Al-Idrisi in his court who could have supplied Anonymus with ancillary information.[70]

A final point of comparison: in terms of structure, style and purpose, the *Historia Sicula* of Anonymus Vaticanus bears little resemblance to the *De rebus gestis Rogerii* of Geoffrey Malaterra. In the most recent analysis of Malaterra's chronicle by Marie-Agnes Lucas-Avenel, she persuasively argues that Malaterra uses a number of literary devices essentially to compose a religious rationalization for Roger's rise and ultimate triumph.[71] For example, he puts long discourses in the mouths of the narrative's two primary protagonists, Robert and Roger de Hauteville (especially the latter in Book II), in order to show that their conquest of southern Italy and Sicily was favored by God. Roger's exhortation of his entourage prior to the Battle of Cerami in 1063 stands out in this regard.[72] There are no equivalent orations

[65] Amari, *Storia dei Musulmani di Sicilia*, iii, 100–101 and 101 note 2.

[66] Malaterra, *Deeds of Count Roger*, Bk. 2, ch. 33, 108 (=*De rebus gestis Rogerii*, Bk. II, ch. XXXIII, 42).

[67] *Anonymi Historia Sicula*, ed. Muratori, viii, col. 760.

[68] *Anonymi Historia Sicula*, ed. Muratori, viii, col. 762; Malaterra, *Deeds of Count Roger*, Bk. 2, ch. 33, 110 (=*De rebus gestis Rogerii*, Bk. II, ch. XXXIII, 44).

[69] Al-Suyuti, *Biblioteca Arabo-Sicula*, ed. A. Amari (2 vols., Turin, 1880–1881), ii, 599.

[70] Al-Idrisi, *Biblioteca Arabo-Sicula*, i, 31–131; *La première géographie de l'Occident*, trans. P. Jaubert, ed. H. Bresc and A. Nef (Paris, 1999).

[71] Marie-Agnes Lucas-Avenel, 'Le récit de Geoffroi Malaterra ou la légitimation de Roger, Grand Compte de Sicile', *ANS* 34 (2012), 169–92.

[72] Malaterra, *Deeds of Count Roger*, Bk. 2, ch. 33, 109 (=*De rebus gestis Rogerii*, Bk. II, ch. XXXIII, 43–44).

in the *Historia Sicula*.[73] Additionally, in Books III and IV of Malaterra, the historian occasionally lapses into verse in order to enhance the epic nature of the Hautevilles' endeavors, such as Roger's seizure of Trapani in 1076[74] and Guiscard's preparations for his 1081 Balkan expedition.[75] In contrast, verse is virtually absent from the *Historia Sicula* of Anonymus. Furthermore, Malaterra utilizes numerous classical references to lionize his central characters and emphasize their heroic qualities. Anonymus also includes some allusions to the authors of antiquity but nothing on the level of Malaterra's borrowings from Sallust, for example.[76] Most crucially, Anonymous was evidently dissatisfied with how Malaterra ended the account and felt compelled to add a denouement to his narrative.[77] In doing so, he apparently misread the monk's intent. Indeed, Lucas-Avenel presents a compelling case that Malaterra composed his chronicle with the specific purpose of legitimizing Roger's accession as the Great Count of Sicily by characterizing his conquest of the island as a restoration to the Christian Church of a land previously lost to the infidels.[78] Accordingly, the Benedictine cleric made the culmination of his chronicle what he considered to be the crowning glory of Roger's career: Pope Urban II's decree granting him the power to act as papal legate for Sicily.[79] Anonymus Vaticanus and Geoffrey Malaterra wrote on the same subject but clearly shared neither the same style nor agenda.

In addition to the *Historia Sicula*'s connections with the Norman court in Sicily and some unique information, yet another sign of the source's significance can be found in the manuscripts containing the work. Caruso and Muratori based their transcriptions of the chronicle mainly on MS Vaticanus latinus 6206.[80] Its exact date is unknown, but its fine Gothic minuscule script would suggest the fourteenth or fifteenth century.[81] Because its narrative extends only to about 1150, the two scholars supplemented the transcription of MS Vaticanus latinus 6206 with readings from the later MS Vaticanus latinus 4936 (fifteenth or sixteenth century) which provides a few more

---

[73] *Anonymi Historia Sicula*, ed. Muratori, viii, cols. 760–62.

[74] Malaterra, *Deeds of Count Roger*, Bk. 3, ch. 11, 140–41 (=*De rebus gestis Rogerii*, Bk. III, ch. XI, 62–63).

[75] Malaterra, *Deeds of Count Roger*, Bk. 3, ch. 14, 145–46 (=*De rebus gestis Rogerii*, Bk. III, ch. XIV, 65–66).

[76] Wolf, *Making History*, 164–68.

[77] *Anonymi Historia Sicula*, ed. Muratori, viii, col. 777.

[78] Lucas-Avenel, 'Le récit de Geoffroi Malaterra'.

[79] Malaterra, *Deeds of Count Roger*, Bk. 4, ch. 29, 213 (=*De rebus gestis Rogerii*, Bk. IV, ch. XXIX, 108).

[80] Caruso, 'Monitum', *Anonymi Historia Sicula*, ii, 828; Muratori, 'Monitum', *Anonymi Historia Sicula*, viii, col. 743; Vatican City, Biblioteca Apostolica Vaticana, MS Vaticanus latinus [Vat. lat.] 6206.

[81] Pontieri, 'Premessa', *Annali Siculi*, ed. E. Pontieri, *RIS*, new ser. 5 (Bologna, 1927–1928), 109–120, especially 112. Note: Pontieri appended the *Annali Siculi* to the end of *De rebus gestis Rogerii Calabriae et Siciliae comitis*.

details of the Hauteville era and continues all the way to 1282.[82] Both are composite manuscripts, containing other chronicles or annals relating to the Norman era of southern Italy and Sicily. The manuscript evidence affirms, in other words, that the *Historia Sicula* was, until the modern era, considered very much a component of the corpus of Italo-Norman historiography.

Nor is the survival of the *Historia Sicula* restricted to the two Vatican manuscripts. It is also found in MS Codex V.G. 31 of the Biblioteca Nazionale di Napoli (seventeenth or eighteenth century) and in three manuscripts of the Bibliothèque Nationale in Paris: MS latin 5911 (sixteenth century), MS latin 6176 (seventeenth century) and MS français 688 (early fourteenth century) (formerly designated MS BN 7135).[83] In short, there are no less than six extant copies of the *Historia Sicula* by Anonymus Vaticanus, a remarkable happenstance, considering that there are but four manuscripts remaining of Geoffrey Malaterra,[84] only one original surviving Latin manuscript of William of Apulia,[85] and no Latin copies of Amatus at all, but only the translation of it into Old French.[86]

The *Historia Sicula* appears, unannounced, towards the end of MS Vaticanus latinus 6206 at folio 290r and extends to 298v, but it is prominently featured in all of the other Latin manuscripts. It begins at the front of MS Vaticanus latinus 4936, for instance, and is unambiguously entitled *Cronica Roberti Biscardi et fratrus ac Rogeri I comitis Mileti* ('The Chronicle of Robert Guiscard and his brother Roger, Count of Mileto').[87] The other three Latin manuscripts begin the same way. Furthermore, MS Vaticanus latinus 4936 underscores that the *Historia Sicula* is exclusively about the House of Hauteville. Its only illustration is a genealogical necklace of fifteen linked spheres spread across the bottom of folios 17v and 18r which contain the names of the family patriarch, his two wives, and each of his twelve sons.[88]

BN MS français 688 provides even more telling testimony of how seriously medieval scholars and scribes took the *Historia Sicula*.[89] Dating from around 1305–1310, the manuscript contains an Old French translation of Amatus of Montecassino commissioned by a certain Count de Militrée.

---

[82] Caruso, 'Monitum', *Anonymi Historia Sicula*, ii, 828; Muratori, 'Monitum', *Anonymi Historia Sicula*, viii, col. 743; Vatican City, Biblioteca Apostolica Vaticana MS Vat. lat. 4936.

[83] B. Capasso, *Le Fonti della Storia delle Province Napolitane dal 568 al 1500* (Naples, 1902), 83–84, note 1; Champollion-Figeac, 'Prolégomènes', *L'Ystoire de li Normant*, i–ii, lxviii–lxx; Loud, 'Introduction', *History of the Normans by Amatus of Montecassino*, 18–19.

[84] Pontieri, 'Prefazione', *De rebus gestis Rogerii Calabriae et Siciliae comitis*, li–lvii.

[85] Mathieu, 'Introduction', *La Geste de Robert Guiscard*, 70–71; Avranches, Bibliothèque Municipale, MS 162.

[86] Champollion-Figeac, 'Prolégomènes', *L'Ystoire de li Normant*, i–ii, lxviii–lxx; Loud, 'Introduction', *History of the Normans by Amatus of Montecassino*, 18–19.

[87] MS Vat. lat. 4936, fols. 1r–27v.

[88] MS Vat. lat. 4936, fols. 17v–18r.

[89] Paris, Bibiothèque Nationale, MS français 688.

Added to it seamlessly on folio 199r is a copy of the *Historia Sicula* done by the same translator.[90] In his translation of Amatus, the translator refers repeatedly to the *Historia Sicula* to fill in gaps in the narrative left by Amatus. To be precise, he used the chronicle of Anonymus Vaticanus to annotate the *Historia Normannorum* on precisely those events absent from the writings of both Amatus and William of Apulia: the troubled relationship between the two Hauteville brothers at the center of the narrative and the details of Sicily's subjugation beyond the capture of Palermo. In reference to Roger's feuds with Robert, for instance, the translator notes: 'This history [*Historia Normannorum*] does not mention how he [Guiscard] quarreled with Count Roger, his brother, and that he went to capture him, but, being unable to take Roger in the city, he pursued him to Sicily'.[91] The reference to Sicily indicates that the translator was relying on the *Historia Sicula* which mistakenly identified Geraci, Sicily instead of Gerace, Calabria as the place where this fraternal drama was played out.[92] The translator also observes that the *Historia Sicula* describes several of Roger's exploits in Sicily not contained in the *Historia Normannorum* of Amatus, like the Battle of Cerami:[93] 'It is to be noted that the other History [*Historia Sicula*] tells of a marvelous victory [Cerami] which Count Roger, the duke's brother, achieved in Sicily before he went to Bari. Nevertheless this History [*Historia Normannorum*] mentions nothing of it.'[94]

The most tantalizing connection between the *Historia Sicula* and other Italo-Norman manuscripts of the era, however, is with the so-called '*Codice Giarratana*' which features one of the oldest and most crucial copies of Malaterra's chronicle.[95] Named for the Marquis of Giarratana who once held it in his private collection, this fourteenth-century manuscript is now in the keeping of the Biblioteca della Società siciliana per la storia patria in Palermo. Affixed to Malaterra's chronicle at folio 29v, without an interval of any sort, is what Giambattista Caruso dubbed the 'Appendix ex Codice Marchionis Farratanae ad ultimum capitulum Libri Quarti Historiae Gaufredi

---

[90] Champollion-Figeac, 'Prolégomènes', *L'Ystoire de li* Normant, lxviii–lxxi; Delarc, 'Introduction', *Ystoire de li Normant par Aimé* (Rouen, 1892), xxxvi; Loud, 'Introduction', in *History of the Normans by Amatus of Montecassino*, 18.

[91] *History of the Normans by Amatus of Montecassino*, Bk. V, ch. 26, 143 (=*Storia de' Normanni*, Bk. V, ch. XXVI, 247–48): 'Non meste ceste Ystoire coment ot brigue avec lo conte Rogier son frere, et coment lo ala prendre. Et, qué non lo pot prendre en la cité, lo persequta en Sicille.'

[92] *Anonymi Historia Sicula*, ed. Muratori, viii, cols. 756–58.

[93] *Anonymi Historia Sicula*, ed. Muratori, viii, cols. 760–61.

[94] *History of the Normans by Amatus of Montecassino*, Bk. V, ch. 28, 146 (=*Storia de' Normanni*, Bk. V, ch. XXVIII, 256): 'Et est de noter que l'autre Ystoire met molt merveillose victoire que fist lo conte Rogier, frere de loc Duc, en Sycille, avant que venist a Bar. Mes ceste Ystoire n'en met noïent.'

[95] Palermo, Biblioteca della Società siciliana per la Storia patria, MS I B 28 [formerly II F 12].

Malaterrae' ('Appendix from the Codex of the Marquis of Giarratana to the last chapter of the Fourth Book of the History of Geoffrey Malaterra').[96] This title stems from the fact that this short segment seemed to pick up the narrative where Malaterra had left off: with the 1098 papal bull of Pope Urban II that authorized Roger to act as papal legate for Sicily.[97] The '*Appendix ad Malaterram*', as it later came to be called, was subsequently renamed simply the '*Annales Siculi*', because most of this short work is a set of annals synopsizing the events of the Kingdom of Sicily to the end of the Hohenstaufen era.[98] These *Annales Siculi* also appear in MS Vaticanus latinus 6206 on folio 298r, immediately following the *Historia Sicula*.[99] It is the first two paragraphs of the *Annales Siculi* that are of critical concern here, for they are the portion which can be characterized as the '*Appendix ad Malaterram*'. They briefly describe what occurred between the death of the Great Count and the succession by his son, Roger II.[100] Intriguingly, these same two paragraphs conform almost *verbatim* to what most scholars consider the final passage of the *Historia Sicula* penned by Anonymus Vaticanus himself. The attached illustration (see Appendix) featuring a side-by-side comparison shows that the two different sources included the very same passage, nearly word-for-word. They are almost identical. Clearly, whoever composed the later *Annales Siculi* must have considered the *Historia Sicula* a worthy source, because he copied the '*Appendix ad Malaterram*' from it. Moreover, that same passage, with only minor variations, is contained in every known Latin manuscript that possesses the *Historia Sicula*. A paraphrased version of it even ends the Old French translation of the chronicle in BN MS français 688.[101] Finally, given that MS V.G. 31 of the Biblioteca Nazionale di Napoli also contains a truncated version of William of Apulia,[102] at least a segment of the *Historia Sicula* can be found in association with copies of all three of the principal Italo-Norman chroniclers. It thus seems that the chronicle of Anonymus Vaticanus was routinely recognized as a conventional component of Italo-Norman historiography.

---

96   *Appendix ex codice Marchionis Jarratannae ad ultimum capitulum Libri Quarti Historiae Gaufredi Malaterrae*, ed. G. Caruso, in *Bibliotheca Historica Regni Siciliae* (2 vols., Palermo, 1723), i, 249–255; ed. Muratori, *RIS* (8 vols., Milan, 1724), v, cols. 603–06; Palermo, MS I B 28, fols. 29v–31v.
97   Malaterra, *Deeds of Count Roger*, Bk. 4, ch. 29, 213–14 (=*De rebus gestis Rogerii*, Bk. IV, ch. XXIX, 106–8).
98   *Annali Siculi*, ed. G. Pertz, in MGH *SS xix*, 494–500; Pontieri, 'Premessa', *Annali Siculi*, ed. Pontieri, 111.
99   MS Vat. lat. 6206, fols. 298v–300r.
100 *Annali Siculi*, ed. Pontieri, 115.
101 Champollion-Figeac, *Chronique de Robert Viscart et de ses frères, L'Ystoire de li Normant et la Chronique de Robert Viscart*, 312–13.
102 Capasso, *Le Fonti della Storia delle Province Napolitane*, 83–84 note 1 and 85 note 1; Mathieu, 'Introduction', *La Geste de Robert Guiscard*, 82–83 and 83 note 1; Naples, Biblioteca Nazionale di Napoli, MS V.G. 31.

The evidence is circumstantial but compelling: the *Historia Sicula* of Anonymus Vaticanus is no mere slavish summary of Geoffrey Malaterra's work. To be sure, Anonymus obviously used Malaterra's chronicle as a template for his own history. After all, if Anonymus was indeed a Sicilian cleric commissioned by the court of Roger II, as scholars have hypothesized, then he would likely have had access to Malaterra's chronicle which featured the king's father. Nonetheless, he quite clearly had additional sources available, because he provides additional details and distinctive accounts. While Anonymus may not rise to Malaterra's level of reliability and breadth, he provides a useful supplementary source for the Normans in the south.

The chief value of the *Historia Sicula*, however, is that it serves to corroborate much of Malaterra's narrative and probably represents what was believed to have occurred by members of King Roger's court a half century later. As such, it should be considered a legitimate part of Italo-Norman historiography which modern medievalists, plagued by a persistent paucity of sources, can ill afford to ignore.

Appendix

Anonymi Historia Sicula a Normannis ad Petrum Aragonensem, ed. L. Muratori (Rerum Italicarum Scriptores, 28 vols., Milan, 1726), VIII, col. 777.	*Annali Siculi*, E. Pontieri (Rerum Italicarum Scriptores, 2nd edn, Bologna, 1928), V, 115 .

Post sanctissimus Comes occulto Dei judicio penitus a virili prole orbatus, fusa ad Deum prece in spe sobolis procreandae uxorem suam cognovit, in eaque filios, & filias generavit. Qui usque ad senectutem honestissimam agens vitam, plurimam aedificatione Ecclesiarum intentus, easque, prout insolita ipsius posteritas adhuc & regit, & conservat, per totam terram suam copiose ditando, & juxta Gallietum religiose, atque decenter ordinando, pius orphanorum protector, & munificus pauperum Christi sublevator extitit. Cumque his, & similibus proficiendo semper in melius, honestae Sanctitatis exemplum cunctis existeret, tandem necessaria humanae conditionis lege naturalem in eo dissolutionem operante, illam illustrem animam tanta collustratione, vel meritorum collegio, ante conspectum Divinae Majestatis expirando delegavit, corpusque eius apud Mellitum in Ecclesia, quam ipse fundaverat honorifice, ut tantum virum decebat, sepultum est. Post hunc Simon, filiorum primogenitus, regimen Consulare accepit: qui per paucos vivens annos, graves ab Apulis irritationes sustinuit. Huic successit ille hominum maximus a Deo dilectus, & benedictus unicus leo, & pacis fundamentum Rogerius, Mundi admiratio, virtutum omnium splendor, & prae Regibus haeres sapiens, & immensus omnia prius tamen Comes, postea Dei nutu, tum incomparabili eius scientia operante dignus, feroces Apuliae, & Capuae Principatus, ad ultimum Rex Siciliae, Tripolis Africae potentissimus, fines suos longe, lateque multiplici terrarum, acquisitione ampliavit; ad cuius laudes, & gesta probitatis singulariter referenda, quoniam Ciceronis eloquentiam insufficientem fuisse reputo, ego qui fere nullus sum, tantae gravitatis onus mihi adhuc incognitum in praesenti temptare formido.

Post haec ***piissimus*** comes, occulto Dei judicio penitus virili progenie orbatus, fusa ad Deum prece in spe sobolis procreandae, uxorem suam cognovit, in eaque filios et filias generavit. Qui, usque ad senectutem honestissimam agens vitam, plurimum in aedificatione ecclesarium intentus, easdem prout insoluta ipsius posteritas adhuc et regit et conservat, per totam terram suam copiose dotando et virorum psalentium religiose atque decenter ordinando, pius orphanorum et viduarum protector ac munificus pauperum Christi sublevator extitit. Cumque his et similibus proficiendo semper in melius honestae sanctitatis exemplum cunctis existeret, tandem necessaria humanae conditionis lege naturalem in ea dissolutionem operante, illam illustrem animam, tanta collustratione, ***ut meritorum agnitione insignitam, ad desiderata beatorum collegia*** ante conspectum Divinae Majestatis expirando delegavit; corpusque eius apud Melitum in ecclesia, quam ipse fundaverat, honorifice, ut tantum virum decebat, sepultum est. Post hunc Simon, filiorum primogenitus, regimen ***consulatus*** accepit. Qui, per paucos vivens annos, graves ab Apulis mutationes sustinuit. Huic successit ille hominum maximus, a Deo dilectus et benedictus, unicus leo et pacis firmamentum, Rogerius, mundi admiratio, virtutum omnium splendor, et prae regibus ***heros*** sapiens et immensus omnia, prius tamen comes, postea Dei multum incomparabili eius sapientia operante, dignus ***dux feracis*** Apuliae et Capuae principatus, ad ultimum rex Siciliae, Tripolis, Africae potentissimus, fines imperii sui longe lateque multiplici terrarum acquisitione ampliavit: ad cuius laudes et gesta probitatis singulariter referenda quoniam Ciceronis eloquentiam insufficientem fuisse reputo. Ego, qui fere nullus sum, tantae gravitatis onus mihi adhuc incognitum in praesenti tentare formido.

5

The Denis Bethell Prize Essay

Christian Community and the Crusades: Religious and Social Practices in the De expugnatione Lyxbonensi*

Susanna A. Throop

The study of crusading religious practices has often focused on practices undertaken at home or at the beginning of a crusade, such as liturgy or the practice of taking the cross.[1] In contrast, the religious practices performed routinely during the crusade itself have been relatively less explored.[2] Yet, analyzing the devotional activities of crusaders while they were actually on

* I am grateful to a number of institutions and individuals for their help. My first thanks are owed to Ursinus College for a 2011 'Summer 2000' grant in support of this research. My colleagues Elizabeth Ho (English) and Philippa Townsend (Philosophy and Religious Studies) at Ursinus are owed particular thanks for helping me to communicate my argument effectively and identifying key readings in the field of religious studies. I am grateful to Julie Hofmann, Nathan Rein, David Perry, Paul Hyams, and Rabia Gregory for their help with particularly ambiguous sections of Latin, as well as to those who attended the 2011 Haskins Society Conference and provided helpful feedback on my paper there, especially Paul Hyams and Richard Abels. Finally, I thank the editors of the Haskins Society Journal for their helpfully incisive feedback. Unless otherwise cited, all translations are my own; I have chosen to emphasize literal clarity rather than eloquence in translating many passages. Of course all errors are also my own, and not the responsibility of the kind souls who have attempted to save me from them.

[1] See, for example, James A. Brundage, '"*Cruce Signari*": The Rite for Taking the Cross in England', *Traditio* 22 (1966), 289–310, and his 'The Army of the First Crusade and the Crusade Vow: Some Reflections on a Recent Book', *Mediaeval Studies* 33 (1971), 334–43. Beverly M. Kienzle, 'Preaching the Cross: Liturgy and Crusade Propaganda', *Medieval Sermon Studies* 53 (2009), 11–32; Christoph T. Maier, 'Crisis, Liturgy and the Crusade in the Twelfth and Thirteenth Centuries', *JEH* 48:4 (1997), 628–57; Kenneth Pennington, 'The Rite for Taking the Cross in the Twelfth Century', *Traditio* 30 (1974), 429–35; Lucy K. Pick, '*Signaculum caritatis et fortitudinis*: Blessing the Crusader's Cross in France', *Revue Bénédictine* 105 (1995), 381–416; Derek Rivard, *Blessing the World: Ritual and Lay Piety in Medieval Religion* (Washington, DC, 2009). M. Cecilia Gaposchkin is now working on a devotional history of the crusades, tentatively entitled *Crusade, Liturgy, Ideology, and Devotion: 1050–1400.*

[2] One notable exception is David S. Bachrach, whose work (cited repeatedly below) has continually highlighted religious practices during war, crusading, and other forms of conflict.

crusade has the potential to illuminate not only the crusading movement but also points of intersection and divergence between that movement and larger cultural trends. Furthermore, although some crusading accounts admittedly provide little information on the religious practices of crusaders, others are more forthcoming. Among these, the Anglo-Norman account of the 1147 conquest of Lisbon during the Second Crusade, the *De expugnatione Lyxbonensi*, is a particularly rich source of information on the daily religious lives of men and women on crusade.

As I will demonstrate, religious practices in the *De expugnatione Lyxbonensi* resonate with ideals and themes active in both contemporary monastic reform and the development of lay piety. Furthermore, they are articulated via the social customs associated with *coniuratio*, a sworn, oath-bound society. A connection between crusading and monastic ideals is hardly surprising, ever since Jonathan Riley-Smith noted that the First Crusaders were in effect 'a military monastery on the move'.[3] For the most part, however, historians' development of this idea has understandably focused on the ways in which crusaders were like monks and/or inhabited a similar ideological universe to that of advocates of reform monasticism.[4] In this article I explore the different, though complementary, connection between crusader religious practices and their conception of community. I will argue that in the *De expugnatione Lyxbonensi* the author's main emphasis is the importance of creating and maintaining a united Christian community in which social and spiritual practices work together to sustain a more perfect society, and that it was this society, in turn, that ultimately enabled individual reform and salvation. In other words, a significant point of connection between crusading, monastic reform, and lay piety is to be found in the daily religious practices themselves, because it was these that played a vital role in both describing and achieving this community.

In what follows I will first outline religious practices in the *De expugnatione Lyxbonensi* and describe how those practices compare with contemporary wartime practices in general.[5] I will then discuss the relationship between

---

[3]   Jonathan Riley-Smith, *The First Crusade and the Idea of Crusading* (London, 1986), 84.
[4]   For example, see William Purkis, *Crusading Spirituality in the Holy Land and Iberia, c. 1095–c. 1187* (Woodbridge, 2008), and 'Religious Symbols and Practices: Monastic Spirituality, Pilgrimage and Crusade', in *European Religious Cultures: Essays Offered to Christopher Brooke on the Occasion of his Eightieth Birthday*, ed. M. Rubin (London, 2008), 69–88; and James A. Brundage, 'Crusades, Clerics and Violence: Reflections on a Canonical Theme', in *The Experience of Crusading 1: Western Approaches*, ed. M. Bull and N. Housley (Cambridge, 2003), 147–56. The reverse point – that monks were, in turn, deeply affected by the medieval culture of war – has been driven home most recently by Katherine Allen Smith in her *War and the Making of Medieval Monastic Culture* (Woodbridge, 2011).
[5]   Since antiquity individuals have recognized that wartime religious practices fall into two categories: those undertaken on campaign and those performed at home on behalf of armies in the field. On this, see David S. Bachrach, *Religion and the Conduct of War c. 300–1215*

these religious practices, monastic reform, the development of lay piety, and *coniuratio*, stressing the common emphasis of all of these on the ideal of Christian community. Finally, I will consider the implications of my argument for our understanding of the purpose of the *De expugnatione Lyxbonensi* as text and of the twelfth-century crusades more generally as action. Before going further, however, a few words describing the text and delineating what I mean by 'religious practices' are in order.

The *De expugnatione Lyxbonensi* was written circa 1147–1148, although the earliest extant manuscript containing the text dates to the 1160s–1170s. Not only was this detailed account of the 1147 campaign to take Lisbon written very shortly after the events it described, it was composed by a clerical eye-witness.[6] The campaign was led by King Afonso Henriques (Afonso I) of the newly-established kingdom of Portugal, along with an assorted cast of crusaders, featuring contingents from the Anglo-Norman world and Flanders as well as Cologne and the Rhineland.[7] Notably, most of these crusaders were from the 'middle ranks of society'—'lesser landowners, knights, burgesses, merchants, and priests'.[8] The author of the *De expugnatione Lyxbonensi* has been convincingly identified as Raol, an Anglo-Norman clergyman who seems to have had some social standing of his own or may have been a papal legate. He composed his account in the form of a letter to a colleague, Osbert of Bawdsey, a cleric connected with the Glanvill family of East Anglia.[9]

(Woodbridge, 2003), 1–2. Here I am considering the first type – religious practices on campaign. For more on the second type – religious practices on the home front – in relation to medieval crusading, see in particular Maier, 'Crisis, Liturgy and the Crusade'.

[6]   Harold Livermore, 'The "Conquest of Lisbon" and its Author', *Portuguese Studies* 6 (1990), 1–16 at 3. Other helpful analyses of the content of the *De expugnatione Lyxbonensi* include Matthew Bennett, 'Military Aspects of the Conquest of Lisbon, 1147', in *The Second Crusade: Scope and Consequences*, ed. J. Phillips and M. Hoch (Manchester, 2001), 71–89; Bachrach, *Religion and the Conduct of War*, 129–35; Giles Constable, 'The Second Crusade as Seen by Contemporaries', *Traditio* 9 (1953), 213–79; Stephen Lay, 'Miracles, Martyrs and the Cult of Henry the Crusader in Lisbon', *Portuguese Studies* 24(2008), 7–31; and Jonathan Phillips, 'Ideas of Crusade and Holy War in *De expugnatione Lyxbonensi*', *Studies in Church History* 36 (2000), 123–41.

[7]   For the best overview of the Lisbon campaign, see Jonathan Phillips, *The Second Crusade: Extending the Frontiers of Christendom* (New Haven, CT, 2007), 136–67. Other relevant studies of the campaign (broadly construed) include: Susan B. Edgington, 'Albert of Aachen, St Bernard and the Second Crusade', in *The Second Crusade: Scope and Consequences*, 54–70; Alan Forey, 'The Siege of Lisbon and the Second Crusade', *Portuguese Studies* 20 (2004), 1–13; Giles Constable, 'A Further Note on the Conquest of Lisbon in 1147', in *The Experience of Crusading 1: Western Approaches*, 39–44; Nikolas Jaspert, '"Capta est Dertosa, clavis Christianorum"*: Tortosa and the Crusades', in *The Second Crusade: Scope and Consequences*, 90–110; Jonathan Phillips, 'St Bernard of Clairvaux, the Low Countries and the Lisbon Letter of the Second Crusade', *JEH* 48 (1997), 485–97.

[8]   Christopher Tyerman, *England and the Crusades, 1095–1588* (Chicago, IL, 1988), 33.

[9]   Hervey of Glanvill served as the constable for the contingent from Suffolk and Norfolk at Lisbon. See Livermore, 'The "Conquest of Lisbon"', and Phillips, *The Second Crusade*, 143.

Although religious practices are more vivid in the *De expugnatione Lyxbonensi* than in some other texts, nonetheless the text is clearly neither a catalog nor a journalistic report, but rather a series of snapshots of certain religious practices that were presumably selected by Raol, a clerical participant, and/or carefully edited by clerical redactors or copyists in East Anglia.[10] We do not have unfettered access to religious practices on the Lisbon expedition, let alone 'crusading religious practices' more broadly, through the text; rather, we have access to the religious practices that were thought to be most significant for narrative or ideological purposes.[11]

Table 1: Religious Practices in the *De expugnatione Lyxbonensi*[12]

Dartmouth Rules	58
Prayers during a storm at sea	60
Blessing, sermon, mass and absolution after arrival at Oporto	68–84
Threat of excommunication during disagreement over Afonso's offer	98–110
Pre-skirmish absolution and blessing	126
Construction of two churches and cemeteries during siege	132–4
Weekly mass and daily distribution of eulogia during siege	134
Blessing of a siege tower, sermon with relic, marking with the sign of the cross before assault	146–58
Processions and circuits of the conquered city, rites of purification and praise	174–80

The question of what constitutes a religious practice has long been debated in many fields, including anthropology, sociology, history, philosophy, and of course, religious studies.[13] Needless to say, modern theory is the product of our own unique historical moment and cannot by itself define medieval phenomena for us. But in thinking about medieval Christian religious practices I have found several points made by modern theorists especially useful, not because they can or should define the medieval evidence, but rather because they provide a thought-provoking context for that evidence. First, because

[10] As Giles Constable has noted, any epistolary work was open for revision from the moment of first dictation through incorporation into a letter collection; see his *Letters and Letter-Collections* (Turnhout, 1965), 51. See my comments below.
[11] My interest was piqued by the initial work for my 'Rules and Ritual on the Second Crusade', in *Medieval Christianity in Practice*, ed. M. Rubin (Princeton, NJ, 2009), 86–91.
[12] Page numbers refer to the *De expugnatione Lyxbonensi*, in *The Conquest of Lisbon*, ed. and trans. C. W. David with new forward and bibliography by J. Phillips (New York, NY, 2001) [hereafter, *De expugnatione*].
[13] As a medieval historian wading into these waters, I found the following works extremely helpful: Catherine Bell, *Ritual Theory, Ritual Practice* (Oxford, 1992) and Talal Asad, *Genealogies of Religion: Discipline and Reasons of Power in Christianity and Islam* (Baltimore, MD, 1993).

religious practices derive significance and meaning from 'interplay and contrast with other practices', they should not be divorced from their specific historical context.[14] Furthermore, they should not be viewed as a kind of action entirely distinct from other actions undertaken by the same actors; in fact, they gain distinction from their imitation of other routine actions. As Catherine Bell puts it, religious practices represent 'the very drawing, in and through the activity itself, of a privileged distinction between ways of acting'.[15] For example, the way that the eucharist imitates a regular meal serves to underline, rather than negate, its distinctiveness. Second, Talal Asad has rightly asserted that medieval Christian religious practices were intimately related to the cultivation of virtue and thus, ultimately, the attainment of salvation. As he explains, based on an analysis of the *Rule of St Benedict*,

Each thing to be done was not only to be done aptly in itself, but done in order to make the self approximate more and more to a predefined model of excellence. The things prescribed, including liturgical services, had a place in the overall scheme of training the Christian self. In this conception, there could be no radical disjunction between outer behavior and inner motive, between social rituals and individual sentiments, between activities that are expressive and those that are technical.[16]

This suggests that when looking at medieval Christian religious practices it may be misleading to presuppose more traditional dichotomies of practical/ symbolic, action/belief, social/individual. Third, as Bell explains, religious practices are actions undertaken in order to effect something. In other words, they are actions designed to promote further action, especially when participants face both indirect access to divine power and a combined emphasis on social and individual salvation, as found in medieval Christianity.[17] Taken together, these points from Bell and Asad steer us away from black-and-white definitions of religious practices as well as from simplistic, one-dimensional explanations of the function of religious practices. They also emphasize the importance of historical context and the impossibility of understanding religious practices outside their specific cultural milieu. Therefore, I have identified religious practices very broadly as behaviors intended to advance the spiritual goals of participants, both as a group and as individuals. As I will show, most of these religious practices performed important social, as well as spiritual, functions.

---

[14] Both Bell and Asad make this point, but the quotation is from Bell, *Ritual Theory*, 90.
[15] Bell, *Ritual Theory*, 90.
[16] Asad, *Genealogies of Religion*, 63. A very similar point, based on an analysis of Augustine's works, has been made by Kienzle, 'Preaching the Cross', 16.
[17] Bell, *Ritual Theory*, 116.

'Changing the will, not the deed': religious practices or crusading practices?[18]

One of the first questions to be answered is whether religious practices in the text could be considered 'crusading' practices; in other words, were these religious practices singular to crusading in some way? When religious practices in the text are analyzed one by one, the answer is no. Religious practices in the text are not a reliable indicator of the crusading nature of the expedition. Put another way, we could not definitively state that the expedition was a crusade by looking at this or that religious practice because most of the practices described in the text have clear counterparts either in wartime Christian practices or in the customary practices of pilgrimage. This interpretive ambiguity confirms the work of other scholars on the slow development of crusade-specific wartime religious practices[19] and the close relationship between pilgrimage and crusade in the twelfth century,[20] and also emphasizes the conservative nature of medieval wartime practices in general.[21] I will argue below, however, that when they are viewed comprehensively, it is clear that religious practices in the text do, in fact, reveal the strong influence of contemporary social and religious trends on the practice of crusading.[22]

Any discussion of religious practices in the *De expugnatione Lyxbonensi* must begin with the communal rules for behavior established by crusade participants at Dartmouth before the fleet sailed, referred to here as the Dartmouth Rules. The decision to set such communal rules for conduct on crusade was not unique; at least one contemporary crusade expedition established, or attempted to establish, a code of conduct upon embarkation.[23] Indeed, at least as far back as the Carolingian period, military sermons had been used to remind soldiers of regulations about their behavior both before and during battle, including restrictions on sexual activity and looting.[24] Similarly, the Dartmouth Rules reflect the importance of right intention

---

[18] The quote is from Bishop Peter Pitões' sermon at Oporto, in which he states: 'You, so it seems, carry arms and the insignia of a military undertaking, but with a different affect, or to say it better, changing the will not the deed, according to the counsel of the apostle ...' (*De expugnatione*, 82).

[19] Maier, 'Crisis, Liturgy and the Crusade', 629.

[20] Purkis, *Crusading Spirituality*.

[21] Bachrach, *Religion and the Conduct of War*, 4.

[22] Such a relationship between contemporary religious practices and crusading ideology is broadly accepted, and most clearly and fully articulated by Purkis in *Crusading Spirituality*.

[23] Philips, *The Second Crusade*, 186. Constable, 'The Second Crusade as Seen by Contemporaries', 240. Social disorder posed a real threat to the success of a crusading expedition and was a significant problem for contingents heading east during the Second Crusade; see, for example, Conor Kostick, 'Social Unrest and the Failure of Conrad III's March through Anatolia, 1147', *German History* 28 (2010), 125–42.

[24] Bachrach, *Religion and the Conduct of War*, 54.

in holy war and echo points made in Eugenius' bull *Quantum praedeces-sores*.[25] Coordinating the movement and behavior of various independent contingents from different regions of Western Europe also posed a severe logistical problem, and Jonathan Phillips is surely correct that there was a strong pragmatic purpose underlying the emphasis on unity evident in the rules.[26] This point finds further support in David Bachrach's observation that the use of religious practices to enforce unity had an effect both on practical camp discipline, and on the less tangible phenomenon of *esprit de corps*.[27]

The *De expugnatione Lyxbonensi* gives us unusually specific details about the content of the Dartmouth Rules. The religious practices set by the Dartmouth Rules were singularly rigorous.[28] Each ship of crusaders was to have its own priest, who was to officiate just as he had done in his parish back home. We know that at various times and places in medieval France and England, parish priests were expected to accompany their parishioners to war.[29] This requirement was surely due at least in part to the commonly held belief, later expressed in Canon 21 of the Fourth Lateran Council of 1215, that Christians should only confess to their own parish priest.[30] The Dartmouth Rules further stipulate that clergy and laity were to hold weekly religious services but separately from each other. Further, every person was to confess and take communion every week. Weekly confession and communion would have been quite exceptional for the laity in the mid twelfth-century. It was not until 1215 that even annual confession was stipulated, and presumably it took even longer for practice to match theory. In addition, the Dartmouth Rules included regulations that, to modern eyes at least, seem to have served social ends, such as guidelines for dispensing justice. Thus, although the concept of

---

[25] Phillips, *The Second Crusade*, 38.
[26] Phillips, 'Ideas of Crusade and Holy War', 134.
[27] Bachrach, *Religion and the Conduct of War*, 38–9.
[28] *De expugnatione*, 58.
[29] Bachrach, *Religion and the Conduct of War*, 92, 154, 156. As a contemporary example, Aelred of Rivaulx in his *Relatio de Standardo* notes that at the 1138 Battle of the Standard, parish priests were dispatched with their communities, and ordered to bring relics, crosses, and banners with them (cited in Bachrach, *Religion and the Conduct of War*, 182). It is worth noting that in the earlier Middle Ages this expectation came from secular leaders. The medieval Church did not issue specific guidelines on pastoral care for soldiers until Innocent III's bull *Ad liberandum* from the Fourth Lateran Council of 1215. See David S. Bachrach, 'The Friars Go To War: Mendicant Military Chaplains, 1216–*c.* 1300', *Catholic Historical Review* 90 (2004), 617–33 at 619–20.
[30] David S. Bachrach, 'The Organisation of Military Religion in the Armies of King Edward I of England (1272–1307)', *JMH* 29 (2003), 265–86 at 268. In England, even before 1215 church statutes forbade priests to hear confessions from strangers unless permission from their parish priests had been granted or there were conditions of dire necessity (Bachrach, 'The Organization of Military Religion', 268 note 8).

regulating behavior was not new, the Dartmouth Rules appear to be unique in the intensity and variety of the religious practices which they prescribed.[31]

As it narrates the progress of the expedition, the *De expugnatione Lyxobonensi* describes more routine religious practices. While sailing, the crusaders encountered a storm at sea and prayed to God in their fear.[32] The practice of praying when faced with natural disaster was not specific to crusade or even to war. As in many hagiographical, autobiographical, and travel accounts, the prayers in the *De expugnatione Lyxbonensi* served to mark a spiritual turning point for many, who 'confessing many sins and acts of negligence with tears and groans, cleansing the conversion (however begun) of their pilgrimage with a flood of tears, celebrated mass in the shelter of a contrite heart'.[33] This passage is conventional in a number of ways: the 'storm at sea' as a moment of spiritual crisis, concern over the role played by personal sins in provoking the crisis, and participation in prayers invoking God's aid and forgiveness. The text also describes the expedition as a kind of *conversio*, an act of turning towards God, equivalent to the taking of monastic vows or vows of pilgrimage.[34]

Routine and unsurprising religious practices continue when the first part of the expedition landed at Oporto and were met by the bishop of the city, Peter Pitões, who indicated that he bore a message from King Afonso Henriques. The first to arrive decided, since it was late in the day and some among them had not come ashore, to defer their answer until the next day, 'so that all those who were in the ships could equally hear the mandates of the king, and receive absolution of their sins and a blessing from the bishop'.[35] Accordingly, early the next morning everyone from the ships met the bishop at the top of a hill in the cathedral cemetery and heard one of the three significant set speeches in the text: the sermon of Peter Pitões.[36] Upon completion of the sermon, mass was celebrated.[37]

The crusaders eventually heard Afonso's appeal after landing at Lisbon, but

---

[31] For further discussion of the Dartmouth Rules and the importance of *coniuratio*, see below.

[32] *De expugnatione*, 60. The view that, despite their fears, the crusaders were not actually at risk of losing God's favor was made clear by the sentence preceding their prayers: 'Therefore all through the night of the Lord's Ascension, divine mercy was a companion and guardian to those in distress, so that [divine mercy] might castigate them with chastisement and not deliver them to death.'

[33] *De expugnatione*, 60.

[34] Giles Constable, *The Reformation of the Twelfth Century* (Cambridge, 1996), 15. The implication of 'conversionem ... utcumque inceptam' seems to be that the expedition was indeed an act of *conversio*, no matter what motives may have originally driven each participant. I discuss further implications of the use of *conversio* below.

[35] *De expugnatione*, 68.

[36] *De expugnatione*, 70–84. The intellectual content of the sermon has been well analyzed. See, in particular, Phillips, 'Ideas of Crusade', 128–32 and Constable, 'The Second Crusade as Seen by Contemporaries', 213–79.

[37] *De expugnatione*, 84.

the discord that resulted from his offer nearly resulted in the excommunication of some contingents. At first glance, this use of excommunication seems
extreme in context, though further examination shows it reflected precedent.
To summarize, when the crusaders began to deliberate over Afonso's offer,
discord arose over issues such as financial considerations and the spiritual
need to complete the pilgrimage to Jerusalem, although it is notable that
the text presents the ultimate underlying cause as envy.[38] A contingent of
Normans and men from Southampton and Bristol broke off from the rest of
the crusaders, led by one William Vitulus (or Viel), a member of a prominent
maritime family that had experienced disappointment during an earlier
military action in Portugal in 1140.[39] The author – clearly favorable to those
who wished to remain in Portugal – tells us that when it became clear that
a unanimous decision would not be reached 'we formed a council to exhort
the wrong-headed, so that either with encouragement and flattering promises
we might keep them with us, or that we might separate them from all of us
and from the holy community of the mother church, as though they were
transgressors of the faith, an oath, and a sworn society [fidei iuramentique
transgressores coniurateque societatis]'.[40] In other words, if unity could not
be maintained through unanimous consensus, then it would be maintained by
the expulsion of the adverse elements through excommunication.

Scholars have remarked on the severity of excommunication in this context,
suggesting that it indicates the importance placed upon the maintenance of
unity.[41] Although this is surely true, more can be said. First, in the aftermath
of the First Crusade excommunication was often aimed at 'renegade'
crusaders, those who did not fulfill their vows.[42] In the *De expugnatione
Lyxbonensi*, however, the offense being punished with excommunication is
not that of foreswearing crusade vows in general (because the break-away
party was not) but rather of abandoning the 'faith, oath, and sworn society'
embodied in the Dartmouth Rules. In this light, it seems that participants
were applying a known and familiar tool (excommunication) in a slightly
unfamiliar way; it is less surprising that excommunication was considered,
than that the Dartmouth Rules were considered of equal, and indeed greater
force, to the crusade vow itself.

Confession prior to battle, usually by individuals, had been a part of
Christian wartime practices since before Carolingian times and continued to
feature in accounts of the First Crusade, but we see something less common

---

[38] *De expugnatione*, 100.
[39] *De expugnatione*, 104. For the previous history of the Vitulus family, see Livermore, 'The
"Conquest of Lisbon"', 8.
[40] *De expugnatione*, 104.
[41] Phillips, *The Second Crusade*, 151.
[42] Brundage, 'The Army of the First Crusade and the Crusade Vow', 335–36.

in the *De expugnatione Lyxbonensi*.[43] The assault through the city suburbs during the siege shows us a form of abbreviated communal absolution instead of individual confession. In the text, Saher of Archelle is sent to bring back the crusader troops at the end of the day, only to find that the situation made such a retreat inadvisable. Saher makes a crucial decision to reengage the enemy immediately: 'all were ordered to come forth quickly from the camps by the lord Saher, while the Bishop of Oporto blessed and absolved all'.[44] The context as well as the grammar of the passage ('episcopo ... benedicente atque absolvente' with the ablative of attendant circumstances) suggests some sort of rough and ready communal absolution and blessing: one can almost see the men running with arms in hand and armor half in place, while Peter Pitões hastily absolves and scatters blessings at high volume. Although this is the only description of pre-battle confession and absolution before the final assault, the image generated of hasty absolutions dispensed at speed seems realistic and implies that participants desired and valued such absolutions.

The crusaders' construction of churches and cemeteries during the siege is worthy of discussion, but not because it breaks with standard wartime practices. The text tells us: 'two churches were constructed by the Franks for the burial of the dead, one on the eastern side by the men from Cologne and Flanders, on the spot where two [men] mute from birth, received the service of speech with the help of God, the other by the English and the Normans on the western side.'[45] Yet these churches and cemeteries – of São Vicente de Fora for the men of Cologne and Flanders and Santa Maria dos Mártires for the Anglo-Normans – were not built to facilitate routine religious practices such as mass, for since the time of Constantine, armies had brought along portable altars for such purposes.[46] Rather, as Stephen Lay has pointed out, the building of the Lisbon churches was based on the belief that fallen soldiers were not simply crusaders but martyrs. To be a crusader was to receive a spiritual reward from the hand of the pope on behalf of God, while to be a martyr was to receive 'a privilege granted directly from heaven'.[47] Thus although the text does not state this explicitly, the construction of these churches and cemeteries seems to suggest a firm belief in the rightness of Christian actions at Lisbon, and an insistence on the direct relationship between crusaders and their God.

In addition, David Bachrach has shown how the construction of commemorative churches or 'battle abbeys' on the home front served to alleviate local concerns about the status of the souls of fallen fathers, husbands, and sons.[48]

---

[43] Bachrach, *Religion and the Conduct of War,* 43–9.
[44] *De expugnatione,* 126.
[45] *De expugnatione,* 132–34.
[46] Bachrach, *Religion and the Conduct of War*, 17.
[47] Lay, 'Miracles, Martyrs and the Cult of Henry the Crusader', 12.
[48] Bachrach, *Religion and the Conduct of War*, 76.

In this light, it is possible to read the construction of São Vicente de Fora and Santa Maria dos Mártires as polysemic: a public attempt to both alleviate concerns about the souls of fallen comrades, and indeed, the souls of soldiers still at risk, and to satisfy the desire for celebration of martyrdom among those more convinced of the certainty of martyrdom. The first motivation was surely not confined to crusading, while the latter was perhaps more crusade-specific. As Bachrach has noted, although it was not uncommon for fallen soldiers to be considered martyrs as far back as late antiquity, nevertheless the crusades appear to have spurred a huge increase in perceptions of martyrdom.[49] That time, energy, and resources were dedicated to this task in the midst of a siege suggests that spiritual reassurance and commemoration were important for the crusaders, as indeed they were for medieval Christian soldiers in other wars.[50]

Right after discussing the construction of the churches, the text indicates that weekly mass had been continuing, as the Dartmouth Rules stipulated. Further, and more exceptionally, as C.W. David noted, the text seems to suggest that a daily distribution of the *eulogia*, or blessed bread, was taking place.[51] The text devotes the most space, however, to describing a portent that some thought cast aspersions on the motives of the Flemings:

For on a Sunday after the completion of mass, the priest saw that the blessed bread [panem benedictum] was bloody, which when he ordered it to be cut with a knife, was found to be permeated with blood, like flesh that cannot be sliced without blood. Indeed after that it was divided into pieces of the same appearance and was seen even for many days after the capture of the city. But some who interpreted this, were claiming that this fierce and indomitable people, desirous of what belonged to others, had not yet lost a thirst for human blood, even though they were then [acting] under the guise of pilgrimage and religion.[52]

In this passage we almost accidentally get a glimpse of weekly mass, and learn that the celebration of mass and communion were taking place within sub-divided regional communities. The apparent distribution of blessed bread over a number of days is striking and not a wartime religious practice that one encounters regularly in medieval texts. While certainly regular masses feature in any number of wartime accounts from the tenth century onwards, it is more usual to find soldiers taking communion just before battle rather than routinely.[53] As previously noted, in daily life it was rare enough for a lay person to take communion once or twice a year.[54] Blessed bread was not

49 Bachrach, *Religion and the Conduct of War*, 148.
50 Bachrach, *Religion and the Conduct of War*, 76.
51 *De expugnatione*, 134 n. 2.
52 *De expugnatione*, 134. Other scholars have commented on the anti-Flemish tone of the passage; see, in particular, Lay, 'Miracles, Martyrs and the Cult of Henry the Crusader'.
53 Bachrach, *Religion and the Conduct of War*, 95–96.
54 See above page 101.

the eucharist, because it had not been consecrated. Nevertheless, why would blessed bread be distributed so regularly?

The social function of mass and communion, and in particular the way these rites served to consolidate unity while at the same time accentuating the differences between the unified and those outside that unity, has been explored by John Bossy.[55] The most applicable point from Bossy's work is that the celebration of communion, as the sacrament that complemented the mass's role as sacrifice, served to cement the bonds of Christian love among those present.[56] Working from this, perhaps the regular distribution of blessed bread in addition to regular celebration of communion simply intensified the sense of joint endeavor and *esprit de corps*. In addition, Bachrach has argued that while pre-battle confession served to purify soldiers and make them worthy of divine aid, pre-battle communion served to strengthen and fortify soldiers in both body and soul.[57] In this light, perhaps more regular distribution of blessed bread can be seen as an attempt to keep the physical and spiritual strength of the soldiers 'topped off', ensuring they would be ready for action whenever necessary; this may have been of particular relevance during a siege, when some encounters with the enemy came too suddenly for any communion to precede them. Due to the repeated encounters with priests necessitated by the practice, it may also have helped to keep the crusaders behaving in morally appropriate ways.

In the religious practices just before the final assault on the city we see much that is standard and predictable, along with one surprise. The text's general outline of the religious practices that directly precede pitched battle conforms to that of other crusading and non-crusading accounts: the preparation of military technology, the blessing of equipment, prayer, the delivery of an inspiring sermon emphasizing God's omnipotence and the Christian's hope of everlasting life in Christ, and finally an assault accompanied by requests for God's aid.[58] The siege tower itself is blessed and sprinkled with holy water, an act of purification symbolically similar to the sacraments of baptism and church consecration. Based on what we know about the blessing of other accoutrements of war, the blessing of the siege tower itself surely served to 'convert a tool of violence into a blessed object', accentuating the unique spiritual merit of the current situation and the special status of participants; the same action transformed the tower into a powerful symbol of God's offensive and protective capabilities.[59]

After the blessing of the tower, a priest (perhaps Raol himself), holding

[55] John Bossy, 'The Mass as a Social Institution 1200–1700', *Past and Present* 100 (1983), 29–61.
[56] Bossy, 'Mass as a Social Institution', 34–35.
[57] Bachrach, *Religion and the Conduct of War*, 95–98, 117–18.
[58] *De expugnatione*, 146–58.
[59] Rivard, *Blessing the World*, 157–64.

aloft in his hand a portion of the relic of the cross of Christ, delivered an inspiring sermon.[60] Relics were seen as conduits to holy power, and the priest called upon his listeners to abase themselves before the relic of the cross, since it was generally believed that the proper way to solicit help from a relic was through humility and/or humiliation.[61] The priest's soldierly audience, like medieval Christians in virtually all contexts, were supposed to believe that they could only conquer through God's will and with his help, making it extremely important to beg for his aid and express their own awareness of his power and their comparative impotence.[62] The priest's sermon clearly conveyed this message, and the audience's behavior signified (albeit superficially) their acceptance of it.

Much has been made of the reported deployment of the relic of the True Cross on this expedition. Some have expressed interest that the phenomenon of taking a piece of the True Cross into battle could so swiftly have moved back to Europe from the Latin kingdoms in the east.[63] Yet, it is worth remembering that, from the time of Constantine I, relics and banners bearing Christian symbols had 'served both as a continuing physical reminder of the support provided by God and the saints to soldiers, and as *loci* of heavenly power on the battlefield'.[64] Crosses in particular (though, certainly, not always relics of the 'true cross') had played important roles in pre-battle exhortations since the Carolingian period. For example, a battlefield prayer from the late 820s, known as the *Benedictio crucis*, 'called upon God to bless the standard of the cross so that it would aid His faithful followers and help to defend them against their enemies. The prayer envisioned a cleric holding up the cross on a banner of some sort before which the king and his men were to kneel and beg God to aid them.'[65] Furthermore, contemporary events make it difficult to claim that the use of a relic of the true cross was a particular sign that this was a crusade. In 1141, for example, Bishop Albero II of Liège ordered city militias to support his siege of the fortress of Bouillon, held illegally by Count Rainald of Bar. The townsmen of Liège insisted that they be preceded into battle by St Lambert, their patron. Two days of rituals took place, including a procession with the saint's body. The procession was headed by a priest carrying a '"portion of the life-giving wood" ... which the anonymous author of the chronicle described as an object of such power that

[60] Livermore, 'The "Conquest of Lisbon"', 7.
[61] Lester K. Little, *Benedictine Maledictions: Liturgical Cursing in Romanesque France* (Ithaca, NY, 1993), 26–30.
[62] Bachrach, *Religion and the Conduct of War*; see also Rivard, *Blessing the World*, 176–77.
[63] Phillips, 'Ideas of Crusade', 138. Phillips cites Allan Murray, '"Mighty against the enemies of Christ": The Relic of the True Cross in the Armies of the Kingdom of Jerusalem', in *The Crusades and their Sources: Essays Presented to Bernard Hamilton*, ed. J. France and W. Zajac (Aldershot, 1998), 217–38.
[64] Bachrach, *Religion and the Conduct of War*, 90.
[65] Bachrach, *Religion and the Conduct of War*, 40.

it would bring victory'.[66] The practice of using blessed crosses and especially of fragments of the true cross would seem, therefore, to be an already well established practice of Christian warfare.

The correlation between the priest's instructions and the behavior of his audience, while notable, is also not exceptional:

'… Behold, brothers, behold the wood of the Lord's cross. Bend your knees, lie down flat on the ground, beat your guilty chests, beg the Lord for help. For it will come, it will come. You will see the help of the Lord above you. Adore the Lord Christ, who on the life-giving wood of the cross spread his hands and feet for your salvation and glory … Amen.' At this utterance all present cried out, with moans and tears, lying flat on their stomachs. Then, at the command of the priest, all stood and were signed with the venerable sign of the lordly cross in the name of the Father and the Son and the Holy Spirit. And thus they began to move the [siege tower] almost fifteen cubits towards the [city] wall, unanimously crying out and begging for God to help them …[67]

The coordination between priest and laity emphasizes that this event was one in which all present understood their roles and fully participated, rather than simply a clerical performance to a passive lay audience. Yet, although this would seem to be a particularly appropriate message in the context of a crusade, in which clergy and laity alike had active roles to play, both the ninth-century *Benedictio crucis* described above and David D'Avray's work on twelfth-century sermons suggests that such active clerical-lay collaboration extended well beyond crusading.[68]

The *De expugnatione lyxbonensi* also records that after the sermon participants were signed with the cross.[69] Christopher Tyerman interpreted this passage as the 'taking of the cross' by participants, yet also argued that the crusaders had surely assumed the cross earlier. To resolve this puzzle, Tyerman speculated that perhaps the act served to boost morale or to incorporate any participants who for some reason had yet to take the cross. Alternatively, he suggested that the reference to 'signing with the cross' may indicate that this was a set sermon designed for crusade preaching that was incorporated into the *De expugnatione Lyxbonensi* in such a way as to leave incongruities.[70]

---

66 Bachrach, *Religion and the Conduct of War*, 173
67 *De expugnatione*, 154–56.
68 D'Avray notes that medieval sermons should be considered 'a cultural phenomenon in which both clergy and laity participated in different ways and degrees' (*The Preaching of the Friars: Sermons Diffused from Paris before 1300* (Oxford, 1985), 64). See also Christoph T. Maier, 'Sermons as Evidence for the Communication between Clergy and Laity', in *Bilan et perspectives des études médiévales (1993–1998)*, ed. J. Harnesse (Brepols, 2004), 223–43.
69 '… venerabili crucis dominice signo in nomine Patris et Filii et Spiritus Sancti consignati sunt' (*De expugnatione*, 158).
70 Tyerman, *England and the Crusades*, 35.

This latter hypothesis seems unnecessary, since the themes in the sermon and the practices associated with it so closely correspond to the rest of the text.[71] Furthermore, the *De expugnatione Lyxbonensi* does not actually tell us that participants 'took the cross' or even crusade-specific vows before their departure from Dartmouth; we do not know if some or all of the participants had or had not 'taken the cross' at this point. Based on the Latin, it is not even clear whether this was a crusade-specific 'taking of the cross' or just a simple blessing with the sign of the cross to conclude. After all, although 'taking the cross' played a role in preparations for the First Crusade, formal practices developed unevenly and often invisibly through the twelfth century, only solidifying in the thirteenth century and later.[72] It seems fair to conclude therefore that signing with the cross was indeed designed to boost morale but was not restricted to crusading alone.

The text's description of the triumphal entry of the crusaders into Lisbon recalls many different traditions but the actions of participants, though deeply symbolic, were not unique to crusades or unusual when compared to other wars.[73] The text's description of the king walking around the high walls of the castle seems to be a form of *circuitus murorum*: a territorial proclamation and a ritual cleansing of space.[74] The reported liturgies – *Te Deum laudamus* and *Asperges me* – confirm that the crusaders sought to attribute victory to God and to purify both the city and themselves.[75]

Here again, the practices accompanying the entrance into Lisbon would seem not to have been particularly new or crusade-specific. Triumphal and thankful celebrations of victory, especially against those of a different faith, survived through late antiquity into the Carolingian period. For example, in 801 Louis the Pious entered the conquered city of Barcelona with a large, priest-led procession. As they went through the gates, all sang psalms and *laudes*, and then proceeded to the Church of the Holy and Victorious Cross to thank God for the victory. Similarly, when Arnulf of Carinthia defeated Viking forces at the Battle of the Dyle in 896, he ordered the celebration of litanies, after which everyone marched in a victory procession, praising God.[76]

---

[71] Phillips, 'Ideas of Crusade'.

[72] Brundage, '"Cruce Signari": The Rite for Taking the Cross'; Maier, 'Crisis, Liturgy and the Crusade'; Pennington, 'The Rite for Taking the Cross in the Twelfth Century'; Pick, '*Signaculum caritatis et fortitudinis*'.

[73] *De expugnatione*, 174.

[74] Sergio Bertelli, *The King's Body: Sacred Rituals of Power in Medieval and Early Modern Europe*, trans. R.B. Litchfield (University Park, PA, 2001), 62–96.

[75] For more on the *Te Deum laudamus* see *The Liturgy of the Medieval Church*, ed. Thomas J. Heffernan and E. Ann Matter (Kalamazoo, MI, 2001); on its use in war, see Bachrach, *Religion and the Conduct of War*, 81.

[76] Bachrach, *Religion and the Conduct of War*, 41.

We turn now to religious practices that seem to be absent from the text. The *De expugnatione Lyxbonensi* fails to mention some wartime religious practices that seem to have been standard in both crusading and non-crusading wars. Perhaps most importantly, the text does not tell us explicitly that the crusaders 'took the cross' or swore crusading vows before departure. This does not mean that vows and the assumption of crosses did not occur. It is nevertheless interesting that while the text does not discuss individual crusade vows and the wearing of the cross, it does outline in great detail the Dartmouth Rules, communal oaths of a slightly different sort.[77] Furthermore, based on both secular army habits as well as crusading practices, it is likely that just before battle the army at Lisbon would have participated in confession (individual or, more rarely, communal) and taken the eucharist,[78] but the text gives us only the off-hand remark about communal blessings and absolution dispensed on the run early in the siege.

In addition, it is noticeable that although there are two hortatory sermons within the *De expugnatione Lyxbonensi* delivered by clergy, there are no pre-battle exhortations delivered by secular leaders; the one speech by a secular leader is given by Hervey of Glanville in an attempt to keep the crusade forces together as they try to decide whether to form an alliance with Afonso.[79] In accounts of secular and crusading expeditions, it is more usual for at least some encouraging speeches to be delivered by secular leaders. It is in no way strange to find bishops and priests giving sermons – that was patently commonplace – but it is interesting that the text does not tell us of any religiously-themed exhortations by secular leaders before battle.

Finally, accounts of crusading expeditions in particular often detail a great number of penitential rites, such as fasting and processions.[80] The *De expugnatione Lyxbonensi,* while certainly conveying the penitential attitude of participants, does not describe any fasting or penitential processions in the lead-up to battle; the one penitential rite we witness before the conquest is the behavior of the crusaders during the early storm at sea, and then after Lisbon is taken we see rites of purification and humble gratitude. Fasting and intercessory processions may well have happened in between, but the text does not report them.

For the most part, though, religious practices in the *De expugnatione Lyxbonensi* conform to medieval wartime religious practices, crusading and otherwise. We could not say with absolute certainty that this expedition was a crusade based on the described religious practices; they are consistent with

---

[77] Namely, *coniuratio*; more on this below.
[78] Bachrach, *Religion and the Conduct of War*.
[79] *De expugnatione*, 104–10.
[80] Bachrach, *Religion and the Conduct of War*, 110–50. Brundage, 'Crusades, Clerics and Violence', 151.

a crusade, but not definitive. Rather, in the text the crusading nature of the expedition is most concretely expressed in the ideas underlying the actions, nicely complementing Peter Pitões' assertion in the text itself that what differentiated a crusade from other wars was intention, not deed.[81]

Yet, if certain religious practices are not included to define the crusade as such, then why does the author of the *De expugnatione* include some, while passing over others – which must have occurred – in silence? If these particular religious practices were described 'for narrative or ideological purposes', [82] what were those purposes – what is the text communicating through its selection of religious practices?

'Diverse but not adverse': monastic reform, lay piety, *coniuratio*, and the importance of community[83]

In his magisterial survey, *The Reformation of the Twelfth Century*, Giles Constable suggests that between 1100 and 1130, the Church shifted from the reform of monastic life and the issues of purity and independence that had dominated during the Investiture Controversy to a growing focus on the spiritual wellbeing of all Christians.[84] Thus, what had begun as an attempt to reform monasticism expanded into an attempt to reform Christian society itself into something more closely resembling the apostolic ideal. Inspired by these ideals, laity and monastics alike developed new and diverse forms of religious *conversatio* and intensified earlier forms of devotion, such as pilgrimage.

Although some contemporaries looked upon these developments with suspicion, in the twelfth century 'the contemporary awareness of growth was paralleled by a recognition and increasing acceptance of a variety of forms of religious life'.[85] Writers such as Anselm of Havelberg, the anonymous author of the *Chronicle of Petershausen*, Otto of Freising, and Peter of Blois affirmed that the new diversity of religious experience did not harm, but rather

---

81 *De expugnatione*, 82.
82 See above page 98.
83 The quote is from Constable, *Reformation*, 87.
84 Constable, *Reformation*, 4.
85 Constable, *Reformation*, 47. On the complex relationship between social reality, terminology, and interpretive schemes (such as the *clericus/laicus* distinction) that both described and influenced that reality, see Otto Gerhard Oexle, 'Perceiving Social Reality in the Early and High Middle Ages: A Contribution to a History of Social Knowledge', in *Ordering Medieval Society: Perspectives on Intellectual and Practical Modes of Shaping Social Relations*, ed. B. Jussen, trans. P.E. Selwyn (Philadelphia, PA, 2000), 92–143, esp. 102–22.

complemented, the unity of the Church, and was indeed part of the divine plan.[86] As James of Vitry would later express it in his *Historia occidentalis*,

> We do not consider religious only those who renounce the world and go over to a religious life, but we can also call 'regulars' all the faithful of Christ who serve the Lord under the evangelical rule and who live in an orderly way under the one highest and supreme Abbot.[87]

What united these different expressions of religious life – what made them diverse but not adverse, in other words – was their common desire to imitate Christ and the apostolic life of the early church.[88]

The author of the *De expugnatione Lyxbonensi* highlights the parallels between the Lisbon expedition, pilgrimage, and reform monasticism in a number of immediate and surface ways. For example, as noted above, the Dartmouth Rules stipulated weekly mass and confession, an extremely high standard for the laity, though not for monks. The separation of men and women echoes the chastity of a religious order, while refraining from costly garments and the establishing of a common purse calls to mind the individual poverty and communal wealth of a monastery. Like members of a monastic house, the Lisbon participants elected their leaders, agreed to their own internal system of justice, and later insisted on taking counsel and making decisions as a group. These practices recall how the value of liberty and local independence were expressed in twelfth-century monastic contexts through the election of a superior, and how the collectivity imposed 'on his or her freedom of action' by insisting on community counsel regarding important issues.[89] Indeed, one is almost tempted to describe the initial agreement of participants as the Dartmouth *regula* rather than the Dartmouth Rules, an impulse further justified by the use of the term *conversio* during the storm at sea to describe the decision to join the expedition. For monastic reformers, the term *conversio* signaled the spiritual reorientation that accompanied taking religious vows, and was also used virtually interchangeably with *penitentia*.[90] Yael Katzir has also suggested that for Second Crusade contemporaries like Bernard of Clairvaux, *conversio* should be translated as 'reform'.[91] *Conversio*

---

[86] Constable, *Reformation*, 48–50.

[87] James of Vitry, *Historia Occidentalis*, cited in and translated by Constable, *Reformation*, 293.

[88] Purkis, 'Religious Symbols and Practices', 70.

[89] Constable, *Reformation*, 176–79.

[90] It is worth remembering that lay brothers were often known as *conversi*. See Brundage, 'Crusades, Clerics and Violence', 154.

[91] Yael Katzir, 'The Second Crusade and the Redefinition of *Ecclesia*, *Christianitas* and Papal Coercive Power', in *The Second Crusade and the Cistercians*, ed. M. Gervers (New York, NY, 1992), 3–11 at 7.

was the counterpart of *conversatio morum*, the change in way of life that also accompanied the taking of religious orders.[92]

These simple parallels in the text will hardly surprise scholars of the crusades or twelfth-century Christianity; we know that as a result of the reform movement, many other different forms of religious life were described in monastic terms, as possessing the same or at least similar spiritual merits as a monastic lifestyle. Pilgrimage, itinerant preaching, and permanent relocation were thought to be forms of eremitism, while crusading was widely seen 'as equivalent, though inferior, to entering a religious house, whose members were also *milites* fighting for the Lord'.[93] The rhetoric of reform, especially 'references to liberty and the spirit of liberty; to solitude and poverty; to the integrity, rectitude, perfection, purity, simplicity, and strictness of the rule; to the imitation of Christ, the apostolic life, and the primitive church; and to exile and peregrination' clearly influenced crusading ideas and texts.[94] Even the outer garb of monks and crusaders had a parallel: crusaders wore the cross upon their shoulders, whilst many considered monastic habits to be 'the cross of Christ', and both groups looked back to Luke 14.27 to provide the scriptural authority for their apparel.[95] It is not surprising that the ideal of a man who led both active and contemplative lives – both as a warrior and as a monk – found extensive development in the twelfth century.[96] Nor is it surprising that those on the First Crusade deliberately adopted monastic goals and some monastic practices, and seem to have clearly identified themselves with members of religious orders.[97]

Indeed, the apparent desire expressed in the *De expugnatione Lyxbonensi* to promote patterns of religious practices that were distinct from the normal rhythms of battle and more constant than the idiosyncratic religious practices often seen in war can also be read as an attempt to describe an active life that was in its very essence penitential. The emphasis upon the crusaders' extremely high standards of routine religious practice (weekly confession and communion), the apparently daily distribution of blessed bread, and the general absence of descriptions of ad hoc practices before the battle (with the obvious exception of the sermon before the conquest of the city), all suggest the author's desire to distinguish the participants in the conquest of Lisbon from their contemporaries as particularly, and regularly, pious. Perhaps even

---

[92] Constable, *Reformation*, 15.
[93] Constable, *Reformation*, 76–77.
[94] Constable, *Reformation*, 125; see also Purkis, *Crusading Spirituality* and 'Religious Symbols and Practices', 77.
[95] Constable, *Reformation*, 190. Purkis rightly notes that the related passages of Matthew 16.24 and Luke 9.23 are frequently invoked in accounts of the First Crusade (*Crusading Spirituality*, 30–35).
[96] Constable, *Reformation*, 290.
[97] Brundage, 'Crusades, Clerics and Violence', 150–51. Maier, 'Crisis, Liturgy and the Crusade', 628. Purkis, *Crusading Spirituality* and 'Religious Symbols and Practices', 77.

the absence of the penitential fasting and intercessory processions, found
in accounts of the First Crusade, should be read not as a lack of piety but
rather as a sign of the way in which, for these people, penance had become
routine and daily, more an essential part of their *conversatio morum* than
singular practices occasioned by crisis. This text thus seems systematically
to construct, through inclusion and exclusion, the image of a penitential
conversatio morum appropriate to a 'monastery on the move', rather than
highlight ad hoc displays of piety, even though chronicles of the First Crusade
had done just that.[98]

A further and more profound link between the *De expugnatione
Lyxbonensi*, reform monasticism, and lay piety may be found in the text's
emphasis on community and cooperation. As prominent reformers repeatedly
made clear, to lead the apostolic life was to embrace the common life (*vita
communis*),[99] and contemporaries repeatedly invoked Acts 2.44 and 4.32 to
remember 'early Christians who had "but one heart and one soul" and "all
things in common"', and to suggest that this was the proper standard for
Christian community life.[100] The value of community lay not only in the way
it restrained individual will, but also in the opportunities it afforded for the
necessary exercise of charity, Christian love of one's neighbor.[101] Further, it
allowed participants to recreate the social environment of the early church,
as they envisaged it. A sharpened emphasis on community was therefore
integral to twelfth-century monasticism and would become significant in the
expression of lay piety later in the Middle Ages.[102] Monasticism thus became
not just a spiritual or religious vocation but 'a social ideal'.[103]

The *De expugnatione Lyxbonensi* makes the link between the Christian
community described in the text and the apostolic life idealized by reformers
crystal clear, especially in the set speeches, but analysis of religious practices
reveals two additional and interrelated points.[104] First, the text repeatedly
signals that unity and community were to be maintained through appropriate
division and representation. Second, on a deeper level, the text shows how
social structures and religious practices were supposed to work together in the

[98]   Bachrach, *Religion and the Conduct of War*, 108–50.
[99]   Chenu, 'Monks, Canons and Laymen', 207, 214, 200. See also, in general, Herbert
Grundmann, *Religiöse Bewegungen im Mittelalter* (Hildesheim, 1961), and Duane V. Lapsanski,
*Perfectio evangelica. Eine begriffsgeschichtliche Untersuchung im frühfranziskanischen
Schrifttum* (München, 1974).
[100] Constable, *Reformation*, 125.
[101] Constable, *Reformation*, 137–38.
[102] Chenu, 'Monks, Canons and Laymen', 213–14.
[103] Constable, *Reformation*, 137.
[104] Constable, 'The Second Crusade as Seen by Contemporaries', 241. To give just one
example, Bishop Peter Pitões refers to the crusaders as 'sons of the primitive church' (*De
expugnatione*, 72). Here my views do not fully align with those of Purkis, who is more hesitant
to see the *vita apostolica* in the *De expugnatione Lyxbonensi* (*Crusading Spirituality*, 82–83).

service of the spiritual goals of both individual and community. In particular, the text demonstrates how the expedition incorporated cooperative bonds (particularly those of *amicitia* and *coniuratio*) and the customary practices associated with those bonds alongside the religious practices outlined above.

The text's treatment of the famed Dartmouth Rules offers an excellent case in point. The text explicitly describes the Dartmouth Rules as 'the firmest pledges of harmony and friendship [*firmissima concordie atque amicitie pignora*]'.[105] The reference to *amicitia*, as well as the invocation of the virtue of *concordia*, indicate that this was an establishment of a medieval cooperative bond.[106] Whether aiming at a religious, economic or political goal, members of cooperative groups shared sworn oaths, a sense of relative equality tempered by clear leadership, and an underlying desire for peace amongst themselves and mutual support against others.[107] Those embarking on the expedition to Lisbon (as depicted in the text) possessed all of these qualities.

The clear reference to *amicitia* at the beginning of the text suggests this was a friendship bond, a formal, structured relationship between equals with clear obligations.[108] However, a few sentences later the text uses another key term: *coniuratio*. As cooperative alliances, *coniurationes* strongly resembled *amicitiae*, but with the key difference that *coniurationes* claimed their own authority; they established rules, including legal norms and procedures for settling disputes and essentially functioned as 'self-created spheres of law and peace'.[109] Not surprisingly, then, it is when describing how the expedition to Lisbon established its own leaders and judges that the text invokes *coniuratio*: 'Two out of every thousand men were chosen and were called judges and sworn men [*coniurati*].'[110] Later, the text describes the expedition explicitly as 'members of a *coniuratio* [*coniurationis socios*]'and 'sworn society [*coniurateque societatis*]'.[111]

Many *coniurationes* aimed at explicitly religious goals, and used the social structure and customs of the *coniuratio* to achieve said goals. Correspondingly, as already noted, the Dartmouth Rules contained stipulations which we might consider primarily social in their scope alongside standards for religious practices. The latter, interestingly enough, emphasized division and delegation in order to promote unity and unanimity, with the ship as

105   *De expugnatione*, 56.
106   Gerd Althoff, *Family, Friends and Followers: Political and Social Bonds in Early Medieval Europe* (Cambridge, 2004), 67–90; Otto Gerhard Oexle, 'Peace through Conspiracy', in *Ordering Medieval Society*, 285–322 at 297.
107   Althoff, *Family, Friends and Followers*, 65. Oexle, 'Peace through Conspiracy', 285–91.
108   Althoff, *Family, Friends and Followers*, 67–90.
109   Oexle, 'Peace through Conspiracy', 293.
110   *De expugnatione*, 56.
111   *De expugnatione*, 100 and 104.

the basic unity of order.[112] Although it is unclear whether each ship was meant to function *like* a parish, or if indeed each ship *was* a parish,[113] the expedition is portrayed as echoing the internal structure of Christendom itself, with parish-like units combining to form a greater whole. The fact that these 'parishes' were on ships was especially appropriate, given the familiar medieval metaphor of a ship for Christian society itself.[114] Ultimately, the community imagined by the Dartmouth Rules with its parish-like divisions served to ensure religious coherence and cohesion on the expedition in the same way that the parochial structure of the Church at a local level was meant to supported overall institutional coherence. Furthermore, the crusaders – again like the Church as a whole – sought to achieve unity not by micro-prescribing universal religious practices for all, but by establishing broad universal guidelines within local structures to buttress the universal faith and mission of the Church.[115] In fact, although this article has analyzed the Dartmouth Rules down into 'social' and 'religious' components, what is striking about the text to modern eyes is the seamless integration of these two types of regulation:

All these people with so many different languages swore firm pledges of unity and friendship. Moreover, they decreed strict laws, to be punished [in kind]: a death for a death, a tooth for a tooth. They forbade altogether magnificent, expensive clothing. Also, women should not go about [alone] in public. The peace should be preserved by all, except for when judgment was handed down for an injury. Each week religious services should be held, one for the laity and another separate for the clergy, unless by some great chance one group should required the other to be present. Each ship should have its own priest, and these priests should conduct their religious affairs just as they had in their parishes. No man of status should retain a sailor or servant in his household. Every week every person should confess and take communion on Sunday.... Meanwhile, two out of every thousand men were chosen and were called judges and sworn men, who, by ordering the constables, could end disputes and distribute money.[116]

The interplay of the social and the religious from sentence to sentence shows concretely how the social structure of a *coniuratio* and intense, reform-inspired religious practices worked together, and how unity could be,

---

[112] This use of division and delegation in order to maintain unity surely relates to what Oexle has identified as a principal notion undergirding medieval society – that of 'harmony through inequality' (Oexle, 'Perceiving Social Reality', 101).

[113] 'Ut singule naves singulos presbyteros haberent, et eadem que in parrochiis observari suo retineret' (*De expugnatione*, 56).

[114] Rivard, *Blessing the World*, 220–21.

[115] *The Liturgy of the Medieval Church*, ed. Thomas J. Heffernan and E. Ann Matter (2nd edn, Kalamazoo, MI, 2005).

[116] *De expugnatione*, 56.

at one moment, maintained by division and representation and by unanimity and lack of distinction at other times.[117]

This dynamic tension between unity and difference, equality and hierarchy, the spiritual and the social, appears in many forms in the text quoted above. Restrictions on rich attire served both to soothe social tensions and to inspire personal humility. The seclusion of women served multiple ends as well, eliminating jealousies and hostilities related to the presence of women, emphasizing the chaste nature of the enterprise, and encouraging the women themselves to contemplate their humility and sinful natures. Electing representative leaders both discouraged the continuation of local allegiances and hierarchies of power which might disrupt the expedition and emphasized the equality of all before God as well as the value of virtue rather than birth or prowess. Likewise, the maintenance of parish-like structures and relationships was at once pragmatic, discouraging disagreement about religious practices and bolstering preexisting social bonds, and spiritual, emphasizing that it was within the Church that the most important relationships and hierarchies, those that are true and lasting, existed. Meanwhile, social and political hierarchies among the laity are downplayed or recreated anew in order to better serve the needs of the expedition.

A close look at the text's Latin reveals that even the vocabulary emphasizes community through a careful combination of the universal and the particular. The importance of community, of unity in diversity, is clearly foregrounded in the first sentence: 'All these people with so many different languages swore firm pledges of unity and friendship.'[118] In the sentences that immediately follow, words with the root *omni-* feature twice, while words with the root I- appear seven times, sometimes in the emphatic combination of '*singule singulis*' or '*singuli singulis*'. Community would thus be maintained by the right participation and placement of each individual within the social world created by the bonds of *coniuratio*. Furthermore, although people needed to be in the right places, those places were not simply based on social, economic or political position, but rather on individual volition and the need to promote religious unity and Christian community.

The importance of preserving this sworn Christian community was again

---

[117] It is worth noting that this is remarkably similar (thought not fully identical) to the concept of *communitas* on pilgrimage articulated by anthropologist Victor Turner. As Rivard explains it, '*Communitas* is a form of social bonding that combines qualities of lowliness, sacredness, homogeneity, and comradeship; it arises spontaneously in all types of groups separated from traditional society; and as the camaraderie it creates often dissolves the governing norms of society instilled in its participants, it is often seen as both holy and threatening' (*Blessing the World*, 136). See Victor Turner, 'Pilgrimage as Social Process', in *Dramas, Fields and Metaphors: Symbolic Action in Human Society* (Ithaca, NY, 1974), 166–230, and John M. Theilmann, '*Communitas* among Fifteenth-Century Pilgrims', *Historical Reflections/Réflexions historiques* 11 (1984), 253–70.

[118] *De expugnatione*, 56.

signaled as the crusading community faced a crisis of dissent within its ranks following King Afonso's offer and debated excommunication. In the text's presentation, this reveals three important facts: first, the dissenters were understood as operating politically but as nonetheless essentially undermining Christian community. Second, the dissenters were portrayed not only as divergent and troublesome but indubitably and fundamentally wrong in their arguments; the dictates of community had, in essence, become a kind of orthodoxy.[119] Third, in a related way, to break the Dartmouth Rules, the code of the community, was on a par with breaking a crusade or pilgrim's vow *per se*. Individual and collective salvation had thus been inextricably interlinked. The threat of excommunication also seems to communicate that if unity could not be maintained through the consent of all, then at least unity could be maintained by redefining the circle of participants, and placing the troublesome individuals outside that new and tighter circle. Community would thus endure in a smaller, more tightly bound form. This is precisely the reason that excommunication was at times invoked as a punishment for breaking a *coniuratio*.[120]

Of course, in the text nobody is ultimately excommunicated, for the words and self-abasing actions of Hervey of Glanvill and his supporters induce the recalcitrant mariners to yield. To summarize the relevant events: facing the resistance of William Vitulus and others, Hervey of Glanvill, a prominent leader amongst the crusaders, attempted to resolve the situation.[121] His speech has been well analyzed by Jonathan Phillips, who has emphasized that Hervey connected 'right intention and unity in both the spiritual and secular senses', as well as stressing contemporary ideas of pride and honor.[122] But the text suggests that Hervey's speech is effective not merely because of his words, but also his actions. Hervey concludes his speech by saying directly to the faction of William Vitulus, 'if you do not wish to be associates [*socios*], then show yourselves to us as lords'. Then, with those words, Hervey tearfully tries 'to humble himself at the feet of William Vitulus, with the best knights and others standing nearby wanting to do likewise. But they [are] not permitted to do this by [William] and his associates standing nearby.'[123] One can practically see the scene and feel the tension: the respected Hervey of Glanvill, at the end of an eloquent appeal, trying to kneel before the by-then surely uncomfortable William.

Or was he, indeed, so uncomfortable? Althoff's analysis of conflict resolution and social practices within cooperative groups suggests that the

---

[119] For an earlier medieval example of this use/effect of excommunication, see Bachrach, *Religion and the Conduct of War*, 71.
[120] Oexle, 'Peace through Conspiracy', 302.
[121] *De expugnatione*, 106–10.
[122] Phillips, 'Ideas of Crusade', 134.
[123] *De expugnatione*, 110.

entire scene was prepared in advance. As he notes, conflicts within cooperative groups were often resolved by public discussions that were preceded by private conversations in which the contents of the public discussion were decided in advance: 'The position taken by the public meeting was therefore already guaranteed'.[124] Thus, it is likely that Hervey's speech was prescribed and expected by all parties. Furthermore, Hervey's self-humbling reads clearly as an act of *satisfactio*, a 'public act of subjugation' designed to give satisfaction (literally) to an opponent and thus end a conflict.[125] Acts of *satisfactio* were also planned and agreed upon in advance before their public performance, suggesting that in this instance, all present knew that Hervey would give a certain speech and then humble himself, and that thereafter William would capitulate.

This voluntary abasement serves at least two purposes: one that we might consider religious/spiritual, and another social. It underlines the humility and willingness to sacrifice one's standing that the Dartmouth Rules encouraged. This action, then, like the Dartmouth Rules, emphasizes correct attitude and spirituality, but also demonstrates a keen awareness of social structures and customs and the need to manipulate them in order to maintain unity. Hervey of Glanvill's apparent willingness to humble himself, to effectively up-end traditional power relationships and recreate a new social hierarchy if necessary, points to the maintenance of community at all costs, and the fact that social structures and customary practices were enlisted to serve spiritual goals.

In the text, Hervey's speech and *satisfactio* are effective, since William and his men agree to stay for as long as provisions would last, at which point, 'All cried for joy, saying "God, aid us".'[126] Unity, signaled by the communal terms 'omnes' and 'nos', is restored. Yet again, however, it is unity through division and representation:

Representatives were selected from among our best men, as one with the men of Cologne and Flanders, through whom the pledge and agreement between ourselves and the king would be defined. They, as one with the king and the archbishop and fellow bishops and the clergy and the laity testified to a confirmed agreement, afterwards proclaimed openly to all.[127]

Again, even the words of this passage emphasize that unity was restored: the adverb 'una' features twice, and the repetition of 'the clergy and the laity' also seems to hint at the total unanimity among those present, while correctly separating Christian society into the two groups.

---

[124]   Althoff, *Family, Friends and Followers*, 163.
[125]   Gerd Althoff, 'Satisfaction: Peculiarities of the Amicable Settlement of Conflicts in the Middle Ages', in *Ordering Medieval Society*, 270–84 at 272–79.
[126]   *De expugnatione*, 110.
[127]   *De expugnatione*, 110.

The construction of twinned churches and cemeteries during the siege further speaks to the use of social distinctions and divisions as a means to spiritual unity. Instead of building one church, which would presumably have had to be situated conveniently for both camps and to accommodate differences in language and local customs, two churches, each with its own cemetery, were constructed. There were pragmatic benefits to this solution: the distance between each camp, its church, and its buried dead was reduced, no small benefit during war when people were both busy and under threat of attack. Perhaps more importantly, language differences and varying customs could be respected, creating less social friction between forces and their priests.[128] At the same time, there was the spiritual significance of the dual constructions as well. By building twice instead of once, organic faith communities were preserved, and local parish relationships, deemed so important in the Dartmouth Rules, were more likely to be acknowledged. Thus, while Anglo-Normans and men from Cologne and Flanders were thus divided in terms of physical space, perhaps language, and local variations in religious practices, they were kept united in terms of their religious faith and the commemoration of their fallen comrades.

Even in the triumphal moment following the conquest of the city, the text reminds us of the delicate relationship between the community as a whole and its constituents. By this point in time the different crusading contingents had virtually come to blows, and as a last effort to ensure peace amongst themselves, they all swore fidelity to Afonso for as long as they were in his territory.[129] In order to prevent personal looting and gratuitous violence, the crusaders decided that only a certain number of armed men would enter the city at first, in order to guarantee an orderly and secure collection of booty and prisoners.[130] However, the Flemings and the men from Cologne broke this agreement (according to the text, whose Anglo-Norman affiliation should not be forgotten) by sneaking extra men into the city to rape, murder, and loot. This prompted the Anglo-Norman author to reflect:

But the Normans and the English, for whom faith and religion [*fides et religio*] remained utterly constant, contemplating what this kind of action might portend, remained quietly in their designated places, choosing to guard their hands from all plundering rather than violate the decrees of faith and sworn society [*fidei et societatis coniuratae statuta*].[131]

For the Anglo-Normans, both their religion and the guidelines of their *coniuratio* restrained them, reminding us of the way in which the Dartmouth Rules serve social and spiritual purposes at virtually the same time. The text

---

128 Bennett, 'Military Aspects of the Conquest of Lisbon', 76.
129 *De expugnatione*, 172.
130 *De expugnatione*, 172–74.
131 *De expugnatione*, 176.

seems to imply yet again that this is the ideal way to maintain the right kind of Christian community: social and spiritual restraints should work together. The fact that the text describes the final looting by the men from Cologne and Flanders as breaking both the *coniuratio* and the moral strictures of Christianity emphasizes that the two were supposed to be working together. Social fidelity buttressed spiritual faith, and vice versa.

The reestablishment of the church of Lisbon – the election of Gilbert of Hastings as the new bishop of Lisbon and the purification of the church itself – offers a fitting endpiece for my discussion. On the one hand, Gilbert's election exemplifies the theme of unity through diversity that has run throughout the narrative. For even as the text narrates that Gilbert was elected by everyone all together, it then carefully delineates the individual participants: 'the king, the archbishop, fellow bishops, all the clergy and laity'.[132] On the other, the occasion of the purification of the temple offers the occasion to restate the fundamentally personal, religious goals of crusading. In recounting the spiritual cleansing of the building, the *De expugnatione* expresses sympathy for the inhabitants of Lisbon and hope for their conversion, but then concludes 'let us consider the uncleanness and impurity of our consciences', thus warning the unwary reader not to think that the purification of the crusaders themselves was complete.[133] These words remind us that the conquest of the city of Lisbon was not the primary purpose of the expedition. Even with the city won, the most important work of pilgrimage and crusade, the redemption of the inner man, was not yet complete; the greater battle had not yet been won.[134]

That this great battle – the conquest of individual impurity and spiritual conversion – was the spiritual goal of participants in the Lisbon expedition, just as it was the goal of other crusaders, pilgrims and professed religious, is a central claim of the *De expugnatione Lyxbonensi* and in its emphases and descriptions it implies that this victory must be accomplished through both social structures (namely *coniuratio*) and religious practices. Just as in a monastery or lay fraternity, participants are shown to utilize a social structure and its customs alongside challenging religious practices, thereby furthering their spiritual goals rather than impeding them. By downplaying, though not eliminating, traditional social distinctions, establishing communal representation and a common purse, hinting at the goal of chastity, and setting high standards for religious practices within smaller 'parish' communities,

---

[132] *De expugnatione*, 178–80.
[133] *De expugnatione*, 184.
[134] This theme, though certainly appropriate for the twelfth century, in fact goes back at least to the last decade of the eighth century. It seems to echo Patriarch Paulinus of Aquileia's treatise for Duke Eric of Friuli (*Liber exhortationis*) which 'stressed that, while the physical battle might end, the struggle to control oneself and live a spiritual life never ended as long as one lived' (Bachrach, *Religion and the Conduct of War*, 56).

the Lisbon expedition creates, in effect, a mobile Christendom with both practical social benefits and great spiritual advantages. Community structure not only allowed for a penitential way of life, it positively encouraged and enabled it: community became a tool for individual salvation.

The emphasis on community in the *De expugnatione Lyxbonensi* also illustrates the way in which reform monasticism could influence the growth of lay piety. As we know, in the long term the trends of the twelfth-century reformation did lead to a reduced conceptual prominence for monasticism. Instead of presenting society as a tripartite construction of monks, clerics, and laity, many portrayed a simpler dichotomy: the laity and the clergy (both secular and regular).[135] Far from excluding the laity from involvement in the Christian community, this new depiction of society effectively called upon all to face the perceived spiritual challenges of the age.[136] Of course, it was not quite that simple. On the one hand, some of the laity did indeed desire to follow members of religious orders down the spiritual path to salvation,[137] and the exercise of penance and the apostolic ideal, although nurtured in reformed monastic circles, were quickly embraced and reinvigorated by the laity.[138] The recuperation of the active life (especially through crusading) also encouraged the laity.[139] On the other hand, reformers were often wary of lay involvement in the Church as a source of potential and, as a result, tended in their own writings to make a clear distinction between a spiritually superior clergy and a subordinate laity, thereby implicitly justifying the demand for freedom from secular control.[140] Thus at the very time when the laity were being inspired by ideals from the reform movement, many reformers were emphasizing the breadth of the gulf between clergy and laity, while still, of course, exhorting the laity to piety.[141]

We see this complicated relationship between monastic reform and lay piety through clerical eyes in the *De expugnatione Lyxbonensi*. Not surprisingly, in

---

[135] Constable, *Reformation*, 321.

[136] Constable, *Reformation*, 326.

[137] André Vauchez, *The Laity in the Middle Ages: Religious Beliefs and Devotional Practices*, ed. D.E. Bornstein, trans. M.J. Schneider (Notre Dame, IN, 1993), xviii. For a unique exploration of how benefactions to monastic houses illuminate the relationship between those houses and their surrounding lay communities, see David A. Postles, 'Religious Houses and the Laity in Eleventh- to Thirteenth-Century England: An Overview', *HSJ* 1 (1989), 1–13.

[138] Vauchez, *The Laity*, 111–12.

[139] Vauchez, *The Laity*, xviii, 62. Constable, *Reformation*, 290.

[140] Vauchez, *The Laity*, 41. This bias in the sources could lead us to think that the laity were opponents of religious reform, when as Constable clarifies 'the contrary was probably closer to the truth' (Constable, *Reformation*, 244). The end result was the closer alignment of monasticism with 'the clergy', rather than holding a separate, third position (Constable, *Reformation*, 321).

[141] Given this, it is not surprising that even while heavily and explicitly echoing reform spirituality, lay fraternities sought to emphasize their own independence from the clerical hierarchy (Vauchez, *The Laity*, 114).

the text the independence of the laity is always contained within ecclesiastical boundaries.[142] Parish structures are maintained, leaving priests in charge of the spiritual welfare of 'their' laity. The most significant annunciations of spiritual ideals and even battlefield exhortations are confined to Bishop Pitões and the anonymous priest. The religious practices undertaken by participants during the siege – mass, absolutions, blessed bread, blessing the siege engine, listening to sermons – all require ecclesiastical leadership, even though they also involve active lay participation. We are not shown members of the laity delivering religiously-themed exhortations, or confessing their sins as individuals, or fasting, or themselves walking in intercessory procession. Put another way, we never see the laity taking the initiative in their religious practices; they are active, but apparently only in following the lead of the clergy. In this regard, the *De expugnatione* expressed the clerical ideal of the time: a lay piety flowering under the proper supervision of the Church. This predictably reflects the chronological context; lay piety did not truly come into its own until the later twelfth and thirteenth centuries, and when it did, it often rejected or significantly altered the kind of Christian community seen in the *De expugnatione Lyxbonensi*.[143] However, I believe it also reflects the clerical identity of the text's author and any redactors/copyists.

This reminds us that what we see in the text is merely one representation of events. Thus we return to the question of why this representation was chosen. And even further: what was the purpose of the *De expugnatione Lyxbonensi*? The usual conclusion, to promote further crusade participation, is unexceptionable.[144] Without contesting that clear and undeniable function of the text, I read the relationship between crusading, reform monasticism and lay piety presented by the text as pointing to a further goal: the promotion of reform ideals with a strong emphasis on appropriate Christian community and the utility of the *coniuratio*, not just for those on crusade but also for those at home.[145]

In addition to the above discussion of the theme of Christian community in the text, looking closely at the genre of the *De expugnatione Lyxbonensi* helps flesh out this assertion. By beginning with a salutation, the text was

---

[142]   In this sense the text's internal evidence corresponds to the overall dynamic identified by Katzir, 'The Second Crusade and the Redefinition', 4.

[143]   Chenu, 'Monks, Canons and Laymen', 213–14, 221–29.

[144]   Phillips, 'Ideas of Crusade', 126.

[145]   This cannot be more than a suggestion. With only one extant manuscript containing the *De expugnatione Lyxbonensi*, there are no grounds for thinking that it was widely dispersed, let alone influential. Further, it has been hard enough to assign a tentative name and identity to the clerical author—we lack the ability to confirm through an analysis of his life that he was indeed a passionate reformer, just as we are unable to pinpoint what edits may have been made (and by whom) before incorporation into the final, and only, manuscript. Yet this suggestion remains plausible and adds further depth to our current understanding of the mid twelfth-century crusading movement.

deliberately framed as a letter home.[146] The current scholarly consensus is that the text we now have started life as a series of rough notes or perhaps some sort of journal, was 'finished' to a degree in the aftermath of the conquest of Lisbon, and then revised again *c.* 1160–1170.[147] The form of a letter was maintained both in the aftermath of the conquest and during later revisions, presumably deliberately.

The choice and maintenance of an epistolary form is not surprising. The eleventh and twelfth centuries witnessed a 'prodigious flowering of letter-writing', perhaps due to increases in literacy, communication, travel, and the influence of classical culture.[148] In particular, missive letters – letters designed to fill no purpose other than communication at a distance – became popular, and many other kinds of works (including sermons, polemical literature, and other persuasive or instructive works) took the form of letters.[149] Different sub-genres emerged in the twelfth century in particular, including crusading letters and letters of monastic vocation 'written to persuade people to enter the religious life'.[150]

To write a letter implies a personal relationship and closeness, a present absence, and a mutual desire for communication. Taken together, this absence and the motive to overcome it are known as the 'epistolary situation' or *Briefsituation*.[151] In the case of medieval letters that were clearly designed for broader dissemination, the individual recipient becomes a conduit to a circle of recipients, all privileged with knowledge deemed vital and important for the broader community; the implication of shared yet private communication is that 'this is too important for me to keep to myself – and you are too important to be kept in the dark'. The broader community is thus invited into the intimate relationship of writer and recipient, giving the broader community a sense of shared information, privilege, and purpose.[152]

What was it that the text was communicating to this broader community,

---

[146]   The only incontrovertible signs of the epistolary genre were a salutation and subscription, though even then, the absence of one or both of these is not conclusive, since letters were copied and recopied (Constable, *Letters and Letter-Collections*, 17–18).

[147]   Livermore, 'The "Conquest of Lisbon"', 1–3.

[148]   Constable, *Letters and Letter-Collections*, 31–33.

[149]   Giles Constable, 'Dictators and Diplomats in the Eleventh and Twelfth Centuries: Medieval Epistolography and the Birth of Modern Bureaucracy', *Dumbarton Oaks Papers* 46 (1992), 37–46 at 37. Constable, *Letters and Letter-Collections*, 14–15. Constable gives examples of such epistolographical treatises by Caesarius of Arles, Peter Damian, Anselm of Canterbury, and Peter the Venerable.

[150]   Constable, *Letters and Letter-Collections*, 15. For additional discussion of medieval letters as historical sources, see Walter Ysebaert, 'Medieval Letters and Letter Collections as Historical Sources: Methodological Questions and Reflections and Research Perspectives (6th–14th centuries)', *Studi medievali* 50:1 (2009), 41–73.

[151]   Constable, 'Dictators and Diplomats', 39.

[152]   As Constable notes, 'An important aspect of the charm – and the power – of letters was

via the artificial intimacy of the letter genre? Certainly part of the message was that the expedition had been a success, and that crusading was, to put it in simplest terms, a good and godly thing; certainly part of the purpose of the letter was to encourage others to crusading in the future. But perhaps, also, the choice of genre was implicitly suggesting that the front line and the home front were united or part of the same effort in some way. Furthermore, perhaps the text was conveying its emphasis on unity through division and representation, and the importance of using social structures and relationships alongside religious practices to further the spiritual health of the individual and the community.[153] After all, these were lessons that could be put into play whether one was on a crusade or not; these were principles that could be applied to local life in the parish as easily as a war camp. To promote individual salvation through an appropriately subdivided Christian community fortified with the social and spiritual virtues of charity, humility, individual poverty – that was clearly a goal many reform-minded clerics would have valued.[154] Moreover, by highlighting the practices and resultant lessons that could be applied back to local life, the text reinforced the message that crusading was yet another one of the 'diverse but not adverse' forms of religious life, that crusading was legitimate and valuable, and as intrinsically connected to the reform Church as pilgrimage or monasticism.

Although the *De expugnatione* was a carefully crafted text, it is not so much a fiction as a text in sustained effort to manage and interpret events. The text does not attempt to eliminate or hide episodes of discord and crisis, as it might were it an invention; instead, it uses them to reinforce the overall message about Christian community. Likewise, the text's descriptions of religious practices were gently shaped, as we have seen, to reinforce themes that were present, albeit perhaps not emphasized, during the crusade itself. Our history, in other words, does not invent events but rather interprets and frames them. Put another way, the text reveals that crusades – actual crusades, not just descriptions in texts – could offer a point of connection between papal and ecclesiastical ideals and popular religious sensibilities. Further, the text suggests that this connection could be deliberately enhanced

that they were addressed at the same time to an individual and to a larger audience and were thus both private and public' ('Dictators and Diplomats', 39).

153 My points here reinforce and expand upon those made by Jonathan Phillips, based on his analysis of the set speeches within the text: 'Raol's prime concerns were these: to show how the crusaders acted with right intention, and to demonstrate that this right intention was firmly underpinned by the preservation of the unity of the crusading force. There were also consistent warnings against envy and greed because they could destroy both right intention and the military capability of the army.' ('Ideas of Crusade', 126).

154 Whether everyone 'at home' would approve of the use of *coniuratio* is another question; many of those outside *coniurationes*, especially authorities, viewed them as dangerous forms of conspiracy. This was not unfounded, since *coniurationes* were frequently used for political rebellion (Oexle, 'Peace through Conspiracy', 287–88).

by those who worked on textual accounts of crusading not only to inspire further crusading but also to advance a concept of a more perfect Christian community back home.

Seen in this light, the *De expugnatione Lyxbonensi* offers solid evidence that the interplay between official reform ideals, wider popular religiosity, and contemporary social structures was less that of contrasting paths than roughly parallel lines heading towards each other and converging. As the *De expugnatione Lyxbonensi* repeatedly informs us, the 'clergy and the laity' worked, or were supposed to work, together on shared goals via the common structure of *coniuratio*.[155] We have long acknowledged that crusading was about creating a religious lifestyle for knights. The *De expugnatione Lyxbonensi* allows us to recognize that it was also about creating a religious lifestyle for and by the broader laity – as individuals and communities – and moreover a lifestyle that extended beyond the boundaries of the expedition into daily life and local society.

---

[155] *De expugnatione*, 56, 110, 179–80.

6

Godric of Finchale's *Canora Modulatio*: The Auditory and Visionary Worlds of a Twelfth-Century Hermit

Monika Otter

Hagiography is by definition about measuring the distance between the human and the sacred: the saint's own distance, but also the hagiographer's and ours. Reginald of Durham's late-twelfth-century life of Godric of Finchale, begun during the saint's lifetime and finished not long after his death, probes all sorts of distances.[1] It is no accident that many of Godric's feats and miracles involve clairvoyance and its auditory equivalent: feats of overcoming spatial or temporal distances in one's seeing and one's hearing. The *Vita* has a precise sense of place, centered on Godric's cell in the forest, but within a concentric circle of larger and larger horizons: the region, the territory of Durham, the sea shore, the ocean, Jerusalem; for Godric was a seafaring merchant before he became a hermit, and also a Jerusalem pilgrim who lived in the Holy Land for several years.

There is not very much scholarly literature on Godric, but interest in him has been constant. There is even a modern novel about him.[2] Historians have long recognized the *Vita*'s value as testimony to many aspects of medieval culture that are rarely illuminated by the narrative sources of the period. It is a life of a man of the people. Pirenne drew attention to Godric's early life as a merchant, as an international trader, and as a man of relatively humble origins working his way up by engaging in trade.[3] Tom Licence and Susan Ridyard have studied him as a lay religious figure, integrated – or perhaps coopted or even coerced – by the monks of Durham into their project of possessing,

---

[1]   The only edition of the text to date is Reginald of Durham, *Libellus de Vita et Miraculis S. Godrici, Heremitae de Finchale*, ed. Joseph Stevenson, Surtees Society 20 (London, 1847). I will cite this edition either by page number or by chapter number (Roman numerals), taking advantage of the work's convenient division into short titled chapters and its detailed analytical table of contents (3–16 in Stevenson's edition).

[2]   Frederick Buechner, *Godric* (New York, 1980).

[3]   Henri Pirenne, *Medieval Cities: Their Origin and the Revival of Trade* (Princeton, NJ, 1974), 116–19.

controlling, and shaping their surrounding territory both economically and spiritually.[4] The monks gained in him a hermitage, a cell with adjacent lands – but they also acquired a revered lay saint who could help their outreach to the laity of the region by modeling a spiritual life appropriate to them. Michael Clanchy has discussed Godric as an interesting example of a layman living on the periphery of monastic and literate culture.[5]

Finally, Godric has received some attention as a musician.[6] The three songs transmitted under his name are the oldest surviving notated music to English texts; indeed, they are among the oldest notated music to survive from England at all. The three songs are each intimately tied to Godric's *Vita*, for each arises from a vision (and 'audition') that is described in great detail; that is, the music, as narrated here and no doubt as experienced by Godric himself, was revealed to him rather than invented by him. The songs apparently enjoyed some popularity, for they are transmitted in other sources. Indeed, some of the texts and all of the music come to us from sources that are independent of Reginald. The notation for 'Seinte Marie' was added to the *Vita* at a slightly later date, and in another source (Roger Wendover's chronicle) the song has acquired a second verse not reported by Reginald. 'Seinte Nicholas' survives only in an independent source. It is worth noting that Reginald, as well as the other sources, was sufficiently interested in the original English words to cite them in full, sometimes together with a Latin paraphrase.[7]

Godric's liminal position on the periphery of monastic practice, monastic liturgy, and monastic knowledge is precisely what interests Reginald in his narrative. It is easy to underestimate the *Vita*. Given its relatively simple Latin

[4]   Tom Licence, 'The Benedictines, the Cistercians and the Acquisition of a Hermitage in Twelfth-Century Durham', *JMH* 29 (2003), 315–29; Susan J. Ridyard, 'Functions of a Twelfth-Century Recluse Revisited: The Case of Godric of Finchale', in *Belief and Culture in the Middle Ages: Studies Presented to Henry Mayr-Harting*, ed. Richard Gameson and Henrietta Leyser (Oxford 2001), 236–50.

[5]   M.T. Clanchy, *From Memory to Written Record: England 1066–1307* (Oxford, 2nd rev. edn, 1993), 239–42.

[6]   On Godric's songs, see the brief entry by Brian Trowell in the *New Grove Dictionary of Music and Musicians* (29 vols., London, 2nd edn, 2001), x, 74. Somewhat dated, but more detailed, appraisals and editions are found in J. Zupitza, 'Cantus Beati Godrici', *Englische Studien* 11 (1888), 401–32; J.B. Trend, 'The First English Songs', *Music and Letters* 9 (1928), 111–28; and J.W. Rankin, 'The Hymns of St Godric', *PMLA* 38 (1923), 699–711. A musicological reconsideration of both the songs themselves and of Reginald's account of Godric's music, based on newer insights into medieval music and without the heavy condescension of these earlier studies towards the 'illiterate' Godric, would be desirable. Helen Deeming, 'The Songs of St Godric: A Neglected Context', *Music & Letters* 86 (2005), 169–85, considers the role of the songs in the promotion of Godric's cult and offers an overview of the manuscript transmission.

[7]   See the detailed summary of the manuscript transmission in Deeming, 'Songs of St Godric', based partly on Zupitza, 'Cantus'; and Alexandra Barratt, 'The Lyrics of St. Godric: A New Manuscript', *Notes and Queries*, new ser. 32 (1985), 439–45.

and its immoderate length (it runs to over 300 printed pages, not including the *Miracula*, and there is an appendix of 'outtakes', stories Reginald did not deem worthy of inclusion but did not want to discard either),[8] one might expect the *Vita* to be an artless, dutiful compilation, more a dossier to be mined for interesting episodes than a literary work in its own right. But Reginald's is an intelligent text, with rhetorical and narrative purposes of its own. Its project, in my reading, is to offer the reader a sophisticated reflection on what might be a layman's proper way of being in the world, accessing knowledge, and experiencing spirituality. In cooperation with his subject, as it were, Reginald traces a layman's way of integrating and constructing his world, a world that is by no means as simple and narrow as older scholarship has sometimes condescendingly implied. For one thing, Godric's life was unusually long even by modern standards – he lived to be over one hundred years old. It also spanned an astonishingly large geographical area, from Scotland to France, Spain, and the Near East, as well as a considerable range of knowledge, spiritual practices and intellectual ambitions.

Parallels are often drawn between Godric and Bede's famous story of Caedmon, so similar in many respects.[9] Like Godric, Caedmon was an illiterate layman operating within the orbit of a monastery. He, too, composed in English, and his surviving song is transmitted bilingually in the learned sources. Caedmon, too, was vouchsafed his song in a vision, and like Godric's music, his song seems to have enjoyed some considerable circulation and popularity. Reginald was no doubt aware of this precedent. Although there is no sign that he specifically modeled his account on the Caedmon story in any particular, Bede was such a canonical and revered figure in twelfth-century England that it is almost impossible his account of the earlier English poet would not have come to mind, especially in his native Northumbria.

One is also reminded of the Life of Christina of Markyate, closer to Godric in time and in many particulars.[10] She, too, is a layperson from a mercantile background, who becomes a hermit in the ambiance of a major monastery (St Albans), who creates a semi-learned liturgical routine for herself, and eventually becomes the nucleus of some kind of satellite community. Like Godric, Christina is locally revered if not venerated in her later life and after her death, and she is personally known to her biographer, who claims, plausibly, to have heard a great deal of the story from her directly.

Reginald also has a personal connection with his subject, inasmuch as he appears to have been partly responsible for the old man's care in his last years. His is not the only early narrative document on Godric. There

8 Reginald of Durham, *Libellus*, 333–70.

9 For a stimulating discussion of Caedmon, in some ways close to my argument here, see Bruce Holsinger, 'The Parable of Caedmon's "Hymn": Liturgical Invention and Literary Tradition', *Journal of English and Germanic Philology* 106 (2007), 149–75.

10 See Clanchy, *Memory*, 191–96, on Christina's literacy and reading.

was a first attempt, now largely lost, by the prior who was also Godric's confessor, bits of which survive in a later condensed version made from it and from Reginald's life.[11] Clearly the Durham community felt that they had a potential saint on their hands, and some details of Godric's life – the people seeking him out, the steps that he takes to safeguard his privacy (e.g., chapter lvii) – appear to point to an incipient cult even in his lifetime. But even though Reginald may already be drawing on another written account within a few years of the saint's death, he is also drawing on personal testimonies as well as on personal contact with his subject. He meticulously distinguishes between what he has heard from others and what he has heard from the saint himself; he also notes whether he heard it only once or multiple times, for Godric evidently was in the habit of repeating his best stories. He frequently cites him verbatim, even for extended passages, and moves deftly between direct speech, paraphrase, third-party report, and his own observations and comments. Reginald's careful modulation of these voices not only serves to establish the scrupulous veracity of his account, but also to interweave his own voice with the saint's – and to carve out a space for Godric's own narration. One gets the sense, skillfully orchestrated by the biographer, of hearing Godric himself speak.

Sometimes the hagiographer's very confusion – the stories he only half understands and whose point he seems to miss – seems to allow a glimpse of Godric's own narratives. The story of the young Godric finding stranded dolphins on a Norfolk beach (chapter iii) is a good example, for it does not fully make sense in Reginald's rendering. He does faithfully convey the upshot, namely Godric's insight that one must not deprive any living being, however humble, of its dying breath. But Reginald muffs the element of danger and escape, of Godric almost being trapped by the advancing tide; and the solution to Godric's dilemma remains somewhat unclear. He did leave with some dolphin meat – did he decide that a dolphin, as a mere 'fish', is exempt from his compassionate rule? Did he wait for the animal to die, or did he take the meat of one of the dolphins that were already dead? The story must have been better and more coherent as Godric told it.

One certainly gets a vivid sense of the hermit's thought patterns, interests, and preoccupations from Reginald's account. For instance, we learn that Godric has a gift for languages, and that he is affectionate towards his family. He might be garrulous by temperament, but he subjects himself to a rigorous regimen of silences. He is given to depression, even over long periods. He is a peasant at heart, tied to the land. He is drawn to animals, compassionate towards them and thoughtfully curious about their awareness and their souls. He seems to have a special fascination with the moment of death, in both animals and humans, seeking to know and even to see how

---

[11] Stevenson's preface in Reginald of Durham, *Libellus*, vii–ix.

the soul leaves the body (chapters iii, xii). He sees ghosts of people known to him in a strangely semi-individuated, ungendered form. For example, his deceased mother's 'spiritus' appears to him as a male figure.[12] Perhaps most importantly, although Godric likes to ponder abstract concepts, he processes them and makes them concrete in vividly visual and auditory terms.

Simply to ascribe these interests and habits of mind to Godric himself would, of course, be naive. All we have is Reginald's text, and whatever impression we get of Godric is heavily filtered and shaped by that text's rhetorical aims and its pre-texts and intertexts, both immediate and remote. But there is a degree of collaboration between the *Vita*'s author and its subject. Towards the end of the *Vita* we are specifically told that Godric 'blessed this book' shortly before dying (chapter clxvi). To think of this collaboration as a kind of joint authorship (as some have proposed for Christina of Markyate) would be going one crucial step too far; but this is a biography that seems to an unusual degree to have incorporated its subject. It is infused with his spirit; perhaps we see Godric in a way not unlike those spectral shapes of the dead and dying that he so frequently encountered.

A central interest of Reginald's *Vita* of Godric, then, is the author's own relationship with the saint, the joining of their voices, and their collaboration if not exactly co-authorship. The *Vita* is deeply and explicitly interested in Godric's status as a layman, beginning even before he is born, with portraits of both his parents as exemplary layman and laywoman, respectively (chapter ii). It is interested, in episode after episode, but also in recurrent metaphors and wordplay, in the saint's visual and auditory experiences, and the way in which they interact. It explores how a lay visionary like Godric not only inhabits his world but constructs it. He does so with his body, for one could describe the basic project of an eremitical life as living out in practice a physical metaphor of one's place in the world; but also with his intellect, with his perception, with his senses, with his voice, in ways analogous to but quite distinct from the monastic world to which his life is contiguous and neighboring – and perhaps also slightly threatening, or at least questioning.

It is in this context of analogy, neighborliness, cooperation, but also rivalry that the question of Godric's literacy or illiteracy becomes most intriguing. He is described as 'illiteratus', untrained in letters, but, as Clanchy observes, he is not really illiterate in the modern sense. As might be expected of a former merchant, he has at least some functional literacy.[13] He owns a psalter (though likely an abbreviated version for laypeople) and uses it.[14] We are even told that as a grown man, after his return from Jerusalem, he went to a local school to improve his reading skills together with the children, apparently

12 Reginald of Durham, *Libellus*, 126.
13 Clanchy, *Memory*, 236.
14 Reginald of Durham, *Libellus*, 43–44.

in deliberate preparation for his planned entry into a religious life.[15] Some
of his feats of 'miraculous' access to learning are of the kind for which we
would today prefer a non-miraculous explanation. How surprising is it that
he should have learned to understand French, having traded extensively on
the Continent and into the Near East (chapter xciv)? How surprising is it that
he should have picked up some Latin (chapter lxxix)? He has studied, even
memorized, his psalter; he has attached himself to a monastery and is trying
to follow, by himself, most of its liturgical practices. How surprising is it that
he recognizes a *litteratus* when he sees one and can call the bluff of a cleric
who pretends to be a layman (chapter cix)?

That the *Vita* insists on treating these incidents as astounding miracles is
perhaps not just the naiveté, as Clanchy suggests, or the arrogance of a *litteratus*
who cannot fathom where or how a layman may have attained knowledge.[16]
Rather, and much more importantly, the *Vita* is trying simultaneously to mark
distance as well as nearness: Godric does not have direct access to learning, to
languages of high culture, to spiritual experience – he is not a monk. And yet
he does have access to all of these, *as if* he were a monk, adapting, working
around, rivaling, and even superseding the modes of access reserved to the
religious. A charming emblem of his quasi-monastic, less-than-monastic, and
more-than-monastic life, of Godric's utter modesty as well as of his claim to
special privilege, is his *tintinnabulum*, the little bell that calls him away from
his agricultural labors to observe the canonical hours (chapter xlvii). His
servants[17] notice with amazement that the *tintinnabulum* will ring by itself at
the required times and knows enough to stop as soon as Godric commences
his prayers. To be sure, his Hours are somewhat makeshift and fall short of
full monastic usage. He does not know all the 'collecta, capitula et cetera
usus' and has put together something 'from the psalms that he had learned
and other prayers'.[18] Unlike a monk, he also struggles to know what time it is
and to tear himself away from his peasant pursuits. Yet, as he smilingly notes,
God himself takes care to call him to prayer – adding, self-deprecatingly, that
God could even move brute animals to praise Him in human speech.

One of the most astonishing examples of this configuration is told twice
in the book, with some slight differences in detail (chapters xli and lxx). It
connects Godric's own, somewhat homegrown version of monastic psalmody
with a kind of eucharistic vision, even a eucharistic performance, that is
usually reserved to ordained priests. The biographer nicely controls his own
involvement in the telling of the episode, moving inward from a neutral
third-person narration to a personal witness ('he told us himself'), to verbatim

---

[15] Reginald of Durham, *Libellus*, 59–60.
[16] Clanchy, *Memory*, 239.
[17] Licence, 'Benedictines', 324. Although his hermitage, unlike similar ones, never evolves
into an official community or priory, over time he does acquire servants and followers.
[18] Reginald of Durham, *Libellus*, 110: ex Psalmis quos didicerat et reliquibus orationibus.

citation of Godric's words, and then back out again to his own distant, evaluating theological commentary. The vision – vivid, even disturbing – literally arises out of Godric's own psalmody and his own book of psalms:

For as he was sitting on the steps of the altar, the liturgical hour completed, he sang to himself, deep in thought, some pleasant piece of psalmody. He had the Psalter open in his lap, but, as he occasionally raised his eyes to the image of the Crucifix, he suddenly saw that the image as well as the cross had become entirely mobile, and that it was bending backwards and forwards with a nodding motion, as if flexibly sensate [*flexuose sensibilem*]. He instantly set aside all other meditations and began to concentrate fully [*totus intendere*] on the sweetness of this vision, raising his eyes and his hands on high. After a little while, behold, a little boy emerged from the mouth of the Crucified, gradually coming out one limb at the time, and it proceeded to the image of Mary as if walking on the surface of the thin air. For there was a wooden statue of the Virgin, on the north side of the altar, but placed on the same beam as the Crucifix, a little farther to the right of the altar. When the little boy arrived there, he rested for some time sitting in the Virgin's lap; she, as if alive in body, appeared to stretch out her hands towards her visitor, wrapped him in her arms, and with a joyful expression cradled and caressed him in her lap. This continued for about three hours; then the boy, the same way he had come, returned into the mouth of the image of the Crucified.[19]

The precise modalities of this vision are further specified, quoting the saint's own description: the boy did not walk on the rood beam between the two statues, but 'more as if rowing, with no footsteps, proceeded through the empty space of the air'.[20] The statue of the Virgin trembles both at the child's arrival and at his departure, so much so that Godric fears that the beam might come down. We then are quoted the saint's own words, in direct speech: 'The boy approached the Blessed Virgin Mary with such lightness and agility,

---

[19] Reginald of Durham, *Libellus*, 99–100: Nam circa gradus coram Altari stratus forte subsederat, et orationis hora expleta, secum aliquid jocundum psalmodiae ruminando decantabat. Libro Psalterii sic in gremio genuum expanso, sed tamen quando alternis vicibus amico oculorum radio ad Crucifixi imaginem reflexo, subito vidit imaginem simul cum Cruce totam fieri mobilem, ac motu nutante saepius recurvari ac inclinari, velut flexuose sensibilem. Qui statim, omnibus ceteris meditationibus intromissis, coepit hujus visionis dulcedini totus intendere, oculosque cum manibus simul ad alta dirigere. Post modicum vero, ecce! ex ore Crucifixi quidam Puerulus sensim membra singula proferendo progreditur, ac gradiendo quasi in aeris tenuis superficie, ad imaginem Sanctae Mariae deferebatur; quae Sanctae Mariae imago lignea quidem exstitit, sed a parte Altaris aquilonali, in eadem trabe tamen qua ipsum Crucifixum constitit, paulo longius a dextro Altaris latere resedit. Quo dum Puerulus advenit, in gremio Virginis aliquandiu residendo quievit; quae, utpote viviens in corpore, manus prolatas contra advenientem videbatur oppandere, ac illum brachiis circumamplectentibus vultu cum hilariori satis blando solamine gremio tenus confovere. Quod per horas fere tres actum est; ac deinde Puer ille eodem tenore, quo prius advenerat, in ore imaginis Crucifixi reversus est.

In the other telling of this episode [chapter lxx], or one very similar to it, the child exits and enters through Christ's side wound.

[20] Reginald of Durham, *Libellus*, 100: sed potius quasi remigio et nullo calcantis vestigio, per aeris spatium inane processit.

with such ready power of motion, bending backwards and forwards, that in
my wretched inexperience I believed that all his joints were infused with
the spirit of life. The boy who thus appeared to me was, without a doubt,
none other but Jesus of Nazareth, the only son of the Virgin Mary.' The
vision, born from song, then changes back into song: 'And that boy, both
as he emerged and as he returned, sang with such a high voice, sweeter
than honey and the honeycomb, gentler than anything I could ever explain.'[21]
The biographer concludes by marveling at Godric's extraordinary privilege:
'Hence, when the man of God heard the voice, he seems to me to have been
raptured beyond all men and almost associated, albeit not equated, to the
dignity of angels. Thus, this man is seen to be a true Israelite, permitted to
see the Lord, whose face the angels desire to behold, in human shape.'[22]

This episode is richly saturated with a number of religious discourses.[23]
The reading of the book takes on a concrete shape as an intense visual and
auditory experience, according to Godric's usual habit of incarnating all
abstract thought into vivid sensual experience, and also of translating the
visual into sound and vice versa. His vision, and his audition, incorporate his
own words and song along with the iconographical material available in the
church: the rood beam with its Crucifixion group, and the superimposition on
it, surely incorrectly but powerfully, of an affective Virgin-and-Child image.
There is the theological theme of the Incarnation, strikingly sexual and oddly
self-performed, as Christ is born of his own mouth, seems to impregnate
Mary, and then emerges after resting in Mary's lap. Both Mary and the crucifix
simultaneously conceive and give birth (moving and trembling violently all
the time). There is a strong claim for the power of psalmody, which becomes
almost eucharistic, performing a sort of transsubstantiation—perhaps made
even bolder (or justified?) by transferring the words that are incarnated from
Godric's own mouth to Christ's; for the boy, the Incarnate Word, emerges
from the Crucified's mouth, and Godric's own singing temporarily migrates
to the boy himself.

This is surely the *Vita*'s most explicit and most audacious statement of

---

[21] Reginald of Durham, *Libellus*, 100–1: Tantae levitatis agilitate ac prompta movendi
facilitate se Sanctae Virginis Mariae imago circumtulit, ac plicando vel reclinando inflexit,
quod imperitiae meae miseria artus illius omnes vitali spiritu perfusos fuisse crediderit. Puer
etiam ipse qui mihi sic comparuit, nullus pro certo alius quam Jesus Nazarenus, Filius Sanctae
Mariae unicus, exstitit. At Puer ille in egrediendo et regrediendo voce altiori et super mel et
favum dulciori, et supra omne quod explicari possit suaviori, cecinit.
[22] Reginald of Durham, *Libellus*, 101: Unde vir Dei dum vocem ejusmodi audivit, supra
hominem raptus pene Angelicae dignitati, ut mihi videtur, quodammodo confoederari, licet
non coaequari, promeruit. Igitur vir iste verus Israelita fuisse dinoscitur, qui Dominum, Cujus
vultum desiderant Angeli conspicere, in forma humana palam videre promeruit.
[23] I have discussed this episode, in a somewhat different context, in 'Entrances and Exits:
Performing the Psalms in Goscelin of St. Bertin's *Liber Confortatorius*', *Speculum* 83 (2008),
283–302 at 290–92.

the power of a saintly layman.[24] Godric is not a priest, not even a monk; he humbly submits to the Durham community for direction and certainly for all his Eucharistic needs. But with his psalmody he can incarnate the Word, and his monastic biographer applauds and assists him through his narration. His quasi-sacramental power, as well as his liturgical practice, is obviously calqued on the monastic versions thereof; it literalizes and concretizes them, thereby parodying them, in the original sense of adopting and imitating their structure and formal qualities. The intent is not to be provocative or challenging, let alone satirical. Godric never appears other than entirely respectful of priestly authority, and he humbly acknowledges his own inadequacies. Reginald always describes Godric's practices as lesser, makeshift, and imperfect versions of their monastic exemplars. And yet, because of these very imperfections and the fact that he can access the divine only by way of a special grace, Godric also surpasses his monastic model and soars far above it.

Godric's visionary, meditative, and musical activities are represented similarly: as a layman's special gift, conceived and experienced in analogy to monastic spirituality, both inferior and superior to it. Godric tends to process theological and abstract thought in terms of vivid visual and/or auditory experience. The two often go together: all of his music, at least as far as the *Vita* tells us, comes to him as part of a vision; and as we have seen in the miracle of the crucifix and the incarnate word, sound for him easily modulates into vision and scenic representation. But if the auditory and the visual are somewhat fungible in Godric's experience, easily morphing and translating into each other, they are not precisely equivalent. Tentatively and somewhat simplistically, one could say that Godric's extraordinary power of vision – his clairvoyance – tends to function horizontally, overcoming and integrating vast geographical spaces; whereas his auditory feats, and also his singing and his musical compositions, perform a vertical integration, connecting him directly to the saints in heaven. His clairvoyance, or long-distance sight, does not typically involve sound.

Our first example of Godric's clairvoyance is not so much a single episode as a recurrent habit. Godric is often described as ranging widely over space and making distant things present not only to himself but even to his entourage. Godric will say things like: 'Before your conversation just now, a little while ago, I was in Jerusalem; and I saw many very astonishing things'.[25] He will go on to describe changes to the city's architectural substance, buildings that have gone up or disappeared since his long-ago visit there – changes that

---

[24] See Caroline Walker Bynum, *Holy Feast and Holy Fast: The Religious Significance of Food to Medieval Women* (Berkeley, CA, 1987), 77 and 227–33, on women and low-status males bypassing clerical authority in eucharistic matters.

[25] Reginald of Durham, *Libellus*, 130: Ante colloquium vestrum, paulo ante, Ierosolimis fui; et ibi multa praemiranda conspexi.

Reginald says were often confirmed to him by more recent travelers. Godric himself speculates on why and how he can see this: 'For as human faces vary for their different qualities, thus it is necessary and indeed natural that people's characters be different and discrete; and as minds have different qualities of mobility, thus their discordant wishes are efficacious to different degrees.'[26] In other words, he just happens to be so gifted that his 'wishes' are 'efficacious' to a high degree, permitting him to see what he wants to know.

At times the metaphoric valence of a vision is so obvious, and articulated so clearly by the seer himself, that a modern reader may ask whether he is 'really' experiencing visions or 'merely' dressing his intended meaning in vivid metaphorical language. But it seems unlikely that Godric (or Reginald) would have distinguished between these options. For example, one of his other frequent feats of clairvoyance concerns ships, which Godric seems to accompany mentally on their journey – a habit surely harking back to his previous life as a seafaring merchant:

Frequently he would interrupt those talking to him and say, 'Brothers, let us pray; for right now a ship is in distress at sea, and a storm that has arisen against them is growing stronger'. After the prayer, he would resume, 'now my ship has landed; with the storm over, it has escaped the acute danger'. He said things of this sort because he saw those foundering mariners as if they were right before him. For, as he assured us, he saw ships traveling at high sea just as clearly with the vision of the heart as he saw people walking on the ground with his own clear eyes.[27]

One might object that, given the dangers of sea travel at the time and the weather on the North Sea and North Atlantic, it was a safe bet that some ship would be in distress at any given time. Perhaps, we might argue, this is not clairvoyance; Godric is simply remembering in prayer his former colleagues and their constant perils. One might also object that Godric's words do not make it clear whether he means a literal ship in real time – how could it come to port so quickly? – or, metaphorically, his own momentary state of agitation. Both objections are valid. But the point is that to the *Vita* – and no doubt to Godric himself – these are distinctions without a difference: his experience of unease, as well as his sympathetic mindfulness of all mariners

[26] Reginald of Durham, *Libellus*, 130: Nam sicut pro diversa qualitate facies hominum immutantur, ita necesse est, quia et naturale, ut diversorum discreti et dispares mores habeantur; ac sicut animi dispares differentes habent motuum qualitates, ita et diversae sunt efficaciae illorum dissonae voluntates.

[27] Reginald of Durham, *Libellus*, 130–31: Saepius colloquentium solebat verba interrumpere et dicere, 'Quaeso, fratres, oremus; quia ecce, navis in pelago periclitatur; et orta tempestas contra eos grassatur.' Factaque oratione, iterum consuevit adjicere, 'Nunc navis mea applicuit; et turbine sedata, pericula saeva evasit.' Talia eloquia conseruit, quia navigio periclitantes quasi coram se positos vidit. Vidit enim, ut nobis asseruit, ita praeclaro cordis contuitu per aequoris alta navigantes, quemadmodum perlucido oculorum radio homines in humo gradientes.

at sea, translates easily and smoothly into a crystal-clear vision of that far-away ship.

In the last ten years of his life, Reginald says, Godric's clairvoyance became practically continuous and gapless within a radius of ten miles: everything in that area was 'to his mind's eye transparent and known, and each thing was plainly visible'. He might see more distant things more intermittently, but he seems to have enlarged his permanent field of vision and powers of attention in this remarkable way. The biographer ends this chapter not with a visual but a musical metaphor, one that is something of a refrain in the narrative, of Godric's heart being played by the Holy Spirit as if it were a harp: 'Just as at the harpist's touch each string brings forth modulations of a separate sound, thus the Holy Spirit will touch the heart strings of spiritual people and bring forth different powers of virtue.'[28]

Just as his clairvoyance connects Godric with the affairs of wider human communities, it is music that adds a vertical dimension to Godric's life, that gives him direct access to the divine. His 'auditions' – visions that incorporate music, and in fact 'teach' him the songs attributed to him – blend with his own musical practice: he joins in the music of his angelic visitors and is enjoined and authorized by them to sing. But he also, in a sense, brings on the visions through his singing, as we have seen in the crucifix episode: they could be described as visual manifestations of his music. Reginald's repeated metaphor of the spiritual harp – Godric as an instrument sounding of itself and/or being played by divine forces ('the organum of the holy spirit resounds through the saint'[29]) underscores the seamless blending of agencies and voices.

The three chapters concerning Godric's extant songs (chapters l, lxiii, and xciii) highlight different aspects of Godric's visionary experience. His prayer and music put Godric in direct touch with the angels and saints. These episodes knit together the human and the angelic, the visual and the auditory, monastic psalmody and Godric's own musical and poetic invention, third-person narration and quoted first-person speech, saint and hagiographer. We increasingly see Reginald's own fascinated involvement, his interventions, his shaping of the interpretation – and even the nature – of what the hermit sees and hears. These interventions, it seems to me, are largely sympathetic, collaborative, and respectful. This reading does not necessarily preclude the more antagonistic reading proposed, for instance, by Licence: in his account, Godric, his religious life, his cell, his land, and his agricultural

---

[28] Reginald of Durham, *Libellus*, 131: omnia quae per decem milliaria circa eum circumpositae erant seu fiebant, cordis ejus oculis pervia et nota erant, et singula aperte patebant ... et sicut ad citharoedi contactum unaquaeque chorda discreti sonitus modulamina efficit; sic Spiritus Sanctus venas cordis spiritualium hominum tangens, diversas virtutum effectivas potentias parit.

[29] Reginald of Durham, *Libellus*, 117: Sic organum Spiritus Sancti modulatur per virum Dei.

production are all somewhat forcibly appropriated by the monastery and subjected to its authority.[30] This is what happened, clearly, to many hermits and other free-lance religious. But the affects involved must remain a matter of conjecture. I would like to echo Ridyard's wise disclaimer: we do not have Godric's own account, and his feelings are inaccessible to us, except perhaps for the intimations of tension and conflict occasionally glimpsed between the lines. What we have is Godric-as-represented-by-Reginald, and with this limitation we must live.[31] But that composite (Godric-as-seen-by-Reginald), I would argue, produces meaning and insight in its own right.

The first of these episodes (chapter 1), finds Godric deep in prayer, much as in the miracle of the moving crucifix. Again, as in the crucifix miracle, he first sees the vision out of the corner of his eye and then is captivated by it. This vision, too, lasts several hours, with Godric trembling and violently agitated, 'as if his spirit wanted to tear itself from its mortal clothing'.[32] Yet his own reaction reassures him that the vision is of divine provenance, for one could not otherwise experience such joy while also fearing for one's life. He sees two young girls, dressed in dazzling white, flanking the altar and looking at each other. After a while they descend and come towards Godric. One identifies herself as St Mary and identifies her companion (who remains silent) as Mary Magdalene. She proceeds to 'teach him a new song, which the Mother of Mercy herself sang before him, as before a boy learning chant, and taught him to sing it in harmonious chant with a musical melody; he sang it many times after her, and he retained the tune of that song all the days of his life'.[33]

In Reginald's description of this musical performance, the liturgical and the para-liturgical, the popular and the monastic, touch and merge. Reginald emphasizes that the song is in English, and it seems, as Rankin notes, apotropaic in nature, like a popular religious charm recited to ward off danger.[34] The episode is preceded by chapters on the dangers and ill-treatment Godric suffered at the hands of thieves and cross-border cattle raiders; and the Virgin specifically instructs him to sing the song as a protection against danger and to soothe and console himself when in trouble. The method by which he is taught the chant both infantilizes and monasticizes Godric – or perhaps more exactly, places him at the threshold, as a child entering the monastery and learning its ways. The musical style also appears to be poised

---

[30] Licence, 'Benedictines'.

[31] Ridyard, 'Functions', 237.

[32] Reginald of Durham, *Libellus*, 117: quod pene videretur sibi animam a terrenis exuviis velle dissolvi.

[33] Reginald of Durham, *Libellus*, 118: Deinde canticum quoddam novum illi edocuit, quod et ipsa Misericordiae Mater coram eo, quasi coram puero discente, praecinebat, et harmonico cantu illud eum musico modulamine cantare docebat, quod ille saepius subsequenter post eam cecinit, et ipsius melodiae canticum cunctis diebus vitae suae retinuit.

[34] Rankin, 'Hymns', 710.

on the boundary between monastic and popular. There seems to be some form of polyphony involved in this vision, although it is not preserved in the notated sources, and it is hard to tell what exactly Reginald has in mind: 'The fabric of the song's words was woven with words of the English language. All these were held together by a rhythmical tenor and with their melody seemed to imitate for the hearers certain musical sounds.'[35] Does this mean that the 'tenor', the accompanying part, was textless and rhythmic, therefore seeming 'instrumental' although it was sung? It may well be that Godric's music followed popular polyphonic styles of his time and place; Gerald of Wales famously remarked that polyphony was widely practiced in the popular music of northern England as well as Wales.[36] It is also conceivable that Reginald, in describing this style of improvisation, consciously or unconsciously approaches it to the composed polyphonic music, new at this time, that is now known to us as *Ars Antiqua* or Notre Dame polyphony, a style that also featured texted upper voices and untexted, or barely texted, 'rhythmical tenors' that hold the entire structure together. If so, we have another example of (mis-) communication and creative encounter between lay and clerical experience.

Although he was not a witness to this episode, Reginald stresses his own proximity to the story: 'He himself told this to me, a sinner, with his own saintly mouth, and with the sweetness of many tears often sang this song to me'. And he adds another sensual detail, describing the holy women's clothes in the saint's own words: '"And to tell you something about an untellable thing", he said, "something that can in any way at all be comprehended with a similitude: their consistency was like the inner skin of an eggshell, which is so tender that if you barely touch it with even the tip of your fingernail, it breaks and detaches from the shell."'[37] This detail involves yet another sense, the sense of touch – perhaps to authenticate the visionary account and distinguish it from a mere dream. But it also graphically illustrates the fragility of the otherworldly vision and the precariousness of its translation into human experience and human language.

The vision related in chapter lxiii features a member of Godric's own family. We were belatedly informed a few chapters before (lxi), that his sister Burgwen had followed Godric into the ascetic life; he had built her a cell at some distance from his, and although they imposed a fairly strict separation

---

[35] Reginald of Durham, *Libellus*, 118–19: Textus vero verborum, quibus canticum illud componebatur, verbis Anglicae linguae contexitur; quae omnia rythmico tenore contexuntur, et melo cantici quosdam sonos musicos audientibus imitari videntur.

[36] Trend, 'First English Song', 118–20.

[37] Reginald of Durham, *Libellus*, 120: 'et ut de re', inquit, 'indicibili dixerim tibi aliquid, quod quoquo modo illarum similitudo possit intelligi, erat illarum figura quasi testulae ovi interior tela, quae quandoque unguinum praeacumine vix prae sui teneritudine de testula confracta expilatur cum quadam artis ingenuae lenitate'.

on themselves, they were very close. (They, or Reginald, were presumably aware of the precedent set by St Benedict and St Scholastica.) Her death, after a lengthy and crippling illness, is devastating to him. Disturbed not to know of her fate after death, he is granted the special favor of a musical vision. He sees the Virgin Mary above the altar, followed by two angelic-looking men in white, who lead Burgwen's spirit between them; he instantly recognizes his sister, 'and rejoicing in his spirit, he instantly concentrated attentively on this sweet vision. As soon as she stood in the middle of the altar, she sweetly lifted up her voice, and with a song of sonorous melody sang this.' The text is quoted first in Latin, then in English: 'Crist and Seinte Marie, sio on scamel me iledde, thaet ic on this hi-herthe ne sculde uuit mine bare fot itreide' (Christ and the Virgin Mary led me thus on a footstool, that I should not tread this earth with my bare foot). Then the two men identified as angels 'loudly lifted up their sweet voices, and with melodious song [canora modulatio] repeated several times: "Kyrie eleison, Christe eleison"'. The distinctive musical element in this vision appears to be percussive. The angels carry books, covered in shiny red leather: 'Singing, they struck these books with their hands, and singing to the Lord with voices of exultation, they agitated their palms alternately and alternately spread open their books' pages'.[38] Here, even more than elsewhere in these musical accounts, one wonders if the description refers to known musical practices: was there percussion in popular and/or monastic chant? Was it conceivable that books would be used percussively? Or does this feature sound as odd to medieval readers as it does to us, underscoring the otherworldliness of this performance? It has been noted[39] that here is some discrepancy between Reginald's account, where the English verses come first and the angels' *Kyrie* is a refrain, and the musical source, which seems to reinterpret the song as a troped *Kyrie*: it clearly stipulates that Soror, the sister, is to repeat her English verset twice, between the three *Kyrie Eleison–Christe Eleison–Kyrie Eleison* verses. This time, there is no direct citation of Godric's words, and no mention of Reginald's involvement; we are merely told that the group then disappeared, leaving no traces where they had stood, and Godric was much consoled.

If Reginald kept himself out of the scene between Godric and Burgwen, he is actually present at the next musical episode, although he cannot see or hear the vision (chapter xciii). The episode is told from his observing point of view, then further elucidated in conversation with Godric himself. (On the other hand, the text of the song, 'Seinte Nicolas, godes drud', which we have

---

[38] Reginald of Durham, *Libellus*, 144: et exsultans spiritu tam jocundae visioni diligenter intendit … voces suavissimas altissime efferunt, et canora modulatione talia saepius repetendo dixerunt, 'Kyrie ꝉ. Xpe ꝉ.' … Canentes igitur talia manu plaudebant, et jubilantes Domino in vocibus exsultationis, palmas alternis motibus iactitabant, et quasi librorum suorum folia alteruterim dispergebant.

[39] Trowell, 'Godric', 74.

from another source, is not reported here.) By this time, Reginald explains, he was one of the monks sent to read mass for Godric on feast days, and on this occasion, at Easter, he stayed overnight. Perhaps he and the other monks had also already begun to take turns caring for the increasingly frail hermit, as is clearly the case in the final musical chapter (clxi). Reginald is awakened in the middle of the night, as Godric 'rejoiced loudly, with his voice raised high, and frequently invoked the name of St Nicholas'. The next morning, he asks Godric to explain, and Godric obliges with a detailed account of what he has experienced, involving three of the five senses: 'I saw with my eyes visions of God [*videns ... vidi ... visiones*] and I saw the Angels of God descend to the sepulcher of Christ.' He hears the angels sing 'sweet-flowing songs of praise, in voices of exultation', and also St Nicholas, who was with them, 'performing the hymn tunes with them with a clear voice'. The angels also 'kept walking around the tomb and ... spread indescribable fragrances of salves and thyme under the tomb and all around'. Godric himself, as he tells Reginald, is swept up by the general rejoicing, and St Nicholas encourages him to sing along: 'he said that it was fitting that the voice of humans of good will should join the Angelic voices'.[40]

Godric's vision is tied to the church's iconography and to the liturgical occasion. The tomb that is the focal point of the vision is presumably an Easter sepulcher in the church. When Reginald asks him about the duration of the vision, Godric measures it by the events of Easter night: 'from nightfall until the morning dawned in the East, the hour in which Christ rose from the dead, and when the Angel, with the sun already up in the sky, rolled back the stone from the tomb'.[41] At the end of Godric's account, both men are overcome by emotion, in a way that stresses their solidarity but also their distance. Reginald weeps as he sees Godric weep, but precisely because he himself is unable to share in the old man's visionary experience: 'because for my sins I was so blind and deaf that I could not hear such things'. And as Godric laments that he is still alive, that he must wait so long for his death, Reginald leaves him quietly, understanding that 'his spirit was embittered'.[42]

---

[40] Reginald of Durham, *Libellus*, 202: Ille igitur voce in altissimis elata clarissime jubilabat, et frequenter Beati Nicholai nomen invocabat ... 'Videns', inquit, 'vidi visiones Dei, et Angelos Dei ad Christi sepulchrum descendere et ibi dulcifluis laudum praeconiis in voce exultationis Domino iubilare ... Sanctus Nicholaus affuit, et melos hymnidicos cum ipsis clarissima voce persolvit' ... Semper interim ipsum sepulchrum circumibant, et dulciflue modulando odorifera unguentorum et inexplicabilia thymiamatum aromata infra illud et circumquaque dispergebant ... dignum esse dicens ut vox hominum bonae voluntatis vocibus consociaretur Angelicis.'

[41] Reginald of Durham, *Libellus*, 202: A primae noctis initio usque in mane oriente diluculo, qua hora Christus resurrexit a mortuis, et orto jam sole Angelus lapidem de sepulchro removit.

[42] Reginald of Durham, *Libellus*, 202: et simul flevi [Reginaldus], qui pro peccatis meis tantum caecus et surdus exstiti, quod talia sentire non potui; 203: quia spiritum illius tunc in amaritudine esse videbam.

That Reginald considers himself knowledgeable about music, and perhaps even musically literate, can be inferred even from his repeated remark that Godric is not.[43] He is certainly interested in music; he takes considerable care to describe Godric's musical achievements in some detail and to preserve his musical legacy. On one occasion, very late in Godric's life, he summons another witness to help him listen as the old man sings, and together the two witnesses make a determined effort to commit his song to memory.[44] It is of course anybody's guess how close the pieces that have survived are to Godric's original invention. The notated tradition commences somewhat later, and, at the very least, there must have been a certain translation process from Godric's 'illiterate' practice into notation, a writing system known to few individuals and almost exclusively tied to the liturgical repertoire, of which Godric's songs partake but to which they do not properly belong. It is also difficult to tell how typical or atypical Godric's performance is for his time and place, or even how typical a given performance is with respect to Godric's usual practice. Not only do we lack context; not only is the meaning of many terms open to question; but Reginald's rhetorical aim of emphasizing the miraculous leaves one guessing whether a particular feature is in fact highly unusual, or whether Reginald is choosing to 'make it strange', to underscore the miraculousness of the ordinary, as he does for instance with Godric's language competence. Things are further complicated by the fact that much of Godric's music, and Reginald's account thereof, comes in the context of visions narrated by the visionary; and by the circumstance that the period of Reginald's own observation coincides with Godric's extreme old age, when Reginald apparently was one of the monks charged with caring for him. The most extended eye- and ear-witness description, in chapter clxi, is dated in Godric's final years, when, close to one hundred years old, he is too weak to keep his eyes open or to sit up in bed without assistance. He is also, one senses between the lines, increasingly ill-tempered: on this occasion, his two caregivers 'cheerfully congratulate him' on his better-than-usual mood.[45] On a similar occasion (chapter xciii, recounting the vision that produces the song 'Seinte Nicolas'), Reginald considers it prudent to withdraw, seeing the old man's 'bitterness of spirit'. The greatest miracle, as Reginald observes, is that the frail centenarian should be able and willing to sing at all, let alone for several hours.[46]

Nonetheless, that description – Godric's extended improvisation on the phrase 'Wilcome Symond' – offers some intriguing hints on Godric's improvisational practice. He begins with textless vocalizations; only after

---

[43] e.g., Reginald of Durham, *Libellus*, 306: Mirandum sane … illiteratum idiotam simplicem notas non simplices, sed innodaciter intricatas, nullo docente, cognoscere.
[44] Reginald of Durham, *Libellus*, 306.
[45] Reginald of Durham, *Libellus*, 307: jocundis illius alloquiis applaudere hilare satis duximus.
[46] Reginald of Durham, *Libellus*, 306.

some time does he add words ('subnexus'), the single English phrase. Reginald explicitly notes that there is no further text; whether he implies that this is uncommon for Godric, or whether it strikes him as unusual in relation to liturgical practice, is not clear. Trowell, in the *New Grove Dictionary of Music* (s.v. 'Godric'), treats 'Wilcome Symond' as a 'lost song' by Godric; but it is also unclear whether there was, in Reginald's or his readers' minds, an identifiable song by that name, or whether this was an *ad hoc* improvisation that did not leave behind a popularly remembered melody (although Reginald does tell us that he and the servant attempted to memorize the tune, presumably in order to write it down or pass it on later). In any event, Reginald is deeply impressed with the quality of Godric's musical invention. The singer incessantly varies the tune ('different notes on each syllable')[47], in phrases described as convoluted and intricate ('innodaciter intricatas'). One wonders whether the simple tunes that have come down to us – for instance 'Seinte Nicolas', also the fruit of an extended vision and a whole night's singing – were in fact so simple, or whether they merely formed the basis for the singer's astonishingly complex improvisations.

That Godric's untutored musicality is in constant dialogue with the liturgical music that is Reginald's background, that it borrows from monastic music and is open to reinterpretation and appropriation by it, is clear to all participants, not least Godric himself. The exchange between the two men on this occasion is particularly enlightening. Finding Godric happier and more communicative than usual, Reginald cautiously questions him about the long performance that he has just witnessed. (It is clear from his narration that such conversations did not always go well.) In the first place, Reginald does not assume that 'Symond' is a religious figure, or at least – half-jokingly perhaps? – leaves open the possibility that he might be an ordinary human acquaintance of Godric's. 'So who is this Simon you kept calling out to?' Reginald asks in effect. 'You did know that we were standing by to serve you if you needed anything?' Godric replies with a question, clearly aiming at a religious interpretation but, at the same time, distancing himself from clerical practice and leaving the choice to Reginald: 'Don't you clerics sing "St Simon, pray for us"?'[48] Reginald, perhaps backtracking from his lighthearted first approach, quickly redefines the frame of reference: there are two apostles by that name, Simon Peter and Simon Zelotes (here identified with Thaddeus), and he did not know which Godric meant. It is only now that Godric, taking up that interpretive offer, settles on Simon Peter, and he makes it clear why. He knows Peter to be the key-bearer, and the symbolism of the keys appeals to him as a characterization of the revelation he has just

---

[47] Reginald of Durham, *Libellus*, 306: semper novi ac disparis cantus melodias quibusque syllabis verborum apposuit.
[48] Reginald of Durham, *Libellus*, 307: et nonne vos clerici in Ecclesia canitis, 'Sancte Symon, ora pro nobis'?

experienced ('Christ disclosed this to me, and he who came down here was, as it were, his porter'[49]). He also seems to read the key-bearer's appearance as an announcement of his impending death: at the end of the vision, Godric sees Peter receding into the light of heaven.[50]

Through the collaborative dialogue between the monk and the hermit, the vision not only receives its interpretation, it also takes on its final shape. This observation is not meant, of course, to call into question the sincerity of Godric's visionary experience but to emphasize that the raw material of the vision – its music, its significance, and even its narrative ark – is shaped ex-post-facto, not unlike the process familiar to most of us, of giving narrative shape to a dream in the act of retelling it. The effort here is dialogic and collaborative, simultaneously tying Godric's vision and music closer to monastic practice, while acknowledging its independence, its parallel but distinct ways of experiencing the divine.

That the words of Godric's songs are in the vernacular, a layman's proper language, distinguishes it from monastic song and places it both higher and lower. On the one hand, Reginald marvels at the simplicity and instant intelligibility of the words: 'words that to a simple listener' – any listener, and/or Reginald himself, for he is the only one present at this point – 'were quite understandable, for he used the English language'.[51] But despite that simplicity ('tamen') he produces an astonishingly intricate song. And the simple words, propelled by the astonishing music, take him directly to things beyond any language at all: Simon Peter, key-bearer to Christ, 'told me wonderful and untellable secrets, which the human mind cannot conceive'.[52] Reginald makes one more attempt to ask what these secrets were but is rebuffed with an unmistakable put-down, which he humbly reports in indirect speech: 'that these things were not explicable in words, and those which were, in part, human, nonetheless could not be retained by my [i.e., Reginald's] heart'.[53] Godric's linguistic and musical experience has neatly bypassed the Latin world of his learned friend. Despite or because of his plain English, he has achieved easy access to the wordless secrets of heaven. Seamlessly, his English songs modulate into the music of the angels.

---

[49] Reginald of Durham, *Libellus*, 308: Haec mihi Christus aperuit; Cujus ipse huc descendens forte bajulus fuit.

[50] For a discussion and numerous examples of such death visions, both in medieval hagiography and in modern thanatology, see Peter Dinzelbacher, 'Mittelalterliche Vision und moderne Sterbeforschung', in *Psychologie in der Mediävistik*, ed. Jürgen Kühnel, Hans-Dieter Mück, Ursula Müller, and Ulrich Müller (Göppingen 1985), 9–49.

[51] Reginald of Durham, *Libellus*, 306: verba, quae auditori simplici satis fuere perceptibilia, nam sermone Anglico usus est.

[52] Reginald of Durham, *Libellus*, 307: mira et inennarabilia mihi secreta retulit quae mens humana non percipit.

[53] Reginald of Durham, *Libellus*, 308: quod illa verbis inexplicabilia forent, ipsa vero quae humana fuerunt jam ex parte a meo corde retineri non potuerunt.

7

Did Portugal Have a Twelfth-Century Renaissance?

André Vitória

Over the seventy-five years since its publication, scholars have continued to adjust and refine Professor Charles Haskins' classic historiographical label 'Renaissance of the twelfth century'. Nevertheless, the concept remains a useful springboard with which to approach, understand, and explain the cultural changes, the accelerations, and the innovations that took place in Western Europe in the course of the twelfth century. Yet, like any other conceptual tool, it has limits in scope that confine its utility geographically and chronologically, as well as qualitative limitations in terms of the particular events and achievements that are its *raison d'être*.[1] Defining events, such as the flowering of dialectic or the coming of age of the study and production of canon law, coincided with each other only in certain places and at given times. Portugal is one place where such a conjunction of events and achievements never occurred. Portugal, in other words, did not have a Renaissance in the way imagined by Haskins for medieval Europe.

This fact should be of some consequence for Portuguese history, since the twelfth century is the country's century of birth. To be born in the age of Abelard, Gratian, or Azo might be auspicious, were it not for the fact that all three – as well as every major intellectual figure of the twelfth-century Renaissance – led their lives and produced their works far from Portugal and without any attestable connection to it. Of course, their work and the work of other leading figures of the Renaissance of the twelfth century did reach Portugal, but it did so unevenly and piecemeal. Gratian's *magnum opus* was known in Portugal by the second half of the twelfth century, as was the theology of St Bernard and Hugh of St Victor, but it is highly doubtful that Abelard's ever was. One need only leaf through the indexes of the most important books written about the Renaissance of the twelfth century to realize that Portugal did not play any part in it. But even if Portugal cannot be ascribed any role in the Renaissance based upon the presence of dynamic

---

[1]   Charles H. Haskins, *The Renaissance of the Twelfth Century* (Cambridge, MA, 1927), chapter 1 esp. 8–11.

learning centres or the intellectual achievements of its people, what about the impact on this peripheral region of Europe of what was being played out elsewhere? Even though active contribution can be ruled out, what about reception? Which were the novelties that reached Portugal, and what were the extent and the effects of their absorption? These are the questions that I will address in what will necessarily be an incomplete sketch of the culture of a kingdom in formation.

The origins of Portugal as an independent kingdom are modest. A small county, it was controlled by a handful of noble families and their respective vassals who owed allegiance to the French count, a vassal of the king of León-Castile.[2] Portugal was also a morphologically irregular territory, dotted with small Benedictine monasteries and a limited urban network structured around five episcopal cities; the Muslim south offered both a threat and the promise of expansion and future riches. The county became a kingdom when the second count of Portugal, Afonso Henriques, succeeded in channelling the ambitions of the Portuguese nobility toward secession from León, offering them a chance to be the elite of the new kingdom and to lead its expansion rather than remaining an intermediate rank in the Leonese aristocracy. This process was set in motion in 1128. By the mid-1140s Portugal was a *de facto* kingdom, and in 1179, six years before the end of Afonso Henriques' long reign, Pope Alexander III finally recognized it as a kingdom in its own right.

This explanation is overly simplistic, but it demonstrates how the birth of the kingdom was inextricably linked with the will and the direct actions of its first king. The kings' ability to rally the nobility round their own designs, to alienate them at crucial moments (as Afonso Henriques did when launching his campaigns against the Almoravids), and to exploit their internal divisions seems to be a persistent trait of the first two centuries of Portuguese history. Periods of aristocratic unrest did occur, and Sancho I, Afonso II, and Sancho II each had to withstand rebellion by some factions of the nobility, but their opposition to the king was never sufficiently coherent and organized to impose the nobility's powers and privileges on him collectively and enduringly. In

---

[2] The count and the king in question are Henry of Burgundy (1066–1112) and Alfonso VI, king of León-Castile, 'emperor' of Spain (d. 1109). Henry, a grandson of Duke Robert I of Burgundy, was Alfonso's son-in-law by marriage with Alfonso's illegitimate daughter, Teresa. He was one of the French noblemen who had answered Alfonso VI's call for military help against the Almoravids in the 1180s and 1190s and was given the marcher territories of 'Portucale' in 1096. His son, Afonso Henriques, was born in 1109 and would become the first king of Portugal. Alfonso VI, conqueror of Toledo (1085) and styled 'imperator totius Hispaniae', succeeded in reuniting and greatly expanding his father's kingdom of León-Castile, pushing the frontier south to the margins of the Tagus. See, briefly, Simon Barton, 'Spain in the Eleventh Century', in *The New Cambridge Medieval History. Vol. IV, c. 1024–1198, Part II*, ed. David Luscombe and Jonathan Riley-Smith (Cambridge, 2004), 171–90; Charles Julian Bishko, 'The Spanish and Portuguese Reconquest, 1095–1492', in *Studies in Medieval Spanish Frontier History* (London, 1980), 396–456 at 402.

fact, the most consistent, articulate, and purposeful opposition to royal power came from the Portuguese bishops, not from the nobility.[3]

By the time of the nascence of the Portuguese monarchy, there was already an established diocesan network in the region where the new kingdom would develop, and this network would expand as the kingdom's borders shifted southward. Unsurprisingly, it is in the cathedrals that we find the first few traces of the novelties that elsewhere in Europe were changing literate culture. In 1185, Fernando Martins, bishop of Porto, left in his will to the cathedral chapters of Porto and Braga[4] a *Decretum*, the whole of the *Corpus iuris civilis*,[5] and *summae* on the *Decretum*,[6] the Institutions, and the

---

[3] See Hermenegildo Fernandes, *Sancho II. Tragédia* (Mem Martins, 2006), 80. The strained and often conflictual relationship between King Sancho I and King Afonso II and factions of the nobility is described in detail in Maria João Violante Branco, *D. Sancho I. O filho do fundador* (Mem Martins, 2006), 232–52, and Hermínia Vasconcelos Vilar, *D. Afonso II. Um rei sem tempo* (Mem Martins, 2006), 97–107, 232–33. Both authors also note the lack of unity within the ranks of Portuguese nobility. Maria João Branco, in particular, identifies a sharp division during Sancho I's reign between a pro-Leonese nobility and one largely dependent on royal service, remarking that these two 'parties' were 'not reconcilable' and 'hence could never have formed a single bloc against Sancho' (Branco, *D. Sancho I*, 249; translation is mine). This divergence of interests and allegiances may be the reason why Portuguese noblemen were never capable of forcing their kings to accept a constitutional pact similar to Magna Carta; they lacked unity and a common resolve. Maria João Branco has recently ventured the hypothesis that Afonso II's statutes of 1211 might have represented just such a pact, but she does not explain why. Although both events were the product of unsettled times, as Professor Branco remarks, it is impossible to overlook the fact that whereas the statutes of 1211 were the initiative of Afonso II and issued by him in the presence of his noblemen and bishops, Magna Carta was imposed on King John by the English barons and part of the clergy on their own terms. See Maria João Violante Branco, 'The General Laws of Alfonso II and his Policy of "Centralisation": a Reassessment', in *The Propagation of Power in the Medieval West. Selected Proceedings of the International Conference. Groningen 20–23 November 1996*, ed. Martin Gosman, Arjo Vanderjagt, and Jan Veenstra (Groningen, 2011), 79–95 at 86–87. On Magna Carta, from a galaxy of studies, see J.C. Holt, *Magna Carta* (Cambridge, 2nd edn, 1992), 25–27, and R.H. Helmholz, 'Magna Carta and the *ius commune*', *The University of Chicago Law Review* 66 (1999), 297–371. The closest we can find to a pact binding the king to a number of obligations was the initiative of the Portuguese bishops who in 1245 compelled Afonso III, whom they had just ushered to power, to swear the so-called Paris oath (see note 52, below), and negotiated a set of concordats with Dinis between 1289 and 1309. Could this be because the bishops were the only political group in the kingdom with enough strength and organization to force the king to compromise?

[4] *Censual do Cabido da Sé do Porto* (Porto, 1924), 385–86.

[5] Including both the *Epitome Juliani* and the more recent and more complete *Authenticum* as regards the *Novels*. For a distinction between the two, see Hermann Lange, *Römisches Recht im Mittelalter. Band I: Die Glossatoren* (2 vols., Munich, 1997–2007), i, 80–85.

[6] These could have been written by any of the following decretists, since their *summae* were all produced before 1185: Paucapalea, Rufinus, Stephen of Tournai, John of Faenza, Simon of Bisignano, or Sicardus Cremonensis. See Johannes Friedrich von Schulte, *Die Geschichte der Quellen und Literatur des Canonischen Rechts von Gratian bis auf die Gegenwart* (3 vols., Stuttgart, 1875–1880), i, 109–45; Isaías da Rosa Pereira, 'Livros de Direito na Idade Média', *Lusitania Sacra* 7 (1964–66), 7–60 at 46–47, note 40.

Code. It is a remarkable bibliographic legacy, especially if we consider that
the references it contains to the Digest and the *Decretum* are presumably
some of the earliest ever for the Iberian Peninsula.[7] These references to
Romano-canonical texts become very common in testaments and legacies
throughout the thirteenth century, though it has proven almost impossible
to locate the works mentioned in modern libraries. But these references do
attest to a connection between scholars from Portugal (particularly from the
archdiocese of Braga and the diocese of Coimbra) and the University of
Bologna that can be traced, according to Ingo Fleisch, as far back as the
third quarter of the twelfth century.[8] This connection was strengthened during
the thirteenth century, and by 1250–60 there was a significant number of
Portuguese scholars at the Bologna *studium*, usually canons or rectors of
churches.[9]

---

[7]   According to André Gouron, the first documentary reference to the *Digest* in Catalonia,
where Roman law spread earlier than elsewhere in the peninsula, dates from 1188. The first
mention of the *Decretum* is from 1192: 'La Catalogne dans le concert juridique européen du
douzième siècle', in *Ius proprium – Ius commune a Europa. El Dret Comú i Catalunya. Actes
del IIIr Simposi Internacional, 5–7 novembre de 1992.*, ed. A. Iglesia Ferreirós (Barcelona,
1993), 19–26 at 21. See below for more information about Fernando Martins.
[8]   See Ingo Fleisch, *Sacerdotium—Regnum—Studium. Der westiberische Raum und die
europäische Universitätskultur im Hochmittelalter. Prosopographische und rechtsgeschichtliche
Studien* (Berlin, 2006), 116–18.
[9]   See Fleisch, *Sacerdotium*, 120–52 for a good survey of Portuguese scholars in Bologna
from *c.* 1180 until the 1260s. Prominent among them was the canonist Menendus Hispanus,
one of Evesham Abbey's legal counsellors in the dispute with the bishop of Worcester. See
Alain Boureau, 'How Law Came to the Monks: The Use of Law in English Society at the
Beginning of the Thirteenth Century', *Past and Present* 167 (2000), 29–74 at 51; Stephan
Kuttner, *Repertorium der Kanonistik (1140–1234). Prodromus corporis glossarum I* (Vatican
City, 1937), 301–3. Also of note was Petrus Hispanus Portugalensis (whom Professor Fleisch
identified with a high degree of certainty as Pedro Salvadores, bishop of Porto), who wrote two
ordines iudiciarii (*Ad summariam notitiam* and *Quoniam utilissimum fori*) and some *Notabilia
in Compilationem Quartam*. See Antonio García y García, *Estudios sobre la canonística
portuguesa medieval* (Madrid, 1976), 104–6; Antonio García y García, 'La Canonística Ibérica
(1150–1250) en la investigación reciente', *Bulletin of Medieval Canon Law. New series* 11
(1981), 41–75 at 58; Kuttner, *Repertorium*, 414–15. Specifically on his two *ordines iudiciarii*,
see Linda Fowler-Magerl, *Ordo iudiciorum vel ordo iudiciarius. Begriff und Literaturgattung*
(Frankfurt am Main, 1984), 136–38, 142–44. One example that may be paradigmatic of the
academic careers of these clerics abroad is that of Dominicus Petri, schoolmaster of Braga. His
life and activities are relatively well documented: he was in Bologna in the 1260s, contracting
debts and promising to pay them (and actually paying some), witnessing legal acts, and buying
and selling legal books, of which he owned a few, along with works of grammar and logic,
as well as a book by Aristotle. See *Chartularium Studii Bononiensis. Documenti per la storia
dell'Università di Bologna dalle origini fino al secolo XV* (10 vols., Bologna, 1909–1939)
[hereafter *CSB*], v, 4, 35, 60, 72, 81, 213; vii, 11, 233; viii, 19, 45, 107–8, 150, 168, 187,
189; x, 182; and Arquivo Distrital de Braga [hereafter ADB], Livro I dos Testamentos, no. 49.
Biographical data from Ana Maria S. Rodrigues et al., *Os capitulares bracarenses (1245–1374):
notícias biográficas* (Lisbon, 2005), 146–49. More information on Dominicus Petri's studies
can be found in Fleisch, *Sacerdotium*, 138–46. See also note 38, below.

The sources available for this period suggest that the study of the new legal science was the earliest and most pervasive medium through which the cultural innovations of the twelfth century reached Portugal, though it was not the only one.[10] In 1175, for example, an anniversary record from the see of Coimbra registers the death of a Master Martinus, canon, who died in Paris and left works on astronomy, arithmetic and medicine to the chapter.[11] It is also possible that John of Seville and Lima, the twelfth-century translator of scientific and philosophical works from the Arabic, was actually Portuguese.[12] Moreover, the intellectual tradition of the two largest monasteries in Portugal – Santa Cruz and Alcobaça – reflects the influence of St Bernard and Hugh of St Victor in its emphasis on the study of Scripture, patristic writings, and hagiographies.[13] Both houses had considerable libraries and were the cultural cradle of St Anthony and also Peter of Spain, the likely author of a paraphrase of Aristotle's *De anima*.[14] Though they are suggestive, these hints allow very little room for extrapolation. Indeed, most of them are redolent of traditional preoccupations rather than new intellectual challenges. For reasons that are still unclear, Portugal, unlike Aragon and the vibrant Castilian city of Toledo, remained on the margins of the translation movement of the twelfth century, and did not produce any philosophical work of note, leaving the cultural landscape of the kingdom looking very bleak.

It is a different picture entirely when we turn to the study and practice of law. The abundant references to legal books and legal scholars were accompanied by a gradual integration of the Romano-canonical system of law into the intricate workings of justice and by a steady rise in litigation. This, I believe, depended on two main factors: the operation of ecclesiastical justice and the development of the Portuguese monarchy and its resultant interaction with the jurisdiction of the Church.

During the twelfth century the Portuguese episcopate largely accommodated itself to the hierarchical organization of the reformed Church,

---

[10] On the importance of the twelfth century as a century of 'legal revival', see James A. Brundage, *The Medieval Origins of the Legal Profession: Canonists, Civilians, and Courts* (Chicago, IL, 2008), chapter 3. Also André Gouron, 'Un assaut en deux vagues: la diffusion du droit romain dans l'Europe du XIIe siècle', in *El Dret Comú i Catalunya. Actes del Ier Simposi Internacional, Barcelona, 25–6 de maig de 1990*, ed. A. Iglesia Ferreirós (Barcelona, 1991), 47–63.

[11] *Liber Anniversariorum Ecclesiae Cathedralis Colimbriensis (Livro das Kalendas)*, ed. Pierre David and Torquato de Sousa Soares (2 vols., Coimbra, 1947), i, 79.

[12] Charles Burnett, 'Magister Iohannes Ispalensis et Limiensis and Qusta ibn Luqa's *De differentia spiritus et animae*', *Mediaevalia, textos e estudos* 7/8 (1995), 221–67. See also José Francisco Meirinhos, 'Ecos da renovação filosófica do século XII em Portugal no tempo de Afonso Henriques: a cultura que vem da Europa e o legado árabe', in *2.º Congresso Histórico de Guimarães: Actas do Congresso* (7 vols., Guimarães, 1995), iv, 164–70.

[13] José Francisco Meirinhos, *Estudos de Filosofia Medieval: Autores e Temas* (Porto Alegre, 2007), 36–37.

[14] Meirinhos, 'Ecos da renovação', 163.

despite a persistent local taste for secular appointments of clerics by the patrons of churches.[15] The influence of Rome certainly became more marked, with its legates and judges delegate, its expanding body of legislation, and channels of appeal. The Portuguese Church was an organized entity before the Portuguese monarchy had even begun to exist, and the first kings of Portugal were keen to take advantage of that circumstance. The bishops, monasteries, and military orders could be excellent allies, more stable and dependable than the unpredictable nobility. Accordingly, Afonso Henriques and his son, Sancho I, pampered the clergy with lands and privileges, and Afonso Henriques swore vassalage to the pope, placing his kingdom under the latter's protection.[16]

Reciprocal privileges were implicit, of course. Owing to his munificence, Afonso Henriques felt justified in appointing bishops to several sees without consulting the pope[17] and intervened in sundry ecclesiastical matters.[18] Sancho I adopted quite the same policy, combining generosity with meddling.[19] Simultaneously, an increasing number of clerics became royal officials and administrators of the king's chancery, treasury, and court, three budding departments whose continuous operation constituted something of an acid test determining the development of a monarchy. Clerics were the first bureaucrats in medieval Europe, and their utility to any secular authority was obvious, since they were literate and familiar with political organization and diplomacy. During the twelfth century and for most of the thirteenth, the Portuguese royal chancery and treasury were in the hands of clerics. The first curial notaries and chancellors were canons,[20] and the administration of the royal treasury was heavily dependent on a few trusted ecclesiastical

---

[15] This matter was still being debated in the Concordats of 1289. *Ordenações Afonsinas* (5 vols., Lisbon, 1984, facsimile of 1792 edition), ii, 15, article 20.

[16] José Mattoso, *Identificação de um país: Ensaio sobre as origens de Portugal (1096–1325). II, Composição* (Lisbon, 5th edn, 1995), 150–52, including a list of the most important royal donations to religious corporations. Afonso Henriques' letter of submission to the pope, of which only copies survive, is published in *Documentos Medievais Portugueses: Documentos Régios*, ed. Rui de Azevedo (4 vols., Lisbon, 1958–61), i.1, item no. 202.

[17] Lisbon, Lamego, and Viseu: Mattoso, *Identificação*, 150.

[18] Examples of royal appointment of clerics to parish and cathedral churches in *Bulário Português. Inocêncio III (1198–1216)* (Coimbra, 1989) [hereafter *BPIn.III*], no. 45, 69–74, and no. 89, 184–95. These documents are also edited in *Die Register Innocenz' III.*, ed. Othmar Hageneder et al. (11 vols., Graz and Vienna, 1964–) [hereafter *Reg. Inn. III*], ii, 95 and vi, 109, respectively.

[19] A few notable examples of royal meddling in church affairs can be found in *Documentos de D. Sancho I (1174–1211)*, ed. Rui de Azevedo et al. (Coimbra, 1979) [hereafter *DSI*], 42; and *BPIn.III*, no. 53, 95–96. For the exchange of possessions with Knights Templar and donation of tithes, see *Reg. Inn. III*, ii, 129 (138). For the persecution and spoliation of clerics and churches, see *PL* 216, cols. 385–86, and *BPIn.III*, no. 154, 295–97; no. 87, 163–80. The dispute between the bishop of Coimbra and the monastery of Santa Cruz appears on pp. 178–79.

[20] Mattoso, *Identificação*, 104–5.

institutions and clergymen.[21] Even the king's court relied on the contribution of clerics, who worked as lawyers and advisors.[22]

Over the first half of the thirteenth century, the nature of this uneasy marriage of convenience became more conflictual, as kings started to claim back what their predecessors had given away. The first herald of change was Afonso II's set of twenty-nine statutes promulgated in 1211, which allowed him to control the application of justice over the nobility and the Church.[23] Three statutes deserve particular attention: the attempt to regulate the vendetta, common mostly among the nobility;[24] the first known example of anti-mortmain laws in Portugal, barring monasteries and churches from acquiring property;[25] and the legal sanctioning of the principle that the plaintiff must follow the forum of the accused,[26] paving the way for the trial of clerics in secular courts. Moreover, the king's court now appeared as a possible venue of appeal from sentences given by secular judges.[27]

These laws were accompanied at a more practical level by the organization of a royal census in the northwest of Portugal, the most densely populated

[21] See Hermínia Vasconcelos Vilar, 'Do arquivo ao registo: o percurso de uma memória no reinado de Afonso II', *Penélope* 30/31 (2004), 25–31. The royal treasury was kept in the monastery of Santa Cruz in Coimbra from 1261 until 1265. Documents concerning its operation are published in Pedro de Azevedo, 'O tesouro de D. Afonso III no mosteiro de Santa Cruz de Coimbra', *Boletim da Segunda Classe da Academia das Sciências de Lisboa* 7 (1912–1913), 230–263. There is evidence that the role of Santa Cruz as repository of the king's treasury went as far back as 1188, as Sancho I's first testament suggests: 'Totum repositum tam panos quam uasa argentea et scutellas et coliares et quicquid in reposito est et panos quos habeo in sancta † ...' (Lisbon, Arquivo Nacional da Torre do Tombo [hereafter ANTT], Cabido da Sé de Viseu, Documentos régios, mç. 1, no. 7; published in *DSI*, 47). A brief overview also appears in Mattoso, *Identificação*, 110–11.

[22] Mattoso, *Identificação*, 107–8.

[23] See Branco, 'The General Laws', for a reassessment of the debate regarding the aims and scope of their promulgation.

[24] *Portugaliae Monumenta Historica* [hereafter *PMH*]. *Leges et consuetudines*, ed. Alexandre Herculano (2 vols. in 3, Lisbon, 1858–68), i.2, 165–66, nos. 4–6, dealing with treason and revenge; *PMH Leges*, i.2, 171, no. 13, dealing with homicide.

[25] *PMH Leges*, i.2, 169, no. 10.

[26] *PMH Leges*, i.2, 170, no. 12. This was a general rule of Roman law. *Corpus Iuris Civilis* II. *Codex Iustinianus* [hereafter *Codex*], ed. Paul Krüger (Berlin, 1877), 3.13.2 (128) and 3.19.3 (129); *Fragmenta Vaticana Mosaicarum et Romanarum Legum Collatio*, ed. Theodor Mommsen (Berlin, 1890), 326. This was incorporated in canon law by Gratian, *Decretum Gratiani*, ed. E. Friedberg, *Corpus Iuris Canonici* (Leipzig, 1879), C. 11, q. 1, c. 15, 630–31 and reasserted in Gregory IX's decretals. *Decretales Gregorii papae IX* [hereafter *Liber Extra*], ed. E. Friedberg, *Corpus Iuris Canonici* (Leipzig, 1881), 2.2.8, 250.

[27] *PMH Leges*, i.2, 167, no. 7. *Pace* Marcello Caetano, who considers that this is not yet proof of the existence of a proper instance of appeal, but only a device for reviewing sentences. In his opinion, it was only with Afonso III that appellate procedures were fully laid out: *História do Direito Português, Volume I: Fontes, Direito público (1140–1495)* (Lisbon, 1981), 400–10.

region in the kingdom and one typified by the strongest aristocratic presence.[28] The census was accompanied by the requirement that all royal privileges should be confirmed by the king and recorded in the newly established chancery register. The surveys, conducted in the summer of 1220, were aimed at determining the extent of the king's possessions and the revenues due to him.[29] They were not yet an attempt to investigate the extent of jurisdictions, as those of 1288 would be, but the confirmations that took place between 1216 and 1221 were clearly intended to ascertain the rights by which property and power were held.[30]

These initiatives doubtless contributed to the surge in political strife between the king and his bishops in the early 1220s.[31] In April 1218, Afonso II allowed all his bishops and the monastery of Santa Cruz, in Coimbra, to tithe the royal revenues obtainable in their dioceses and properties.[32] Later in the same year, however, a bitter dispute with the bishop of Lisbon resulted

---

[28] The most important noble families in the kingdom hailed from the northwest of Portugal, which was the heart of the old, pre-existing county of Portucale. The rest of the territory was conquered, and since conquest was monopolized by the king, those noble families were never able to have the same kind of presence or influence there. For centuries, therefore, the northwest would remain more characteristically seigneurial than the central or southern part of the kingdom, which were more urban and where most of the royal domains were concentrated.

[29] *Portugaliae Monumenta Historica. Inquisitiones*, ed. Alexandre Herculano (2 vols. in 3, Lisbon, 1858–68) i.1, 1–287 (for the region known as Entre Douro e Lima only). A new transcription is being prepared by the Instituto de Estudos Medievais (FCSH-UNL).

[30] See the formulary of the confirmations in Afonso II's chancery register: ANTT, Chancelaria régia, Chancelaria de D. Afonso II, liv. 1, fol. 43. It is published in João Pedro Ribeiro et al., *Memoria para a historia das confirmações regias neste reino com as respectivas provas colligidas pelos discipulos da aula de diplomatica* (Lisbon, 1816), doc. 1 in the appendix. On the 'confirmações gerais' during Afonso II's reign, see Abiah Elisabeth Reuter, *Königtum und Episkopat in Portugal im 13. Jahrhundert* (Berlin-Grünewald, 1928), 15–16. Concurrent with these measures was the elaboration, between 1220 and 1229, of an inventory of all churches from five dioceses in Portugal and one in León, with special mention of those that were under the king's patronage or where the latter had collation. See the transcription of this list by Instituto de Estudos Medievais (FCSH-UNL) in: http://bit.ly/9sZfII (shortened URL), 1–51.

[31] For a general overview of these royal initiatives, see Reuter, *Königtum*, 14–20. See also Vilar, 'Do Arquivo ao Registo', 19–50, with valuable pages on the creation of a royal chancery register; Maria João Branco, 'Escrita, Ley y Poder Regio: la cancillería regia y los juristas del rey en la construcción de un nuevo concepto de realeza en Portugal (1211–1218)', in *1212-1214: El trienio que hizo a Europa. Actas de la XXXVII Semana de Estudios Medievales de Estella. 19 al 23 julio 2010* (Pamplona, 2011), 343–71.

[32] The royal charters containing these donations are published in António Domingues de Sousa Costa, *Mestre Silvestre e Mestre Vicente, juristas da contenda entre D. Afonso II e suas irmãs* (Braga, 1963), notes 107 (diocese of Braga), 146 (diocese of Porto), 147–51 (dioceses of Coimbra, Tui, Évora, Lamego, Viseu) and 153 (diocese of Lisbon). The charter concerning the diocese of Guarda, recorded in the chancery register (ANTT, Registo da chancelaria de D. Afonso II, fol. 40v), remains unpublished. See Branco, 'Escrita, Ley y Poder Regio', 363–66, 371, who considers that with this move the king was safeguarding the future (his political future, surely, by buying allegiances) rather than recompensing the past 'más para prevenir el futuro que para compensar el pasado'.

in Afonso being accused of depriving his church of its revenues and taxing it excessively, of sympathizing with Jews and appointing them to royal offices, and of forcing women into the canons' chambers in order to accuse them of concubinage.[33] By the end of 1220, Afonso II was in dispute with the archbishop of Braga and was accused by Honorius III of coercing clerics into secular courts and requiring military service and other illegal exactions from them.[34] The archbishop had to leave the kingdom, in what would become an increasingly common course of action for Portuguese prelates.

Multiple factors converge to make the years that follow Afonso II's policy shift such a rich period in terms of legal challenges over jurisdiction, especially between king and clergy.[35] Royal encroachment, starting with Afonso II, and the Fourth Lateran Council's rulings on clerical taxation and reorganization of episcopal resources[36] must have fuelled much of the determination with which property was defended and the king's prerogatives upheld.[37]

---

[33] Vatican City, Archivio Segreto Vaticano, Registra Vaticana (Honorius III), 12, fols. 139–40 (ep. 184), *Optamus filii karissimi*; published in Costa, *Mestre Silvestre*, note 218. As for clerical concubinage, bearing in mind the impressive record of Spanish clergymen on that particular count, one wonders whether the bishop of Lisbon might not be rewriting tales of canons actually caught *in flagrante* by royal officers. That concubinage was associated with the clergy in Spain and Portugal papal legate John of Abbeville discovered during his visit in 1228–1229 (see below, note 36); this reputation was perpetuated in the fourteenth-century semi-autobiographical narrative *Libro de Buen Amor*, a set of tales of love attributed to Juan Ruiz, archpriest of Hita. As for the king forcing women into the canon's chambers, we have only the bishop of Lisbon's word for it. On the difficulties of moralizing the Spanish clergy after the Fourth Lateran Council, see Peter Linehan, *The Spanish Church and the Papacy in the Thirteenth Century* (Cambridge, 1971), especially 2–3, 29–30.

[34] Vatican City, Archivio Segreto Vaticano, Registra Vaticana (Honorius III), 11, fol. 60v (ep. 301: *Gravi nobis*); published in Costa, *Mestre Silvestre*, note 205.

[35] On conflicts of jurisdiction due to growth of goverment, see John Watts, *The Making of Polities: Europe, 1300–1500* (Cambridge, 2009), 264–70. Although addressing the topic specifically for the fourteenth century, it contains valuable insights for an understanding of jurisdictional conflicts in general.

[36] On the enforcement of the canons of the Fourth Lateran Council in the Iberian Peninsula, the legacy of Cardinal John of Abbeville, and the reactions it provoked, see Linehan, *The Spanish Church*, chapters 2 and 3; Peter Linehan, 'A Papal Legation and its Aftermath: Cardinal John of Abbeville in Spain and Portugal, 1228–1229', in *A Ennio Cortese*, ed. Italo Birocchi et al. (3 vols., Rome, 2001), ii, 236–56.

[37] Evidence for this is the obsession of the Portuguese bishops and the larger monastic houses in the kingdom with securing papal confirmations of privileges, and indeed of any documents that might prove useful for supporting their claims. This is observable in the donation giving the church of Porto temporal power over the city of Porto, which was confirmed successively by Popes Innocent III, Honorius III, Gregory IX, and Clement IV: Arquivo Histórico Municipal do Porto [hereafter AHMP], Autos e sentença, A-PUB/5514, 37–41. On the constant requests made to Zamoran judges to arbitrate the disputes of Portuguese churchmen, see Peter Linehan, 'The Case of the Impugned Chirograph and the Juristic Culture of Early Thirteenth-Century Zamora', in *Manoscritti, editoria e biblioteche dal medioevo all'età contemporanea. Studi offerti a Domenico Maffei per il suo ottantesimo compleanno*, ed. Mario Ascheri and Gaetano Colli (Rome, 2006), 461–513.

This change in the dynamic between king and Church, I believe, is significant not only to the socio-political history of Portugal, but also to its cultural history and the way in which some of the broader legal innovations of the twelfth century had a specific impact there. At the dawn of the thirteenth century, Portuguese clerks might not be deconstructing *quaestiones* in the Parisian style, but they were certainly learning every aspect of legal procedure and immersing themselves in the new science of law, because needs were pressing. The proliferation of legal books in private clerical libraries throughout the thirteenth century, to which I refer above, must be a sure sign of that. More concrete evidence can be found in litigation and legislation, especially in what seems to be one of the main tenets of royal policies until the fourteenth century. Pope Alexander III, when recognizing the independence of Portugal and the royal status of Afonso Henriques, required that the new kingdom should be kept undiminished; this came to be seen as a defence of the inalienability of the royal fisc.[38] Capable jurists like Silvester or Vincentius Hispanus[39] found no difficulty in converting this general stipulation into the backbone of a conscious policy of strengthening and expanding royal

[38] The bull is published in *Monumenta Henricina* (15 vols., Coimbra, 1960), i, no. 9, 18–21, especially at 19. For a brief overview of this topic, see Maria João Violante Branco, 'The King's Counsellors' Two Faces: A Portuguese Perspective', in *The Medieval World*, ed. Peter Linehan and Janet L. Nelson (London, 2001), 518–33 at 526–27. The argument for the inalienability of the royal fisc was used by Afonso II's lawyers against his sisters on the matter of the testamentary dispositions of King Sancho I, which included the creation of landed estates for his daughters. The particulars of this dispute, which lasted from 1212 to roughly 1220 (although a final agreement was only reached in 1223), are treated in detail in Costa, *Mestre Silvestre*, 29–39.

[39] Two canonists of note, Silvester and Vincentius both taught at Bologna and both reached the top prelatures of two Portuguese dioceses. Silvester was archbishop of Braga from 1229 until 1244, and Vincentius was bishop of Guarda from 1226 until 1248. Vincentius, in particular, was an active glossator, having written glosses and *apparatus* on Gratian's *Decretum*, the first and third *Compilationes Antiquae*, the decrees of the Fourth Lateran Council, and the decretals of Gregory IX, among others. On Silvester, see Kuttner, *Repertorium*, 12, 18, 355, 359; Stephan Kuttner, 'Bernardus Compostellanus Antiquus: A Study in the Glossators of the Canon Law', *Traditio* 1 (1943), 277–340 at 310 (notes 6–8); Stephan Kuttner, 'Glosses of Silvester on the Decretal "Pastoralis"' (as part of the Bulletin of the Institute of Medieval Canon Law), *Traditio* 22 (1966), 474–76; García y García, *Estudios*, 106–8. On Vincentius, see Kuttner, *Repertorium*, 374 (note 2) and index on 535; Stephan Kuttner, 'Wo war Vincentius Hispanus Bischof?' (as part of the Bulletin of the Institute of Medieval Canon Law), *Traditio* 22 (1966) 471–74; Gaines Post, '"Blessed Lady Spain" – Vincentius Hispanus and Spanish National Imperialism in the Thirteenth Century', *Speculum* 29 (1954), 202–9; García y García, *Estudios*, 108–12 (with a very thorough list of bibliographical references on 112–13, note 24). There is arguably no work by any other Portuguese medieval canonist comparable to that of Vincentius Hispanus, with the possible exception of Johannes de Deo's, who wrote numerous introductory textbooks on canon law: A. D. Sousa Costa, *Um mestre português em Bolonha no século XIII, João de Deus. Vida e obras* (Braga, 1957); García y García, *Estudios*, 113–17 (with abundant bibliographical references on 117–18, note 28).

power.[40] I do not argue that the birth of the modern state was an inevitable development, but considering the history of Portugal from the beginning of the thirteenth century until the 1350s, it is indeed royal power that grows more conspicuous and overarching. Much of its growth was made possible as a result of legislation and legal confrontation. Such a course of development seems fitting for a kingdom that originated in an act of usurpation, and for a dynasty whose main political concern was legitimization.

Afonso II claimed to rule for the welfare of the kingdom and to protect the weak from the abuses of the strong.[41] He made himself visible and accessible to his subjects both through his officials, whose alleged misbehaviour he tried to keep in check,[42] and through direct appeals to his court. Within fifty years, his son Afonso III would produce over 200 statutes and consolidate the pathways through which his justice was enforced,[43] in much the same way that Joinville describes Louis IX judging, delegating, and thus exercising his rule, with the knowledge that 'no realm was ever lost, nor passed to the lordship of another, except by default of right'.[44] Unlike the *Établissements* or Beaumanoir's *Coutumes*, however, the statutes of Afonso III were not part of a private compilation but were real legislation created in order to be applied throughout the kingdom.[45] Besides addressing several matters of public and private law, these rules placed great emphasis on Romano-canonical procedure: the division of legal actions into different stages, fixed standards for witnessing and determining the quality of proofs, and so on. At about the same time that these legal rules were being produced, a cleric from Braga or Porto wrote a *Summa dictaminis* with formularies for the legal documents that episcopal notaries were expected to write.[46] A little earlier,

[40] See Branco, 'Escrita, Ley y Poder Regio', 348, 359–70.
[41] Welfare of the kingdom ('prol do reino'): *PMH Leges*, i.2, 172, no. 15; 176. Protection of the weak ('mezquinhos'): *PMH Leges*, i.2, 164, no. 2; 172–73, no. 16.
[42] On malfeasance perpetrated by royal officials and other commanded surrogates acting typically as lords and on the development of a 'justice of accountability', see Thomas N. Bisson, *The Crisis of the Twelfth Century: Power, Lordship, and the Origins of European Government* (Princeton, NJ, 2009), 316–49, but especially 322–23.
[43] With the institution of royal judges throughout the kingdom, for example (*PMH Leges*, i.2, 163–64, no. 1). No laws could be effective without people on the ground to interpret and apply them, as John of Abbeville, papal legate to Spain, remarked in 1229: 'Parum est in ciuitate ius esse nisi qui illud tueatur existat: nec prodesset iura insurgere contra malos, si deesset iurium executor.' See Pedro Sáinz de Baranda, *España Sagrada: La Santa Iglesia de Barbastro en sus estados antiguo y moderno,* (51 vols., Madrid, 1747–1957), xlviii, 325.
[44] 'onques réaume se perdist, ne chanjast de seigneurie à autre, mez que par défaute de droit' in *Mémoires de Jean sire de Joinville, ou Histoire et chronique du três chrétien Roi Saint Louis*, ed. M. Francisque Michel (Paris, 1881), 17. See Magnus Ryan, 'Rulers and Justice, 1200–1500', in *The Medieval World*, 503–17 at 503–4.
[45] The establishment of justice between the parties seems to have antedated the creation of laws as a requirement for ruling. See Ryan, 'Rulers and Justice', 508, following S. Gagnér.
[46] *Summa dictaminis secundum quod notarii episcoporum et archyepiscoporum debeant notarie officium exercere*, published in Ludwig Rockinger, *Briefsteller und formelbücher des*

Pedro Salvadores, the Bologna-trained bishop of Porto from 1231 until 1247, had written two brief *ordines iudiciarii*, and his mastery of Romano-canonical procedure was evidenced in a dispute with King Sancho II over tithes, to which I will refer below.[47] These elements suggest that in this field of intellectual endeavour Portugal did not diverge from other regions of transalpine Europe, as procedural law was a major channel for the diffusion of the Romano-canonical legal system, due to its accessibility and practical utility.[48]

Familiarity with Roman and canon law increased, a consequence of the rise in litigation that occurred as frictions and clashes between individuals and institutions became more frequent. The first half of the thirteenth century was an active period in terms of legal practice. Royal surveys, the royal confirmations of privileges, and the gradual fine-tuning of royal justice all proved very distressing to a large section of the clergy and exacerbated disputes with the monarchy over the limits of spiritual and temporal jurisdictions. More people struggled for a fair share of the resources available: besides the king, the traditional clergy and the nobility, there were the rising urban oligarchies and the mendicant orders, all growing in number. With confrontation soaring at all levels of the social hierarchy – king against bishops, bishops against their chapters, bishops against mendicants, noblemen against clerics, urban elites against bishops and noblemen – the need for justice and peace was acute.

Sancho II lost his throne ostensibly because he failed to deliver justice and appease the myriad conflicting parties that shattered social peace.[49] He was not a 'good king'. Fourteenth- and fifteenth-century chronicles portray him as weak and negligent, surrounded by bad advisors,[50] lacking the character and the strength to quell the unrest that afflicted the kingdom:

… because of his lack of character and bad advisors, the whole land was nearly lost, and bad deeds were rife … thenceforth the situation of the whole realm worsened, in such a way that strong and weak alike killed and plundered, stole and burned, fearing

---

elften bis vierzehnten jahrhunderts, Quellen zur Bayerischen und Deutschen Geschichte 9 (Munich, 1863), 525–92. On the possible identity of Dominicus Dominici, see García y García, 'La Canonística Ibérica', 120–22; and Fleisch, *Sacerdotium*, 74–77.

[47] See note 9 above, for details about the identification of Bishop Pedro Salvadores with the canonist Petrus Hispanus Portugalensis.

[48] See André Gouron, 'Un assaut en deux vagues', 61–62.

[49] Fernandes, *Sancho II*, part 4 *passim*. Innocent IV referred explicitly to a failure of justice ('saecularis defectum iustitiae') in the bull of deposition of Sancho II (cf. *Liber Sextus Decretalium*, ed. E. Friedberg, *Corpus Iuris Canonici* (Leipzig, 1881), 1.8.2 (972–73)). This prompted Johannes Andreae's comment that 'Si ille, qui praeest, est negligens et remissus, debet superior illi dare idoneum coadiutorem.'

[50] *Livro de Linhagens do Conde D. Pedro*, ed. José Mattoso, *Portugaliae Monumenta Historica*, New series (Lisbon, 1980), ii.1, 128 ('he had bad advisers, thenceforth he did not do justice'); *Crónicas Breves e Memórias Avulsas de S. Cruz de Coimbra*, ed. Fernando Venâncio Peixoto da Fonseca (Lisbon, 2000), 72 ('he did not provide justice'). Translations are mine.

not the evil by which the realm was thus being destroyed. And he [the king] let all these things go unpunished, not seeking to make justice, because of the weakness of his heart.[51]

His successor, Afonso III, would strive to be the king Sancho II never was, even if he had to break promises and dash hopes in order to do so.[52]

In the more conflictual yet increasingly regulated society that emerged during the first half of the thirteenth century, the use of Roman and canon law as sources of jurisprudence and due process became a tangible reality even in the lower strata of society. In 1231, three judges delegate were appointed by Pope Gregory IX to hear and judge the complaint of the lepers of the city of Braga (which was then an episcopal domain) against two laymen concerning ownership of an oven. It is no small measure of the triumph of papal justice in the thirteenth century that even in the periphery of Western Europe nothing was apparently too insignificant to a determined litigant willing to take his grievance to the papal curia – and consequently to the realm of the *ius commune*.[53]

In 1237 when, according to Bishop Pedro Salvadores of Porto, unspeakable crimes scourged his diocese,[54] it was with technicalities that the same bishop quarrelled with Sancho II over the right to tithe goods arriving in Porto by boat.[55] In this dispute, Gregory IX's new decretal collection is often cited, to prove, for example, that when the name of a judge delegate is not expressly mentioned in the appointment, it is because the appointment is

---

[51] *Crónica de Portugal de 1419*, ed. Adelino de Almeida Calado (Aveiro, 1998), 119–20. Translation is mine.

[52] Most notably the Paris oath of 6 September 1245 (see Costa, *Mestre Silvestre*, note 554), in which Afonso III promised to restore many of the ecclesiastical liberties and immunities that had been violated during Sancho II's reign. In 1250, on being asked by the archbishop of Braga and the bishops of Porto, Viseu, Lamego, Coimbra, and Guarda why he had not fulfilled his promises, the king impudently replied that the said oath was meant to be fulfilled provided that it was within his power to fulfil it, and only if doing so did not constitute a danger to his body and soul, nor a contradiction of the laws of the kingdom. ANTT, Cabido da Sé de Coimbra, 1.ª incorp., docs. particulares, mç. 14, no. 42, membrane 1 (bottom) (published in *PMH Leges*, i.2, 185–89).

[53] ADB, Gaveta das Propriedades Particulares, no. 749.

[54] 'For there is an endless number of brigands, who, neither fearing God nor respecting men, turn monasteries and churches devoted solely to worship and service of God into dens of thievery, castles for soldiery, stables for their beasts, and public houses for infamous and dissolute women. And plundering the tenures and estates of clerics and farmers, and even those of monks, they kill their tenants by the sword in front of the altars, or burn them along with the clerics. And all warnings and excommunications prove ineffective to tame such misdeeds. For who can hear that babies are torn up from their mothers' breast, while others are thrown upon rocks, drowned in rivers, if their parents, after being stripped of all they had, fail to rescue them with some – albeit modest – ransom, crying and praying for mercy – who can hear this and not be consumed with pain?' Published in Costa, *Mestre Silvestre*, note 516. Translation is mine.

[55] Arquivo Distrital do Porto [hereafter, ADP], Mitra da Sé do Porto, Pergaminhos, no. 7.

made *ex officio*, and the task can therefore be transferred to another.[56] This was intended to ward off an *exceptio* made by the king's proctor which cited titles in the *Digest* on delivery of possession or property,[57] transference of jurisdiction[58] or the proper way of disinheriting one's offspring[59] to contend that a judge delegate could not be appointed *ex officio* but in his own name, and since one of the three judges delegate had since excused himself from all hearings, it was not within his power to transfer to another judge a jurisdiction he no longer held.[60] Sancho II's proctor had a very good reason to make this *exceptio* besides delaying the proceedings: he was convinced that the replacement judge was partial to the bishop of Porto and would tip the scales in the latter's favour, as one of the two other judges was also sympathetic to the bishop.[61]

The creative use of Roman property and disinheritance laws to try to invalidate a thirteenth-century papal appointment of a judge delegate is one example of the abstract and technical role that learned law came to play in the resolution of disputes. Though formal and procedural in nature, this knowledge had a real impact on the affairs of men by stalling disputes or winning them on procedural irregularities. It established when certain kinds of proof were admissible and when they were not[62] and divided a legal

---

[56] *Liber Extra* 1.29.14; in ADP, Mitra da Sé do Porto, Pergaminhos, no. 7, membrane 1 (bottom).

[57] *Corpus Iuris Civilis* I. *Digesta* [hereafter *Digesta*], ed. T. Mommsen (Berlin, 1872), 41.1.20 (646–47), in ADP, Mitra da Sé do Porto, Pergaminhos, no. 7, membrane 2 (bottom). On the meaning of *traditio* according to Roman law, and its distinction from *mancipatio*, see W.W. Buckland, *A Text-Book of Roman Law from Augustus to Justinian* (Cambridge, 3rd edn, 1963), 226–32; H.F. Jolowicz and Barry Nicholas, *Historical Introduction to the Study of Roman Law* (Cambridge, 3rd edn, 1972), 143–56.

[58] *Digesta* 50.17.54 (Momm., 869), in ADP, Mitra da Sé do Porto, Pergaminhos, no. 7, membrane 2 (bottom).

[59] *Digesta* 28.2.2 (Momm., 373), in ADP, Mitra da Sé do Porto, Pergaminhos, no. 7, membrane 3 (top).

[60] These arguments are given by Sancho II's proctor, a certain J. Gonsalvi, who can be plausibly identified as João Gonçalves Chancinho, canon of Coimbra and *curialis* of Afonso III, who left several law books in his will, including *summae* and *brocarda*. See Pereira, 'Livros de Direito', 23–5; and the biographical note in José Artur Anes Duarte Nogueira, *Sociedade e Direito em Portugal na Idade Média* (Lisbon, 1994), 502.

[61] 'cum possent per hec de facili duo iudices remanere qui ipsum regem ad instantiam Portugalensis episcopi expensis et laboribus fatigarent' (ADP, Mitra da Sé do Porto, Pergaminhos, no. 7, membrane 4, bottom).

[62] See the statutes of Afonso III: *litis contestatio* and dilatory exceptions (*PMH Leges*, i.2, 277, nos. 111–12; 277–78, no. 114; 285, nos. 145–46), countering of malicious dilatory trickery (*PMH Leges*, i.2, 278, no. 118; 289, no. 157), probative strength of sworn statements and body injuries (*PMH Leges*, i.2, 284, nos. 140–41; 298, no. 186) and presumptions of felony (*PMH Leges*, i.2, 296–97, no. 182, expanding on the Roman principle that one witness amounts to no witness (*Codex* 4.20.9 (Kr., 158); *Digesta* 22.5.12 (Momm., 292)), expressed in *PMH Leges*, i.2, 227, no. 22).

action into specific phases with deadlines and rules. Even when rejected, the *ius commune* shaped new law. Thus, Afonso III chose to ignore these legal conventions with regard to a title in the *Code* on restitution of property seized unlawfully in the course of a lawsuit, as he considered it to be at odds with the essence of the statute he was creating.[63] A lawsuit could be opposed, as in a dispute in Coimbra in 1250–1251, on the grounds that it was harvest time and a title in the *Digest* exempted vintners from appearing in court while busy harvesting.[64] The opinions of Azo, Accursius, Hostiensis or Innocent IV – to name but a few – were routinely rallied to support different points of law and used to supplement the legal collections. By the mid-thirteenth century, 'lawyering' had become a craft, and the lawyer a skilled professional who had to meet certain standards in order to practise and who was under the close and constant scrutiny of his peers.[65]

Although tailoring old laws to fit new conflicts was a common way of solving legal conundrums, the solutions themselves could be wildly different and lead to bitter disputes, since what one lawyer saw as a cogent and precise analogy was often considered far-fetched and insubstantial by another. In the same legal action where the wine harvest argument was presented, the plaintiff (a knight) was accused of not having specified the particulars of the lawsuit in the first summons and of wanting to do so at an inappropriate stage when the *litis contestatio* had already taken place. This irregular pleading, it was argued, was against the law and done only to cause the monastery (the defendant) further inconvenience and expenses.[66] This position was based on a title in the *Digest* ruling that a banker (*argentarius*) who withheld details when requested was to be punished, because he would be acting deceitfully (*dolo malo*).[67] Needless to say, the knight's proctor did not share this interpretation. In his view, the knight had never been asked to give details other than those contained in the papal rescript and since the title in the *Digest* referred only to details withheld when requested, it did not apply. In a snide remark, he added that the opposition's proctor's interpretation of the title was 'extremely superficial'.[68]

---

[63] *Codex* 8.4.7 (Kr., 332); cf. *PMH Leges*, i.2, 328, no. 223.

[64] *Digesta* 2.12.1 (Momm., 25). This reason was presented by one of the parties in a dispute between Vincentius Didaci, knight, and the convent of Lorvão concerning the church of Abiul: ANTT, Mosteiro de Lorvão, cx. 89, rolo 2, membranes 3–4.

[65] In the dispute cited above, note 64, for example, the suitability of Vincentius Didaci's proctor to represent him is openly questioned by the opposing party because he was a priest, and according to *Decretum Gratiani* C. 5 q. 3. c. 3 (Fr., i, 547–48) and C. 21 q. 2 c. 5 (Fr., i, 855), priests were not allowed to litigate. See ANTT, Mosteiro de Lorvão, cx. 89, rolo 3, membrane 5.

[66] ANTT, Mosteiro de Lorvão, cx. 89, rolo 3, membrane 1.

[67] *Digesta* 2.13.8 (Momm., 27).

[68] This tension between almost boundless freedom to make creative analogies, and a more substantial approach to the textbooks became a source of disagreement among legal scholars

I would risk saying that no other area in the broad spectrum of twelfth- and thirteenth-century literate culture ever attained in Portugal the level of diffusion and influence that Roman and canon law did or kindled the same intellectual fire. Although it flowered mostly in the thirteenth century, its appeal could already be felt by the end of the twelfth century, though mainly through the administration of ecclesiastical justice. In 1182, Bishop Fernando Martins of Porto, mentioned above as the owner of several law books, was one of the judges delegate who arbitrated a dispute between the archdioceses of Braga and Compostela concerning their boundaries.[69] The report on the enquiry that was to be forwarded to Pope Lucius III allows one to follow the arguments adduced by both sides and the documentary sources that supported them. They probe deeply into the early history of the Hispanic church, into the times of the Suebi and the Visigoths, in what was essentially a matter of antiquity and precedence. But under this cloak of antiquarianism new ideas and ways of thinking were already smouldering: the *Code* and Gratian's *Decretum* are cited a few times to address matters of prescription and restitution.[70] One particular maxim is evoked, a maxim that would have a long and distinguished life up to the present: when a plaintiff is unable to prove what he claims, the defendant must be absolved.[71] This is an early sign of the direction that the future would take.[72]

---

from the thirteenth century onward. See Kees Bezemer, 'The Infrastructure of the Early *Ius Commune*: The Formation of *Regulae*, or its Failure', in *The Creation of the* Ius Commune: *From* Casus *to* Regula, ed. John W. Cairns and Paul J. du Plessis, Edinburgh Studies in Law 7 (Edinburgh, 2010), 57–75 at 66–70. Here Jacques de Revigny and Pierre de Belleperche are presented as exponents of the two trends. On the method of the medieval civilians more generally, James Gordley, '*Ius Quaerens Intellectum*: The Method of the Medieval Civilians', in *The Creation of the* Ius Commune, 77–101, especially 80–93.

[69] Report published in Carl Erdmann, *Papsturkunden in Portugal*, Abhandlungen der Gesellschaft der Wissenschaften zu Göttingen, phil.-hist. Kl., Neue Folge, 20 (Berlin, 1927), 266–82, doc. 91. On the documentary evidence used in the hearing and registered in the report, see Maria João Branco, 'Constructing Legitimacy and Using Authority: The Production of Cartularies in Braga during the 12th Century', in *Erinnerung, Niederschrift, Nutzung: Das Papsttum und die Schriftlichkeit im mittelalterlichen Westeuropa*, ed. Klaus Herbers and Ingo Fleisch (Berlin and New York, 2011), 31–62, especially 47–61.

[70] *Decretum Gratiani* C. 16 q. 3 c. 13 (Fr., i, 793) and C. 6 q. 3 c. 3 (Fr., i, 562); also *Codex* 2.52.7 (Kr., 116) and 7.39.8 (Kr., 312).

[71] See Erdmann, *Papsturkunden in Portugal*, 282, referring to *Codex* 2.1.4 (Kr., 92). An example of evolved, rational methods of proof, according to R.C. van Caenegem, 'Methods of Proof in Western Medieval Law', in R.C. van Caenegem, *Legal History: A European Perspective* (London, 1991), 71–114 at 82.

[72] Another case of the early reception of the new legal science (and a near contemporary to the Braga-Compostela dispute) would be that of a certain 'magister decretista Petrus'. He is mentioned in the record of an 1195 dispute, heard by King Sancho I, between the abbot and monastery of Lorvão and the knight Gomes Nunes concerning the appointment of a priest to the church of Abiul. Master Petrus, who is described as recently arrived from the Roman curia but whose exact role in the king's court is not revealed, tried to cajole the king (unsuccessfully) into giving him the church, claiming that he held a benefice to that effect granted by the bishop

To return to the rhetorical question that started this essay, it is clear that Portugal did not have a twelfth-century Renaissance nor took any active part in it. But it is also clear that at least one of the grander intellectual and institutional achievements of the age – the development of legal thought and procedure – did have a considerable and lasting impact there. The study and practice of Roman and canon law constituted the focal point where the new kingdom's needs for political and judicial organization met and were, to a certain extent, answered by the cultural innovations of the twelfth century. They became key instruments in the political crisis that marked the first half of the thirteenth century, and their dominance would be almost complete within the following hundred years, when the kings Dinis and Afonso IV succeeded in using the concepts and procedures of law to reduce the Church's temporal jurisdiction and increase the monarchy's political power. The constant in this narrative, then, is the steady growth of learned law as a source of jurisprudence, a political tool, and a distinct language. To speak this language meant being able to use Roman and canon law precepts to sort out actual problems, and thus render service to a king, a bishop, an abbot, even the lepers of Braga, perhaps by eventually taking the case to Rome and arguing it there. Though fought in the world of ideas, these wars had practical, palpable consequences.[73] They could lead to rewards, and a career could be built upon them, but they also fostered a degree of intimacy with abstract thinking of a fairly high order. In this respect, Portugal was in tune, if not with the latest fashion, then with the fundamentals of what was being created elsewhere; in the area of law, in other words, the Renaissance may have felt in that European *finis terrae* a bit less like the distant affair it unquestionably was. These considerations, while not exactly providing any new understanding of what the Renaissance of the twelfth century was, raise important questions about its repercussions over time and far from its centres. It cannot be compared to a uniform wave, spreading its novelties uniformly over the whole of Europe; rather the Renaissance was more like stones dropped into a pond that created ripples, but ripples that weakened and lost intensity as they reached the pond's periphery. The result was a decline in completeness and originality of intellectual endeavour, perhaps also an increased dependence on local socio-political circumstances, and most certainly a much slower timeline for the arrival of each individual novelty. Professor Haskins painted a picture of the cultural changes and achievements of the twelfth century with such convincing and masterful strokes that it has remained a powerful image to this day. Considering the effects of those

---

of Coimbra. See *DSI*, 339–40; also Maria João Violante Branco, 'Poder real e eclesiásticos. A evolução do conceito de soberania régia e a sua relação com a praxis política de Sancho I e Afonso II', PhD dissertation (Lisbon, 1999), 235–37.

[73] For the relationship between legal practice and ruling, see Ryan, 'Rulers and Justice'.

changes and achievements on the periphery of Europe, and how they in turn generated change and enabled new achievements, may allow us to flesh out that big picture through time and space, making it clearer, richer, and even more compelling.

8

Internal and External Audiences: Reflections on the Anglo-Saxon Archive of Bury St Edmunds Abbey in Suffolk

Sarah Foot

Violent disorder broke out in various parts of England during the political turmoil of 1326–7 and included particularly severe rioting in the monastic towns of Abingdon, St Albans, and Bury St Edmunds in Suffolk. In January 1327 agitators from London roused the townspeople at Bury to conspire to attack and destroy the abbey of St Edmund. An armed mob forced entrance through the gates of the abbey on 14 January and seized and imprisoned the officials of the convent and several monks. They carried away all the treasures of the abbey, including the charters,[1] muniments, and papal bulls from the sacristy and the treasury. Accounts of the legal process that followed the riots show the magnitude of the abbey's losses: in one, the monks alleged that the rioters had carried off three copies of a charter of King Cnut in their favour and four copies of a charter in Harthacnut's name.[2] So denuded were the archives that the abbot had to pay the king to stay a suit against him in the royal courts, since he claimed the deeds he would have used for the defence of his case had been stolen by the rioters.[3]

---

[1]   The word charter is used here to mean any document recording the transfer or confirmation of property rights or privileges. The research behind this paper has been done in preparation for a new edition of the Anglo-Saxon charters of Bury St Edmunds in Suffolk, undertaken collaboratively with Dr Kathryn Lowe, for publication with the British Academy. I am grateful to Michael Bentley, Bruce O'Brien, Teresa Webber, and an anonymous reviewer for comments on an earlier draft of this paper.

[2]   C.W. Goodwin, 'On Two Ancient Charters in the Possession of the Corporation of King's Lynn', *Norfolk Archaeology* 4 (1855), 93–117, at 94n, citing the account given in the Werktone Register: London, BL, Harley MS 638, fols. 116r–118v; Rodney M. Thomson, *The Archives of the Abbey of Bury St Edmunds*, Suffolk Records Society 21 (Woodbridge, 1980), no. 1281. The text was printed by William Dugdale, *Monasticon Anglicanum*, ed. John Caley, Henry Ellis and Bulkeley Bandinel (6 vols. in 8, London, 1817–30), iii, 108–9n.

[3]   'Depredatio abbatiae sancti Eadmund', ed. Thomas Arnold, *Memorials of St. Edmunds Abbey*, RS 96 (3 vols., London, 1890–96), ii, 327–54, at 33. See Albert Goodwin, *The Abbey of St Edmundsbury* (Oxford, 1931), 52; Mary D. Lobel, 'A Detailed Account of the 1327

Rebels targeted Bury's archives again during the Peasants' Revolt in 1381. This time, however, they sought not to destroy the deeds but rather to consult them for evidence to substantiate some of their own claims. Like the authors of *cahiers de doléance* produced by the third estate in France in 1789, the rebels believed that the burdens of taxation and obligation had fallen less heavily on earlier generations, and that the abbey's earliest charters would confirm their view. They thus demanded that the monks produce, 'in the sight of the commons', the charters of liberty for 'the vill which Cnut, the founder of the monastery had once granted'. The monks duly brought out before the guildhall all the charters they could find and showed them to the mayor, the aldermen, 'and a whole crowd of villeins'. When the rebels declared themselves unhappy with the documents produced by the abbey, the monks agreed to search their charters again to find the evidence for the liberties which St Edmund's claimed; further, they promised that if they found none, they would produce new ones to serve the purpose.[4]

An abbey's muniments – not just its recent records but the more ancient title deeds carefully preserved in its archives – thus clearly could speak to more than one possible audience in fourteenth-century England. Yet earlier generations of monastic archivists at Bury and at other English abbeys such as St Albans (which was also asked to produce ancient documents by rebels in 1381)[5] scarcely designed their archival policies and arrangements for safe-keeping with the needs of inquisitive and rebellious townspeople at the forefront of their minds. Rather, the crucial task of creating and preserving the institutional memory of a religious community about its collective past and identity drove the development of monastic (and cathedral) archives. As the example of Bury St Edmunds shows, these archives, once formed, had, like books, *sua fata*.[6]

One of the five wealthiest monastic houses in England, the Benedictine abbey of Bury St Edmunds in Suffolk owed much of its economic prosperity in the later Middle Ages to its vast landed endowment and its extensive rights. It jealously guarded the documentary witnesses to the granting and confirma-

Rising at Bury St Edmund's and the Subsequent Trial', *Proceedings of the Suffolk Institute of Archaeology and Natural History* 21 (1933), 215–31 at 216.

[4]   Thomas of Walsingham, *Chronicon Angliae*, ed. Edward Maunde Thompson, (London, 1874), 303; Stephen Justice, *Writing and Rebellion: England in 1381* (Berkeley CA, 1994), 47.

[5]   Justice, *Writing and Rebellion*, 47–48, 256–58.

[6]   Several recent studies have explored the role of charters and cartularies in construction monastic identities. For example Patrick Geary, *Phantoms of Remembrance: Memory and Oblivion at the End of the First Millennium* (Princeton, NJ, 1974); Amy G. Remensnyder, *Remembering Kings Past: Monastic Foundation Legends in Medieval Southern France* (Ithaca, NY, 1995); Karine Ugé, *Creating the Monastic Past in Medieval Flanders* (York, 2005). See also Charles Insley, 'Remembering Communities Past: Exeter Cathedral in the Eleventh Century', in *Cathedrals, Communities and Conflict in the Anglo-Norman World*, ed. Paul Dalton, Charles Insley and Louise J. Wilkinson (Woodbridge, 2011), 41–60.

tion of those privileges, which extended not just over the *banleuca*[7] but also encompassed the *sac* and *soc* of liberty of Bury, a large rural tract of eight-and-a-half hundreds over which the abbot held extensive economic, jurisdictional, and governmental authority.[8] Desirous of preserving these valuable privileges, the abbey placed considerable reliance on the documentary evidence for the extent and nature of the lands and freedoms granted to it in previous generations; the monks therefore accumulated an impressive archive of title deeds extending back into the pre-Conquest period. The extant collection of thirty-nine cartularies and registers from Bury (more than survive from any other medieval English abbey) reveals much about the medieval community's systems of record keeping as well the administration and exploitation of its estates during the high and later Middle Ages.[9] To many of those concerns, however, the Anglo-Saxon archive appears at best only tangentially relevant, and decreasingly so to generations further away from the Norman Conquest. One may wonder why successive archivists continued to preserve these texts so long after the lifetime of those involved in the original transactions, and may ask what motives drove them to make fresh copies of material that appeared at best outdated, if not frankly redundant, at least for dispositive purposes. Considerations beyond the pragmatic must have inspired later medieval scribes to create fresh copies of texts dating from before 1066.

Like other medieval monastic houses in England (and indeed elsewhere in Western Europe) Bury saw the preservation of its earliest muniments as a means not just of preserving its past but of consolidating its own institutional sense of self. At periods of political trauma or (as in the eleventh century) dislocation, the archival record played a critical role in expressing and preserving memories of the abbey.[10] For example, one of the Bury archivists' overriding motives may have been the desire to perpetuate the memory of the abbey's royal benefactors; that the rebels of 1381 believed that Cnut had founded the abbey speaks to the success of that endeavour. This essay tries to tease out some of the other possible motives that may have inspired Bury's monks to continue recopying such documents in the later Middle Ages through an exploration of the various audiences, internal and external to the abbey, envisaged by draftsmen and copyists of Bury's Anglo-Saxon charters, privileges, and other written deeds.

Each Anglo-Saxon monastic archive is unique. Bury's distinctiveness lies not only in the extraordinary number of its extant medieval cartularies but

---

[7] I.e., the area within a one-mile radius of the abbey church, including the town and its fields over which the monks held a secular franchise as well as the claimed exemption from all episcopal authority.

[8] M.D. Lobel, 'The Ecclesiastical Banleuca in England', in *Oxford Essays in Medieval History presented to Herbert Edward Salter* (Oxford, 1934), 122–40.

[9] Thomson, *Archive*, 1–6.

[10] Geary, *Phantoms,* 81–114*;* Insley, 'Remembering Communities Past', 41–42.

also in the nature of the documents preserved from the Anglo-Saxon period, most of which were written in Old English. Just over fifty separate items of pre-Conquest date survive from Bury, making this an archive of medium size in comparison with other collections of Anglo-Saxon charters. Yet, unlike most other English pre-Conquest archives, that of Bury St Edmunds Abbey contains few documents in the form of Latin diplomas.[11] Five extant texts purport to record royal grants to Bury; a single private grant to the abbey dated 962 also looks suspiciously like a royal charter. Two other surviving Latin royal diplomas in favour of different beneficiaries relate to land that came later into Bury's possession; presumably the abbey acquired both these texts when the monks obtained the lands to which they served as title deeds.[12] All the remaining extant pre-Conquest documents were written in the vernacular: eighteen royal writs issued by Edward the Confessor, all but one of which seem to be authentic,[13] and seventeen Old English wills.[14] Only one Old English will making a post-mortem bequest to Bury St Edmunds is known apart from that group kept in the abbey's own archives: the will of Wulfgyth (mother of Ketel, whose will was among those preserved at Bury), from the archive of Christ Church, Canterbury; Wulfgyth bequeathed two ornamented horns to St Edmund's.[15] Additionally, the monks preserved some further Old English documents, describing a variety of gifts to and exchanges with the abbey.[16] The prevalence of the Anglo-Saxon vernacular in this archive is of particular significance given the generally precipitous decline in Old English as the language of record after 1066 elsewhere.[17]

Whether the abbey once held more Latin diplomas than the eight now known must remain uncertain. Most of the entries of donations to the abbey recorded in the lists of benefactors to Bury found in several of the abbey's cartularies were clearly compiled with reference to the relevant documenta-

---

[11] For discussion of the shape and content of early medieval archives elsewhere in Europe see Georges Declercq, 'Originals and Cartularies: The Organization of Archival Memory (Ninth–Eleventh Centuries)', in *Charters and the Use of the Written Word in Medieval Society*, ed. Karl Heidecker (Turnhout, 2000), 147–70 at 148–53.

[12] The royal grants to Bury are Sawyer, *Charters*, 507, 980, 995, 1045, and 1046; the private grant to the abbey is Sawyer, *Charters,* 1213; the two royal diplomas to other beneficiaries: Sawyer, *Charters*, 483, 703.

[13] Sawyer, *Charters*, 1068–1085. The sole entirely spurious writ is Sawyer, *Charters*, 1070, a text apparently created by scribal error conflating the texts of Sawyer, *Charters*, 1069 and 1078. K.A. Lowe, 'Sawyer 1070: A Ghost Writ of King Edward the Confessor', *Notes and Queries* 50 (2003), 150–52; see also Richard Sharpe, 'The Use of Writs in the Eleventh Century', *Anglo-Saxon England* 32 (2003), 247–91 at 265.

[14] Sawyer, *Charters*, 1483, 1486, 1489, 1490, 1494, 1499, 1501, 1516, 1519, 1521, 1525–1525a, 1526, 1527, 1528, 1529, 1530–31, and 1537.

[15] Sawyer, *Charters*, 1535. Ketel's will is Sawyer, *Charters*, 1519.

[16] A.J. Robertson, *Charters*, nos. 92, 93, 97, 100, 104 and 119.

[17] Bruce O'Brien, 'Forgery and the Literacy of the Early Common Law', *Albion* 27 (1995), 1–18 at 4.

tion, for they frequently reproduced the wording of the endorsements of single sheets, or rubrics from cartulary copies. But a handful of recorded benefactions relate to grants for which there is no longer any evidence a written record had once existed.[18] It cannot now be established whether any of those referred to grants made via Latin diplomas. Given the difficulties which St Edmund's experienced with its immediate neighbours later in the Middle Ages, we might readily imagine that the monks lost some of their early deeds; indeed, we may express some surprise at the extent to which pre-Conquest deeds survived at all.

Complex and varied impulses governed the preservation of original documents and the making of later copies in monastic and cathedral archives. Perhaps most important was the need to conserve in a permanent form the memory of what property had been given to a church or monastery and by whom.[19] Indeed, many written records of conveyances claimed specifically to defend against the forgetfulness of later generations. As a charter of King Æthelred dated 995 in favour of a layman, now preserved in the archives of Abingdon, asserted: 'Whatever is transacted by men of this world to endure for ever ought to be fortified securely with ranks of letters, because the frail memory of men in dying forgets what the writing of letters preserves and retains.'[20] Written testimony gave fixed and verifiable form to records of transactions originally enacted in oral performance;[21] they evoked for later generations the acts that had made the transaction binding, preserved the names of those involved in case of later dispute, and added the weight of a church's sacred authority to protect against future challenge.[22] Many charters addressed themselves directly to the Almighty and invoked his wrath in anathemas that requested eternal punishment for any who attempted to subvert the donors' original intentions.[23] By incorporating documents into highly visual rituals of conveyance at the time when land grants were made, the Church could help the (largely unlettered) laity to recognize the validity of

---

[18] Listed by C.R. Hart, *The Early Charters of Eastern England* (Leicester, 1966), 248–49.

[19] Compare Remensnyder, *Remembering Kings Past*, especially 19–41 and, for the creation of documentary records in contexts involving conflict, 215–88.

[20] Sawyer, *Charters*, 883. Compare Laurent Morelle, 'The Metamorphosis of Three Monastic Charter Collections in the Eleventh Century (Saint-Amand, Saint-Riquier, Moutier-en-Der)', in *Charters*, ed. Heidecker (Turnhout, 2000), 171–204.

[21] Franz Bäuml, 'Varieties and Consequences of Medieval Literacy and Illiteracy', *Speculum* 55 (1980), 237–65 at 249.

[22] Warren Brown, 'Charters as Weapons: On the Role Played by Early Medieval Dispute Records in the Disputes they Record', *JMH* 28 (2002), 227–48 at 229.

[23] Michael Clanchy, *From Memory to Written Record: England 1066–1307*, 2nd edn (Oxford, 1993), 146. Several vernacular texts in Bury's archive contain sanctions protecting their provisions from future interference, for example Sawyer, *Charters*, 1213, 1483, 1490, 1499, 1519, 1521, 1525–29, 1531, 1537. See more generally B. Danet and B. Bogoch, '"Whoever Alters This, May God Turn His Face from Him on the Day of Judgement": Curses in Anglo-Saxon Legal Documents', *Journal of American Folklore* 105 (1992), 132–65.

the written word. When they stored charters in altars, or preserved copies of particularly precious texts in Gospel Books, they contrived visibly to connect those documents tangibly with the divine.[24] In the second half of the eleventh century, the monks of Bury made a copy of arguably their most valuable charter (a grant of privileges in the abbey's favour granted by King Cnut), onto a blank leaf in one of the abbey's pre-Conquest gospel books, adding copies of other key documents (including a papal privilege and a charter of William I) on subsequent folios.[25] The sacred contents of the book (and its connection with the altar) thus served to protect and validate the secular matters recorded in the texts; in the same way, charters were sometimes stored in shrines with the relics of saints.[26]

Couched often in formulaic language, charters fix particular versions of events, telling narratives about how specific rights or portions of land came to belong to the recipient of a grant. Their record of the transaction (and sometimes recitation of the previous history of the estate) may well have run counter to alternative views about the property's ownership: that claiming of a property's narrative formed part of a charter's purpose. Charters were not written merely to prevent failures of memory but to ensure that a correct version of events was the one recollected.[27] They speak as much to the future as to the present audience who witnessed the original transaction and whose names were recorded as witnesses to the deed. Thus, while the monks of Bury valued these records as proof of their title to the lands and privileges they conveyed, their safe preservation mattered equally to those whose generosity the texts recounted. Charters 'guard the memory' of donors, too, as Warren Brown has argued; 'that memory upheld the donor kindred's claim to the prayers of the recipient community and the favour of the community's patron saint'.[28] Texts bound not only the parties to the original transaction

---

[24] Susan Kelly, 'Anglo-Saxon Lay Society and the Written Word', in *The Uses of Literacy in Early Medieval Europe*, ed. Rosamond McKitterick (Cambridge, 1990), 36–62 at 43–44.

[25] London, BL, Harley MS 76, fols. 138–41 ('the Bury Gospels') datable to the first half of the eleventh century. The charter in Cnut's name, discussed below, is Sawyer, *Charters*, 980. Compare the copying of various charters relating to Christ Church, Canterbury to the so-called MacDurnan Gospels (London, Lambeth Palace Library, MS 1370), a gospel book that once belonged to King Æthelstan which he gave to Christ Church. See also the York Gospels (York, Minster Library, Additional MS 1) onto the last six leaves of which were added nine different texts in Old English including surveys of estates in Yorkshire, sermons by Archbishop Wulfstan, some bidding prayers, and a list of sureties.

[26] Francis Wormald, 'The Sherborne Cartulary', in *Fritz Saxl 1890–1948; A Volume of Memorial Essays from his Friends in England*, ed. D.J. Gordon (London, 1957), 101–19 at 106–8; Clanchy, *From Memory*, 154–56.

[27] S. Foot, 'Reading Anglo-Saxon Charters: Memory, Record or Story?', in *Narrative in the Early Medieval West*, ed. Elizabeth M. Tyler and Ross Balzaretti (Turnhout, 2006), 39–65 at 62–63.

[28] Brown, 'Charters as Weapons', 229; compare Insley, 'Remembering Communities Past', 49–54.

but also future generations, obliging the descendants of a donor to continue to defend the community's rights to the donated property in order to protect their ancestors' souls.[29]

As with other monastic foundations, Bury's monks made careful record of the names of lay and ecclesiastical donors to the abbey, fulfilling their side of these reciprocal arrangements by ensuring that they and their successors would remember and pray for those who had made gifts to St Edmund. Compilers of these benefactor lists clearly used the abbey's archive of charters and other documents to create their records, for they frequently quoted from the endorsements or cartulary rubrics to individual texts that specified the land which an individual had given. They did not create such lists to make an inventory of what the monks owned, but rather to remember those on whose generosity the community depended for its material well-being. Similarly, there was a close connection between the documentary record of the lands of Christ Church, Canterbury and that church's liturgical commemoration of its benefactors, as Robin Fleming has demonstrated.[30]

If we now consider not just which documents survive from before the Norman Conquest, but the number of separate copies made of each individual text dating from the Anglo-Saxon period, we begin to discern a possible hierarchy of significance in these texts from the perspective of the abbey's later medieval archivists. The most frequently re-copied charter was that granted to Bury by Cnut in the early 1020s (Sawyer, *Charters*, 980). Counting in descending order the number of copies made we next find two charters in the name of Edward the Confessor (Sawyer 1045 and 1046); one granted by Edmund of Wessex in 945 (Sawyer 507); two writs that Edward the Confessor gave to the last pre-Conquest abbot, Baldwin (Sawyer 1084 and 1085); the earliest of the Confessor's writs that made reference to the grant of Mildenhall in Suffolk to the abbey together with the valuable liberty of the eight-and-a-half hundreds (Sawyer 1069); and a royal diploma in the name of Harthacnut (Sawyer 995). All of these texts, with varying degrees of plausibility, conveyed important lands, rights, and privileges to the abbey. In addition to creating multiple cartulary copies, the monks therefore sought to have these texts 'inspeximussed' and enrolled by successive monarchs. Does their careful preservation tell us anything about the audiences for which they were either first created or later recopied?

Specific present and future audiences were envisaged; indeed they were addressed directly in Anglo-Saxon royal diplomas. Couched in the first person and often in the present tense, charters record a king's conveyance of a title to land and privilege to a specific beneficiary, in this case the abbey

---

[29] Brown, 'Charters as Weapons', 230; Declercq, 'Originals and Cartularies', 160–65.
[30] Robin Fleming, 'Christ Church Canterbury's Anglo-Norman Cartulary', in *Anglo-Norman Political Culture and the Twelfth-Century Renaissance*, ed. C. Warren Hollister (Woodbridge, 1997), 83–155 at 102–6.

at Bury. In this way, charters speak directly to the parties involved in the original transfer, and to those whose names are appended at the end of the text as witnesses consenting to the conveyance.[31] But a future audience is also explicitly anticipated and directly addressed in the sanction or anathema, which threatens dire and eternal penalties for those who seek to infringe the terms of the grant. Furthermore, the text of a charter speaks implicitly to an imagined future court at which any subsequent dispute would be heard. Serving effectively as title-deeds to the lands or privileges to which they refer, these diplomas were designed, and frequently used, as evidence in disputes over land-ownership and the tenure of privileges; in conception and execution their texts were meant to outlive all the original parties to the transaction they recorded.[32]

Writs, too, had both an explicit and immediate audience – the shire court and such of its officers as the king mentioned by name or status in the address – and an implicit future one. Many contain brief statements warning against the undoing of the arrangements made known via the writ. For example, several of those that Edward the Confessor gave to Bury conclude with an admonition not to take away from the abbey any of the things granted to it (in one case addressing that warning specifically to future bishops) or in more general terms, not to do the abbey any wrong.[33] Charters and writs might thus serve as defences for the protection of the abbey's lands, rights, and special privileges.

As statements of a testator's intentions for the distribution of his possessions after his death, wills also spoke to an audience in an imagined future time and can also be seen as expressions of distant hope rather than

---

[31] The first recourse for students of Anglo-Saxon charters remains Frank Merry Stenton, *Latin Charters of the Anglo-Saxon Period* (Oxford, 1955). The series of papers that Pierre Chaplais wrote for the *Journal of the Society of Archivists* between 1965 and 1969 are conveniently collected in *Prisca munimenta: Studies in Archival and Administrative History presented to A.E.J. Hollaender*, ed. Felicity Ranger (London, 1973), 28–107.

[32] Kelly, 'Anglo-Saxon Lay Society', 44–45. The parties in disputes often took their diplomas (books) with them to the court in order to support their side of the argument, as for example in the settlement of the long-running dispute over the ownership of a minster at Cookham in Berkshire settled at a council at *Clofesho* in 789, in Sawyer, *Charters*, 1258, or among the transactions described in the text known as the 'Fonthill letter' in Sawyer *Charters*, 1445. See Simon Keynes, 'The Fonthill Letter' in *Words, Texts and Manuscripts*, ed. Michael Korhammer (Cambridge, MA, 1992), 53–98, and Nicholas Brooks, 'The Fonthill Letter, Ealdorman Ordlaf and Anglo-Saxon Law in Practice', in *Early Medieval Studies in Memory of Patrick Wormald*, ed. Stephen Baxter et al. (Farnham, 2009), 301–17.

[33] Sawyer, *Charters*, 1068; compare Sawyer 1069, 1073, both more general exhortations, also 1071 and 1072. For the role of writs in dispute settlement see Patrick Wormald, 'A Handlist of Anglo-Saxon Law-Suits', *ASE* 17 (1989), 247–81, no. 89 (also printed in Sawyer *Charters*, 1077, describing a dispute between Bury and a certain Semer over land in Norfolk), and nos. 66–67, 74, 79, 86–87, 92–93, 95. See also Florence E. Harmer, *Anglo-Saxon Writs* 2nd edn (Stamford, CT, 1989), 46–47.

immediate expectation. For some, that future may have seemed imminent, if a will were drawn up during serious illness or in old age. But others wrote of their future intentions while still in full health, as did Ketel Alder who, though sound of body, drew up his will and deposited it at Bury before setting off on a potentially dangerous pilgrimage.[34] Whether the future uses to which such texts were put were, in fact, those anticipated or desired by the original parties is, of course, far from clear. For example, Leofgifu, a widow and a substantial owner of land in Essex and Suffolk, left one of three copies of her will at Bury for safe-keeping, but since several of the lands she bequeathed seem not to have come into the hands of the intended beneficiaries after her death, we must wonder whether her will was ever in fact executed.[35] But in each of these examples, the testator clearly envisaged an audience, and frequently one extending beyond the family or religious community directly involved in the transactions.

With these considerations in mind, let us look more closely at some of Bury's pre-Conquest deeds, starting with a Latin royal diploma, the most prized of all the texts in Bury's pre-Conquest archive, the grant from Cnut to the monastery of Bury. This document survives not only in multiple later medieval copies but as an eleventh-century single sheet, a display version clearly made to have considerable visual impact. Written in an attractive and skilful Anglo-Caroline book hand, the text is beautifully laid out on the parchment by somebody with considerable aesthetic sensibilities. Cnut, 'king of the whole island of Albion and of many other nations', declares that the monastery called *Badriceswurðe* shall always be inhabited by monks and free from all domination of the bishops of that shire; he confirms the monks' freedom to elect their own abbot, directs the town's inhabitants to pay Danegeld to the abbey, and gives to the monks a fishery and royal rights to fish locally, together with an annual gift from his queen of 4000 eels. Finally the king pronounces an anathema on any man attempting to deprive this house of its freedom or to bring back seculars, *clerici*, to the foundation. After the witness list, there follows an Old English summary of the Latin, reiterating the abbey's freedom from the domination of any bishop of the shire and the abbey's rights to taxation. Although the text bears no date, its witness list dates from 1022 x 1023. It seems most likely that the charter was, or purported to be, the record of a grant made by Cnut when he reorganized the early secular community at *Beodricesworth* and turned it into a regular Benedictine community. That reform is customarily dated to 1020 on the

---

[34] Sawyer, *Charters*, 1519; see Julia Crick, 'Widowhood in pre-Conquest England', in *Widowhood in Medieval and Early Modern Europe*, ed. Sandra Cavallo and Lyndan Warner (London, 1999), 24–36, at 30–31. Bury preserves the wills of two other laypeople drawn up before making pilgrimages, that of Ælfric Modercope (Sawyer, *Charters*, 1490) and a woman, Sifflæd (Sawyer, *Charters*, 1525).

[35] Sawyer, *Charters*, 1521.

basis of number of late Bury sources.[36] Yet, despite the care with which this document was created, it cannot be the original single-sheet version of a diploma granted by Cnut (for its hand has been dated to the third quarter of the eleventh century), nor does the bulk of the text as preserved here appear to be authentic. Even so, the Latin text might have been modelled in part on a genuine charter in Cnut's name, perhaps one in Bury's favour. The least suspicious elements of the grant are the final clauses granting the fishery and eels; that genuine instrument might have involved those gifts, but otherwise we cannot establish any of the terms of that putative grant. The addition of an Old English summary does not inspire confidence; quite what purpose it was meant to serve is also uncertain, other than perhaps to ensure that the critical phrase about the abbey's historic freedom from episcopal interference was accessible to an English-speaking audience with little Latin.[37]

What did the new text offer the monks of Bury that, presumably, Cnut's supposed original diploma had not? The crucial sentence from this point of view (and, it would appear, from the viewpoint of the later medieval abbey) relates to the freedom of the monastery from all domination of the bishops of the shire. This is the earliest text surviving from Bury to make claims about the abbey's independence from the control of the local episcopate. Bury does not appear to have had difficult relations with the East Anglian bishops at any point before the Norman Conquest, indeed the local bishop seems to have played a part in the reorganization of the community in Cnut's reign.[38] Problems only arose after the Conquest when, as part of a wider movement to relocate English bishoprics in more prominent places, Herfast, bishop of Elmham, tried to move his see from the remote and insignificant town where it languished to the place where the shrine of St Edmund was flourishing.[39] The disadvantages of such a move from Bury's point of view, and particularly from that of its Norman abbot, Baldwin, are obvious. Had Herfast been successful, Bury would probably have lost its status as an independent Benedictine monastery and become a cathedral priory, with Baldwin demoted to the status of prior. Bury's successful resistance of this attempt owed much to the foresight of Abbot Baldwin, in whose strategy the forged charter in Cnut's name played a central role.

---

[36] Antonia Gransden, 'The Legends and Traditions Concerning the Origins of the Abbey of Bury St Edmunds', *EHR* 100 (1985), 1–24 at 13–18; Tom Licence, 'The Origins of the Monastic Communities of St Benedict at Holme and Bury St Edmunds', *Revue bénédictine* 116 (2006), 42–61 at 52–58.

[37] Compare the creation of foundation charters in 1076 for the Flemish house of St Amatus at Douai discussed by Ugé, *Creating the Monastic Past*, 146–59.

[38] David N. Dumville, *English Caroline Script and Monastic History: Studies in Benedictinism, A.D. 950–1030* (Woodbridge, 1993), 31–34; Licence, 'Origins', 53–55.

[39] T. Licence, 'The Norwich Narrative and the East Anglian Bishopric', *Norwich Archaeology* 45 (2007), 198–204.

After Baldwin failed to make Archbishop Lanfranc publish the papal bull that he had obtained in 1071, which removed his abbey from the jurisdiction of any English bishop and placed it under the direct protection of the Roman see, he took his case before the king's council at Pentecost in 1081.[40] According to a lengthy narrative account of that council produced at Bury after the event, Baldwin showed the court charters from King Edmund, King Cnut, Harthacnut and Edward the Confessor, all of which gave him freedom from episcopal interference. The king thus found for the abbey on the basis of that written evidence (and also as a result of the oral testimony of the abbot of Ramsey, who was able to swear that Bury had never been the site of a bishopric, even in the murky past). Although the bishop spoke eloquently, he was unable to produce any documentation to back up his case or any witnesses for his cause other than the man who had kept his predecessor's dogs.[41] Baldwin prevailed as a direct result of the quality of the textual materials he could produce as evidence of the abbey's freedoms.

In this situation, we find both a context in which this high-quality single-sheet could have been forged, to be produced as in evidence before the court in 1081, and one answer to our question about audiences after 1066 for the abbey's pre-Conquest royal diplomas. While purporting to speak internally to the members of the newly-reformed Benedictine abbey in 1020, the charter in Cnut's name appears in fact to have been designed in William's reign to warn an external audience, including the current and future bishops of East Anglia, against seeking to interfere in Bury's historic independence. Although none of the other deeds Baldwin took to the court on the same occasion gave quite the same liberty, collectively they made a powerful case for the extent of the abbey's rights over the town. These rights, the abbey claimed, dated back to the time of Edmund of Wessex and his grant of privileges in 945, that conveyed to Bury all the land that lay around the resting-place of King Edmund. Baldwin could produce a charter in Edmund's name (perhaps a single sheet, for we know such a version survived into the Middle Ages although we now have only later copies). This text, too, had been confected with great skill on the basis of a genuine charter of that king's, but it is also not above suspicion. The charter purports to give the abbey at an implausibly early date a title to the area of the *banleuca*, by granting that 'all the land around that place should be held by the monastery in perpetuity' without specifying any particular number of hides. It comes

[40] Antonia Gransden, 'Baldwin, Abbot of Bury St Edmunds, 1065–1097', *ANS* 4 (1982), 65–76 at 70.

[41] D. Bates, *Regesta regum Anglo-Normannorum: The Acta of William I (1066–1087)* (Oxford, 1998), no. 39; Herman, *De miraculis sancti Eadmundi*, ed. Thomas Arnold, *Memorials of St Edmund's Abbey*, RS (3 vols., London, 1890–96), i, 65–66; Gransden, 'Baldwin', 71. By contrast, the dispute between Christ Church and St Augustine's Canterbury over the rights to the port at Sandwich was settled by oral testimony, O'Brien, 'Forgery', 9.

with a set of vernacular bounds which conveniently circumnavigate the town in a neat circle starting on the southern side.[42] This diploma, also, spoke to present and future audiences outside the abbey. Baldwin may have taken a third single-sheet charter in the name of Harthacnut to Winchester in 1081; the earliest extant version of that text is a late-twelfth-century single sheet, that perhaps reflects a later attempt to improve the wording of the privileges it purported to give to Bury.[43]

If Baldwin thus had two (possibly three) newly-created single sheets to bolster his case for the monastery's holding the *banleuca* and remaining free from episcopal oversight, he needed to work less hard to demonstrate Bury's right to the eight-and-a-half hundreds. Edward the Confessor had made a series of grants to Bury conveying the sokes (franchise) of a group of eight-and-a-half hundreds in Suffolk to successive abbots of St Edmund's, of which the most recent followed Baldwin's own appointment as abbot of Bury. The single-sheet text of the writ for Baldwin still survives but, like all Bury's other pre-Conquest writs, it provided evidence only of the temporary alienation of the rights by the king and would have lapsed on his death.[44] Perhaps uncertain of the reception of such a deed at William's court, Baldwin went further and created two Latin charters in the Confessor's name granting the same privileges to the abbey, apparently modelling those diplomas on his (genuine) Old English writ.[45] Together all these texts gave time-depth to the abbey's crucial claims to extraordinary liberties and freedom from episcopal control. Their external significance thus far out-weighed any utility they might have had as records for internal consumption at Bury.

We have already seen how well these royal diplomas served their purpose in ensuring Baldwin's victory over the bishop in the court case of 1081. The monks continued to value them by making new versions of their texts (enhancing the value of the one in Cnut's name yet further by copying it into a prized gospel book as we have already seen) and having them 'inspeximussed' in the later Middle Ages to ensure that successive kings and bishops continued to note the distinctive privileges which they granted. But Bury was not the only house to make multiple copies of its deeds in the years after the Conquest. Compare, for example, the two Canterbury houses of Christ Church and St Augustine's and their repeated recopying of documents relating to the ownership of rights relating to the port of Sandwich.[46] We

---

[42] Sawyer, *Charters*, 507; Lobel, 'The Ecclesiastical Banleuca', 129–37; Sharpe, 'Use of Writs', 256.

[43] Sawyer, *Charters*, 995.

[44] Sawyer, *Charters*, 248. Privileges granted in writs lapsed also on the death of the beneficiary, hence the renewal of the same rights by Edward to successive abbots.

[45] Sawyer, *Charters*, 1045 and 1046. The verbal similarities between the first of these and the Old English text of the forgery in Cnut's name are so close that they cannot have been created independently; see Harmer, *Writs*, 141, n. 2; Sharpe 'Use of Writs', 246.

[46] O'Brien, 'Forgery', 5–10.

need not doubt that in all liturgical commemoration of benefactors to Bury St Edmunds, the monks' gratitude to those kings who had proved so generous and sensitive to the monks' needs, Cnut above all, would have found ample expression.[47] In the aftermath of the Norman Conquest that had created such instability of tenure and rights, all English religious houses sought to use their archives to protect their own property and rights, placing especial value on their claim to the support of royal donors.[48]

Although the most copied of the deeds from Bury's Anglo-Saxon archive, these few royal diplomas and privileges do not reflect the full range of pre-Conquest texts preserved by the abbey's later medieval archivists; they also preserved a number of vernacular deeds relating to the affairs of local laypeople, as already mentioned. Yet only two cartularies between them preserve all the extant documents from Bury's pre-Conquest archive: the so-called Sacrist's register (Cambridge, University Library, MS Ff 2. 33) and the 'White Register' (London, British Library, Additional MS 14847). Both seem to have been compiled during the time of Abbot John of Northwold (1279–1301) and that of his sacrist, William of Hoo (1280–94) and both descend, by different means, from a third, now-lost cartulary that John of Northwold had himself compiled in the later thirteenth century.[49] In their record of this vernacular material, these two cartularies supply important linguistic evidence about the development of Old English after the Norman Conquest, but they also cast fresh light on later medieval archival policy at Bury. For example, only two of the wills preserved in the abbey's archive were copied into any Bury manuscript other than the White Register and the Sacrist's Register.[50] A third survives as a single sheet and in later cartulary copies in the archive of the other religious house that benefited from its provisions: Christ Church, Canterbury.[51] That the bulk of Bury's numerous

---

[47] Compare Robin Fleming, 'History and Liturgy at Pre-Conquest Canterbury', *HSJ* 6 (1994), 67–83; see also Geary, *Phantoms of Remembrance*, 81–114; Remensnyder, *Remembering Kings Past*, 100–7.

[48] O'Brien, 'Forgery', 10–11. For examples of southern French houses that placed special value on royal founders and benefactors see Remensnyder, *Remembering Kings Past*, 150–211; and for instances of Flemish houses that re-imagined their pasts in the eleventh century see Ugé, *Creating the Monastic Past*, 72–92, 112–36, 145–58.

[49] K.A. Lowe, 'Two Thirteenth-Century Cartularies from Bury St Edmunds', *Neuphilologische Mitteilungen* 93 (1992), 293–301; Thompson, *Archives*, 19–20.

[50] The will of Bishop Ælfric (Sawyer, *Charters*, 1489) survives also as a single-sheet, of which antiquarian copies were made: Oxford, Bodleian Library, Gough Berks. 20, fol. 14r–v; Bodleian Library, James 24, 72–73. An additional copy of Sawyer 1527, the will of Thurketel of Palgrave, survives in a fifteenth-century cartulary (London, British Library, Additional MS 45951, fol. 1r) which collected a full history of the Palgrave estate.

[51] The will of Æthelric (Sawyer, *Charters*, 1501), survives as a single sheet in the Canterbury archive, Canterbury, D&C, Chart. Ant. B. 2, and in two Canterbury Registers: Canterbury D&C, Reg A. fol. 141v and Canterbury D&C, Reg E, fol. 43r as well as in an antiquarian copy: London, British Library, Stowe MS 853.

cartularies do not include copies of any statements of post-mortem bequest seems to imply the obsolescence of most of these texts as practical deeds by the time the cartularies were made. So what, beyond antiquarian interest, might have motivated John of Northwold and his copyists to keep recopying this group of texts?

At first glance, looking for utilitarian purposes underpinning the recopying of vernacular texts by scribes who clearly struggled in places to comprehend the language in which they were written seems futile. The information these documents conveyed had little contemporary practical relevance to Bury's affairs by the thirteenth century, and indeed most conferred relatively small benefits to the abbey. Other factors must, therefore, have motivated the sacrists to make fresh versions. One explanation may rest in Bury's status in the later Middle Ages. The abbey had complete jurisdiction over the *banleuca*, including exclusive testamentary rights in the town.[52] Rather than proving their wills in one of the usual ecclesiastical courts (the archdeacons', the bishops' consistory or the archbishops' prerogative courts), the townspeople of Bury brought them before the sacrist's court.[53] It fell to the sacrists to keep copies of their probate registers (and all Bury's late medieval registers have survived, except for the one for the years 1483–90).[54] Against this background, we can readily see how sacrists who had charge of contemporaneous record-keeping might have thought their responsibility extended to the making of fair copies of earlier documents in their care, including the pre-Conquest wills. Although a late-medieval audience for these texts, written as they were in an archaic vernacular, was likely to have been at most the highly restricted one of sacrists and their scribal assistants, no doubt these men recognized the evidential value of what they were copying from their direct experience in the proving of wills in their own day. The copies provided additional confirmation of the historicity of the abbey's testamentary rights.

Yet, the possibility exists that successive scribes recopied earlier written documents for purely antiquarian reasons, simply because they were there. A wider group of medieval monks at Bury beyond those who worked for the sacrist may have valued these archaic texts for their historicity as tangible relics of the abbey's past, memories captured in writing. By recopying these vernacular deeds, and modernizing their language to conform more closely to contemporary speech, the archivists showed their appreciation of the witness the documents bore to the devotion of earlier generations of the abbey's neighbours to the shrine of St Edmund and its custodians. Their continued place in the archive also continued to serve the needs of the lay donors, long

---

52 Lobel, 'The Ecclesiastical Banleuca', 122–40.
53 Robert Dinn, '"Monuments Answerable to Mens Worth": Burial Patterns, Social Status and Gender in Late Medieval Bury St Edmunds', *JEH* 46 (1995), 237–55 at 239–40.
54 Listed by Dinn, 'Monuments', 239 at note.

beyond their lifetimes. Several of the wills Bury preserved included explicit statements about the testators' wishes for the safe-keeping of their written statements after death, specifying Bury as just one holder of a text copied in duplicate or triplicate.[55] Making fresh copies was one way of continuing to honour the wishes of the dead, ensuring their devotion would not be forgotten. Each new act of writing re-articulated the pious sentiments expressed by testators in life, reaffirmed their generosity to St Edmunds (and, in many cases, to other religious communities in the eastern region), and brought their names back into the minds and onto the lips of a new generation of monks, to be remembered afresh in prayer.

There survives one further category of document in Bury's archive: miscellaneous lists. Other Anglo-Saxon monastic archives preserve lists of various sorts (relating to books, vestments, relics, liturgical vessels, estate surveys, or itemized statements of dues or rents payable or of the serfs on a particular estate).[56] The vernacular often appeared a more appropriate medium than Latin for the recording of such information. Such lists were written down, and recopied, for rather different reasons from those that led to the creation of fresh copies of the more formal charters and other texts already considered. They thus raise different questions about their pragmatic function and about the audiences for which they might have been intended, both at the time of their first copying and in the future.

A Bury manuscript dating from the last third of the tenth century and containing a bilingual copy of the Rule of St Benedict has inserted at its end an additional quire, prepared and ruled to match the rest of the manuscript, on which are recorded thirteen separate notes.[57] (See Appendix and Figures

---

[55] For example the will of Thurketel (Sawyer, *Charters*, 1527), of which three copies were made: one kept at Bury, one in the care of the bishop of Elmham and the third held by the testator. Also Sawyer, *Charters*, 1516, the will of Edwin, which specified copies to be kept at Bury, St Benet at Holme and one with the testator.

[56] For example the lists of gifts given to Exeter preserved in a preliminary quire added to the front of the 'Leofric Gospels' (Oxford, Bodleian Library, MS Auct. D. 2. 16) or the inventories of vestments and treasures at Ely included in the *Liber Eliensis*, ed. E.O. Blake, Camden 3rd series (London, 1962), bk ii, cc. 114 and 139, pp. 196–97 and 223–24; bk iii, c. 50, pp. 288–94. For estate surveys, see Robertson, *Charters*, nos. 109–10. For discussion of the preservation of charters and inventories together at Exeter see Insley, 'Remembering Communities Past', 50–55.

[57] Oxford, Corpus Christi College, MS 197, fols. 106v–109r (A.D. 1045 x 1065–s. xii¹) in Robertson, *Charters*, no. 104. Compare to London, British Library, MS Faustina A.x, part B, fols. 102–51, another bilingual copy of the Rule of St Benedict dating from the early twelfth century, to which were added several vernacular texts including the only extant copy of Æthelwold's 'Account of the Establishment of Monasteries' under King Edgar and various medical recipes and charms. A book particularly, and specifically, for the use of monks (or in the case of Faustina A. x, perhaps nuns), N.R. Ker, *Catalogue of Manuscripts Containing Anglo-Saxon* (Oxford, 1957; repr. 1990), item 154, at 195, the Rule of St Benedict occupied a special place in a monastery's library.

1–4.) The same mid-eleventh-century hand recorded the first six notes, all of which relate to the abbey in the time of Abbot Leofstan (1044–65) or that of his predecessor. A second group comprises four separate memoranda: three statements of Baldwin's charitable generosity to the monks of the abbey (given in both Latin and Old English versions) and an Old English memorandum quantifying food-rents from some of Bury's manors. All these date from the time of Abbot Baldwin, 1065–97/8.

Several factors made a copy of the Rule which ordered the monks' common life a suitable repository for the recording of these memoranda. This was a book much valued by the monks (and thus one they would keep safely) but also one in regular daily use. As the Rule itself prescribed, it was often to be read in the community, so that none of the brothers could offer the excuse of ignorance.[58] The Rule offered an obvious place in which a new abbot might choose to note the condition of the abbey at his arrival and make an inventory of the books and vestments he had found in the church, which is what the third note provides.[59] On the other hand, several of the notes, especially those relating to pittances provided for the supply of the monks, had greater relevance to the convent than to the abbot. Can one envisage a tidy-minded archivist seeking to impose some order on an ill-assorted jumble of texts by writing them all out in a clean copy in one place? Perhaps he saw his act of recording them as a defence against the forgetfulness of future generations. There is no evidence that any of these matters had been the subject of dispute, but their writing might have been to prevent argument in the future. Bearing in mind the size of Bury's endowment in the mid-eleventh century, it seems unlikely that this selection represents the total number of agreements over the payment of food-rents made to the abbey. One must thus wonder why these records, and only these, appeared worthy of inclusion. Whatever the first scribe's motives, we cannot determine any organizing principles behind the decisions he made about the order in which he copied the notes. If the first items are correctly understood to be contemporaneous notices of the possessions and rents of the abbey in Leofstan's time, it would seem more logical to place the third note, about Leofstan's appointment, first. This, and the apparent dislocation of the fifth memorandum from its rightful place, may indicate that the scribe made his fine copy from a collection of separate memoranda, each perhaps preserved on some ephemeral surface such as a wax-tablet or parchment cut-off. Further exploration of the contents of the

---

[58] *Rule of St Benedict*, trans. Timothy Fry (Collegeville, MN, 1981), 288–89.
[59] Equally, were the abbot himself not responsible for the decision to preserve this material, the abbey's copy of the Rule was a location that might just as readily have occurred to a tidy-minded archivist among the monks. Other Anglo-Saxon monasteries in the period also added documentary records to their important ecclesiastical books in this period; Rebecca Rushforth, 'The Eleventh- and Twelfth-Century Manuscripts of Bury St Edmunds Abbey', unpublished PhD thesis (University of Cambridge, 2003), 18.

memoranda may help to shed some light on the question of their function, and intended audience.

The first note is a compound record of the annual food-rent payable to Bury by four tenants of an estate at Newton in Suffolk where Bury held two carucates at the Conquest.[60] It records an agreement as to the precise amount of produce payable made between Ætheric and 'the abbot', a statement of a new, higher contribution imposed by Abbot Leofstan, and then notes the amounts to be paid by three others: Brihtric, Leofstan and Thurstan. All four of these names occur also in the third note in connection with various liturgical books and vestments kept in the abbey. If the men so named in both memoranda are the same (and while the last three names are not uncommon, it seems beyond coincidence to find all four named together twice), it is unlikely that these were lay tenants of a Bury estate. Brihtric was indeed given the epithet '*pr*', which might indicate he was prior of the abbey, but may simply mean he was a priest (*preost*).[61] Might this note refer to food-rents payable to the abbey by monks from lands they had retained after their entry into the cloister, or lands which the named men had once owned, but which now belonged to the whole congregation? All four seem, from their ownership of mass-books and vestments, to have been ordained to the priesthood; they might have joined Bury's community before its reform into a Benedictine abbey, when their retention of personal property would have been less exceptional. Alternatively we might better understand these items not as belonging to these men individually, but assigned for their use from the monks' communal property. Whatever the precise interpretation of this compound memorandum, its audience is clear: the text had a particular meaning for the four men who were required to have ready on 4 September each year the specified quantities of produce (bushels of malt and wheat, oxen, sheep, bacon, loaves and cheeses) and the abbots who would ultimately receive these for the support of their community. This is an internal document of no significance outside the abbey (and probably meaningless beyond the tenants' lifetimes, as other arrangements would presumably have been made with their successors).

Second, completely unrelated to the first, there follows an enumeration of various small holdings of Bury's in north-west Norfolk. Once again this list seems to have a narrow audience, restricted to the abbey and conceivably to the men who owned these small holdings. A statement of the abbey's own

---

[60] LDB 360r, *Domesday Book Suffolk*, ed. Alex Rumble (2 vols., Chichester, 1986), i, 14:32 [hereafter *DB Suff.*].

[61] A Brihtric *praepositus* was mentioned in some versions of the abbey's benefactor lists as having been responsible for acquiring for Bury a third part of the estate at Barton, for example that printed by F. Hervey, *Pinchbeck Register relating to the Abbey of Bury St. Edmunds* (2 vols., London, 1925), ii, 283.

reckoning of its holdings, this record could not have provided legal proof of
their ownership of land in this region.

The third is the longest of these memoranda. After a preamble to which
we shall return, it reports the appointment of Abbot Leofstan to Bury by
King Edward the Confessor and lists the items the new abbot found inside
the church and the treasurehouse (*in madmhus*), these being liturgical books
and vestments for the community, together with some sets of vestments and
liturgical objects apparently belonging to individual monks who are named.
Interpreting this memorandum is straightforward: it relates to the particular
event of Leofstan's appointment in 1044 and gives us some insight into his
attempt to master the possessions within his new dominion. Although it may
plausibly be connected with the notes that follow it, there is no obvious
connection between this long memorandum and the two much briefer ones
that had come before, beyond the reference to Leofstan in the first.

In style, the third memorandum also differs from its predecessors.
Ultimately, it turns into a straightforward list, although it begins with a
remarkably florid introduction: 'May the noble name of our Lord the Saviour
Christ be honoured forever to all eternity'. Remarking that the Lord had
formed the company of angels and also created man after his own image,
the text goes on to report that 'in these days, He has given to King Edward
the island of Britain, just as in the past He gave it to his kinsman,[62] the
noble and honourable St Edmund, who now dwells in heaven, and that the
same King Edward has now given the monastery of *Bædericeswyrðe* to
Abbot Leofstan, to take charge of everything, inside and out'. Although this
opening resembles the proem to a Latin charter, I have been unable to find
any extant text on which it might have been modelled directly; perhaps it
was translated from a now lost charter, possibly one conferring the abbacy
of Bury on Leofstan. Had such a charter once existed, the copyist of this
memorandum did not choose to preserve much of it, for immediately after
the statement that Edward gave his kinsman's monastery to Leofstan to take
charge of everything both inside and out, the text continues with an inventory
of what the new abbot found inside the abbey: in the church a set of ten
service books; in the treasure house a collection of vestments. In origin, that
list constituted a document quite separate from the text used to supply its
impressive preamble.

The rest of the third memorandum comprises an impressive list of the
communal vestments in the treasury of the vestry, a collection rather larger
than that listed from mid-eleventh century Exeter but much smaller than that

---

[62] That Edward the Confessor liked to see himself as St Edmund's kinsman is apparent from
the writs he gave to Bury in which he styled himself as the martyr's kin. See Sawyer, *Charters*,
1073, 1074, 1078 and 1084.

recorded at Ely in a similar period.[63] There follows a fascinating list of the books, vestments, and liturgical vessels owned by particular members of the community. Among the latter, Brihtric stands out as the best equipped cleric, having access to all the essential objects he would need for the celebration of mass at, or indeed away from, the abbey. If he were, as the benefactor-lists might imply, the abbey's prior (*praepositus*), his duties may have taken him regularly away from the abbey. Given all of these elements, we may readily surmise the audience for this memorandum: the monks of Bury themselves. As already argued, that they should choose to keep it inside a copy of the Rule of St Benedict also makes sense.

The fourth note makes a statement about the nature of Bury's lands at the time of Leofstan's arrival: what, in other words, he found 'without' when he surveyed his new domain. Having described the town, the memorandum goes on to itemize food-rents due to the abbey, listing a total of thirteen months' payment.[64] Such a record had an obvious practical value for the abbot, perhaps even more so for the monks who depended on these rents for their own nourishment. Indeed, we might imagine that should tenants of any of the manors listed have contested their obligations, a list of this kind might have been produced in support of the abbey's demand for food-rent. The fifth note, stating that Abbot Leofstan had thirty books of his own and then

---

[63] Robertson, *Charters*, 194–95. For Exeter's eleventh-century inventory see Patrick W. Conner, *Anglo-Saxon Exeter* (Woodbridge 1993), 226–35; and a twelfth-century inventory from Ely: *Liber Eliensis*, bk iii, c. 50, ed. Blake, 293–94.

[64] These are the manors which singly or in groups were said to pay one month's food rent to Bury. Worlingworth (LDB fol. 368r; *DB Suff.* i, 14:103; for the original grant of Worlingworth to Bury see Sawyer, *Charters*, 1489) with (Monks) Soham (LDB 368r, *DB Suff.* i, 14:102); Palgrave (Sawyer, *Charters,* 1213 and 1527; LDB 361r, *DB Suff.* i, 14:45) with Thorpe (Westhorpe: LDB 370r, *DB Suff.* i, 14:132); Redgrave (LDB 360v–361r; *DB Suff.* i, 14:42); Rickinghall (Sawyer 1219; LDB 360v; *DB Suff.* i, 14:46) with Stoke (Ash: LDB 369v, *DB Suff.* i, 14:122, 125) and Brockford (LDB 361r, *DB Suff.* i, 14:47); (Great) Barton (LDB 361v; *DB Suff.* 14:48); Rougham (Sawyer , *Charters*, 1219; LDB 362r, *DB Suff.* 14:51); Elmswell (LDB 364v, *DB Suff.* 14:73) with Woolpit (Sawyer, *Charters*, 1219; LDB 362v, *DB Suff.* 14:55) and Groton (LDB 359v, *DB Suff.* i, 14:25); Cockfield (Sawyer, *Charters,* 1483, 1494 and 1486; LDB 359r–v, *DB Suff.* i, 14:24) with Chelsworth (Sawyer, *Charters,* 703, 1494 and 1486; LDB 368v; *DB Suff.* i, 14:109); Whepstead (Sawyer, *Charters,* 1526; LDB 356v, *DB Suff.* i, 14:3) with Bradfield (LDB362a; *DB Suff.* i, 14:52); Horningsheath (probably Horringer in Thingoe hundred: Sawyer, *Charters*, 1526, LDB 356v, *DB Suff.* i, 14:2) with Risby (LDB 356v; *DB Suff.* i, 14:1); Lackford (LDB 357r, *DB Suff.* i, 14:7) with Herringswell (LDB 358v; *DB Suff.* i, 14:18); Runcton with Culford and Fornham. This Runcton is probably not to be identified with the South Runcton in Clackhouse hundred in Norfolk where Bury did hold land at the Conquest, but rather with somewhere now not identifiable nearer to the other two places with which it paid: Culford, in Bradmere hundred, Suffolk (Sawyer, *Charters,* 1225, LDB 364r; *DB Suff.* i, 14:70) and one of the Fornhams in Thedwestry hundred, in all of which Bury had an interest. At both Fornham, All Saints and Fornham, St Martin the abbey held one carucate of land: LDB 357v, *DB Suff.* i, 14:9; LDB 361v–362r, *DB Suff.* i, 14:50. At Fornham, St Genevieve the abbey held 2 carucates as an outlier: LDB fol. 362r, *DB Suff.* i, 14:53.

explaining the food rent payable by a thirteenth estate at Pakenham, seems to be displaced because it would more logically have come with Leofstan's inventory of the things he found inside.

At the top of the next folio, still in the hand of the first scribe, is a laconic sixth note unrelated to any of the preceding text. It explains the condition of an estate at Egmere in Greenhoe hundred in Norfolk 'when Cole left it'; enumerating the stock, the state of the arable, and items that presumably were to be paid in a food rent. Egmere did not lie among Bury's possessions at the Conquest, nor can this note be linked with any statement of food rents just discussed. In his will, datable to 1023 x 1038, Bishop Ælfric of Elmham had bequeathed 30 acres at Egmere to Ælfwine, his priest at Walsingham, leaving the rest to Ufi the prior.[65] In Domesday Book, Egmere was said to be held before 1066 by Æthelmær, bishop of Elmham.[66] The bishop plainly held Egmere, not Bury.

Perhaps Bury had leased the land from the bishop; if so, this note might somehow relate to the terms of the lease. But it does not record the lease itself, since it fails to describe the entirety of the estate (reckoned at three carucates in Domesday Book), or to list the annual food-rent payable to the bishop from the leased land. Rather, it explains the situation on the Egmere estate at one particular moment, that is, at the moment when Cole left it. Perhaps Cole (his name represents the Anglo-Scandinavian name Koli) farmed the estate on the abbey's behalf, in which case the note may provide an inventory of what the abbey's representative found when he went out to Egmere to investigate its condition after Cole's departure. Alternatively, it may be that Cole, not the abbey, was the tenant of Egmere, leasing from the bishop. If Cole were the abbot of Bury's man, this note could be understood as the report that he made to the abbot, his lord, when he left the land, a formal record that he had fulfilled the obligations placed on him and one that he would want the abbot to keep safely on his behalf, in case he should have future difficulty with his landlord, the bishop of Elmham. A group of chapters in Ine's law-code deals with men who wanted to give up their tenancies and specifies the conditions relating to their departure. If a man had three hides, he was to show one-and-a-half hides of sown land on his departure. The 160 acres that Cole had sown of the Egmere estate represented one-and-a-third carucates of the full three carucate estate, only slightly less than the amount specified in West Saxon codes.[67] Should this second interpretation prove correct, it would help to explain both why this note was copied with the

---

[65] Sawyer, *Charters*, 1489.

[66] LDB fol. 192v; *Domesday Book Norfolk*, ed. Philippa Brown (2 vols., Chichester, 1984), i, 10: 11.

[67] The Law Code of Ine, cc. 64–6, in *Die Gesetze der Angelsachsen* (3 vols., Halle, 1903–1916), i, 118–19; see also Rosamond Faith, *English Peasantry and the Growth of Lordship* (Leicester, 1997), 76; and Thomas Charles-Edwards, 'The Distinction between Land and Moveable Wealth

others in this manuscript, and for whom it may have been written. Further, it raises the possibility that Cole's lord was Abbot Leofstan, and that it was the connection with this abbot that caused the first scribe of these memoranda to record the note here.

There follow four discrete memoranda, three statements relating to Abbot Baldwin's generosity to his monks (made first in Old English and then in Latin) followed by a final vernacular memorandum quantifying the food-rents paid by the thirteen manors already listed under the fourth note. Just as one might associate all of the first six to the time Abbot Leofstan, the second group may plausibly all be linked to the time of Baldwin's abbacy, 1065–97/8. They speak to three audiences: the monks, the abbey's reeves in Bury, and their tenants.

Collectively, the memoranda preserved at the end of Bury's copy of the Rule of St Benedict reveal much about the administration of the abbey of Bury St Edmunds as a corporation. They shed some light on the practicalities of running this large and complex organization and its need to keep track of the income it could expect from its lands on which the community was dependent for its subsistence. In particular, the focus over the supply of food-rents for the support of the monks from manors in their possession shows the preoccupation of successive abbots in the period immediately before and after the Norman Conquest with ensuring the regular supply of adequate provisions. Charitable gifts for the funding of commemorative feasts (whether paid in money or in kind) speak likewise to a concern with the monks' table. In that context, the inclusion of what may seem to a modern reader more like an *ad hoc* arrangement over rent (the first note) or the yet more opaque statement of the condition of one particular small estate (the sixth note about Egmere) may appear more logical. Pragmatism might similarly explain the inclusion of the inventories of books and vestments in the midst of these records of food-rents and charitable payments. Those particular notes can be more closely dated than any of the others, since they were apparently compiled at the time of a new abbot's appointment when it made sense to compile a survey of the resources available for the spiritual as well as the temporal well-being of the community. A decision to preserve such miscellaneous notes in one of the abbey's most treasured possessions, its copy of the Rule by which its collective life was ordered, was a good one, for this was surely one of those books the monks were most likely to try to save in the event of fire or flood and one stored in the safest part of the monastery, least accessible to thieves. Bearing in mind the predominance of Old English among these memoranda, one may wonder whether it was also the fact that this manuscript provided a vernacular text of the Rule as well

in Anglo-Saxon England', in *English Medieval Settlement*, ed. Peter H. Sawyer (London, 1979), 97–104 at 103.

as the Latin that drew it to the first scribe's attention when he sought out a suitable place in which to record these notes. The Old English of the book thus may have offered a structure for archiving Old English documents.

For a modern readership, the memoranda provide evidence about the running of Bury St Edmunds as an economic unit and shed a different light from the majority of the records in its archive, which reflect rather its religious history and political and social status within Suffolk and beyond. That they do so is in large measure because they were both originally composed and copied in this manuscript with a quite other audience in mind from that envisaged by the authors of the rest of the abbey's muniments. These notes were written primarily for an internal audience of the community of monks living at the shrine of St Edmund and their successive abbots. Some had relevance to the tenants of Bury's estates, but there is no wider audience beyond those directly connected with the abbey to whom they were addressed. The monks compiled none of these defensively, envisaging a potential future audience in legal dispute; none indeed would constitute adequate proof of the provisions to which it relates. Even so, although some are clearly time-specific (those datable to the point of Leofstan's appointment, or that describing the state of Egmere when Cole left it), they may all implicitly speak not just to the contemporary audience for which they were crafted but to an imagined future one of successive generations of monks at Bury.

For historians, handling (and editing) such texts requires the application of rather different skills from those used for the treatment of more conventional texts in an Anglo-Saxon archive. The central question that the British Academy Committee on Anglo-Saxon Charters urges on the editors of each volume is that of authenticity, but this is scarcely the right question to ask of memoranda such as these. Nor is the question of form a particularly helpful one, since these were not formal, legal documents: they followed no pre-existing templates or formulae but were crafted as each individual author thought fit.

Pursuing the question of audience has helped to clarify why and how these miscellaneous notes look so different from the rest of the wider archive in which they were preserved and to explain something of their function. We saw how several of the small number of Latin royal diplomas in the abbey's archive were recopied – and substantially improved in the process – in order to serve the abbey's needs in its disputes against the bishops of Elmham and, at times, against the townsfolk. Since the monks appear to have had fewer such Latin title-deeds than did many other monastic houses, they seem to have determined to make the most of those they did own, by bringing them regularly to the attention of successive monarchs as the proofs of their particular privileges. The events of 1327 demonstrated how prudential it was that the abbey kept multiple copies of some of their most precious deeds as a defence against the risks of loss, whether through natural disaster (fire or flood) or the rapacity of the abbey's immediate neighbours. In the absence of evidence that pre-Conquest Bury held any other Latin diplomas than those now known, it is impossible to determine how selective their recopying policy might have been. Whether the abbey once had written witnesses to different versions of its past which it chose not to retain and to remember cannot now be determined, of course. The later copies of those texts that did survive spoke to some of the imagined future audiences that their original draftsmen may have envisaged, but subsequent generations found it expedient to adjust the original wording better to suit contemporary needs. The beautiful display copy of the charter in Cnut's name demonstrates with what skill such an improved document could be executed. In continuing to recopy their collection of writs, the monks of Bury apparently ignored the fact that these texts had no evidentiary value beyond the death of the original parties.[68] Again, they made fresh copies to reach new external audiences – the king and his council – and those modernized versions served not just as records of a remembered past but as continuing testimony to the extraordinary liberties which the monks enjoyed.

Different considerations lay behind the recopying of vernacular texts recording gifts made by individual local lay people to the abbey or statements of their intended disposition of property after their death. By preserving these documents as a group in successive registers, archivists in the sacristy contrived to create an unparalleled collection of statements of testamentary intent reaching back to the mid-tenth century, and so to provide time-deep justification for Bury's continuing prerogative in proving wills in the later Middle Ages. Yet the act of recopying these and other texts from lay benefactors had a potentially more important mnemonic function, for it served to reconnect each subsequent generation of monks at Bury with the individual donors whose generosity had enhanced the abbey's possessions in earlier centuries. We might almost see this as a prayerful act, a partial fulfilment of the monks' obligations in the reciprocal exchange of tangible and intangible gifts.

That none of the memoranda with which this discussion ended survives outside the manuscript of the Rule of Benedict has perhaps already been explained. If these actions had once been recorded on other media, there can have been no need to preserve those ephemeral objects once the notes had been preserved in fair copy in this manuscript. It remains uncertain, of course, how well this collection of memoranda represents the total number of such records made at Bury in the eleventh century. Only one other similar text now survives from the archive: a note of an agreement between Ordric the cellarer and 'every man in Bury St Edmunds occupying a house on his own land', who should pay one penny to the cellarer on St Peter's day (29 June) at the beginning of the harvest, when summoned to the saint's reaping. The

---

68 Sharpe, 'Use of Writs'.

only men to be exempt from this obligation were St Edmund's servants, the *cnihtas*, and the priests in the monastery who sing at the altars.[69] Of direct relevance to all those encompassed by its terms, this text has a more obvious audience external to the monks and was more copied than the memoranda we have been discussing, surviving in three separate registers.[70]

Whether the bureaucratic scribes in the Bury scriptorium simply made fair copies of anything they could find is not clear, but I hesitate to assume so, remembering the size of Bury's land-holdings at the Conquest and the consequent need to organize the food-rents payable from each of them (or at least the commuting of that payment in kind to a monetary rent). It is tempting to ascribe to Abbot Leofstan personally the decision to make a clean and permanent copy of the lists of books, vestments, and supplies that he enumerated on taking up office. Yet the other memoranda, especially those recording gifts made *ad uictum monachorum* mattered more to the monks for whose provision they were granted than to the abbot. A cellarer on whom fell the obligation to arrange food supplies would have had an obvious interest in using records about both food rents and pittances. That no eye outside the abbey need see the texts made the monks' own Rule an ideal repository.

Taken together, the documents preserved in Bury's pre-Conquest archive served to create and, over successive generations, to reinforce the monks' understanding of their shared past, particularly the extent to which they owed to the generosity of kings and local nobles their identity as the community of St Edmund and the lands, rights, and privileges which they enjoyed as a congregation. This collection of Anglo-Saxon charters, writs, and wills bears witness to an integrated and thoughtful archival policy designed both to memorialize the abbey's past and to ensure its future material security, its privileges, and its independence from episcopal interference, while continuing to fulfil the obligations of prayer for its benefactors.

In the political confusion of fourteenth-century England, the prudence of successive archivists in preserving multiple copies of Bury's key royal charters (and in having had the foresight to have these multiply 'inspeximussed') bore fruit. For, although the abbey suffered losses, the monks were not deprived of all the proofs of the exceptionality of their rights and privileges.[71] In this collection of pre-Conquest documents they did indeed find what a thriving community needed for its collective spiritual and material well-being, as well as the means by which to preserve its corporate memory for the benefit of future monks.

---

[69]   Robertson, *Charters*, no. 119, ed. and trans. at 220–21 with relevant notes at 471–72.
[70]   Cambridge, University Library, Additional MS 6006, fol. 51 (the so-called *Liber de consuetudinibus* of Bury, a thirteenth-century manuscript); Cambridge, University Library, MS Ee. 3. 60, fol. 161 (the *Registrum vestiarii*, known as the Pinchbeck Register) and Cambridge, University Library, MS Gg. 4. 4, fol. 317, for the *Registrum cellerarii* I.
[71]   Lobel, '1327 Rising', 230–31.

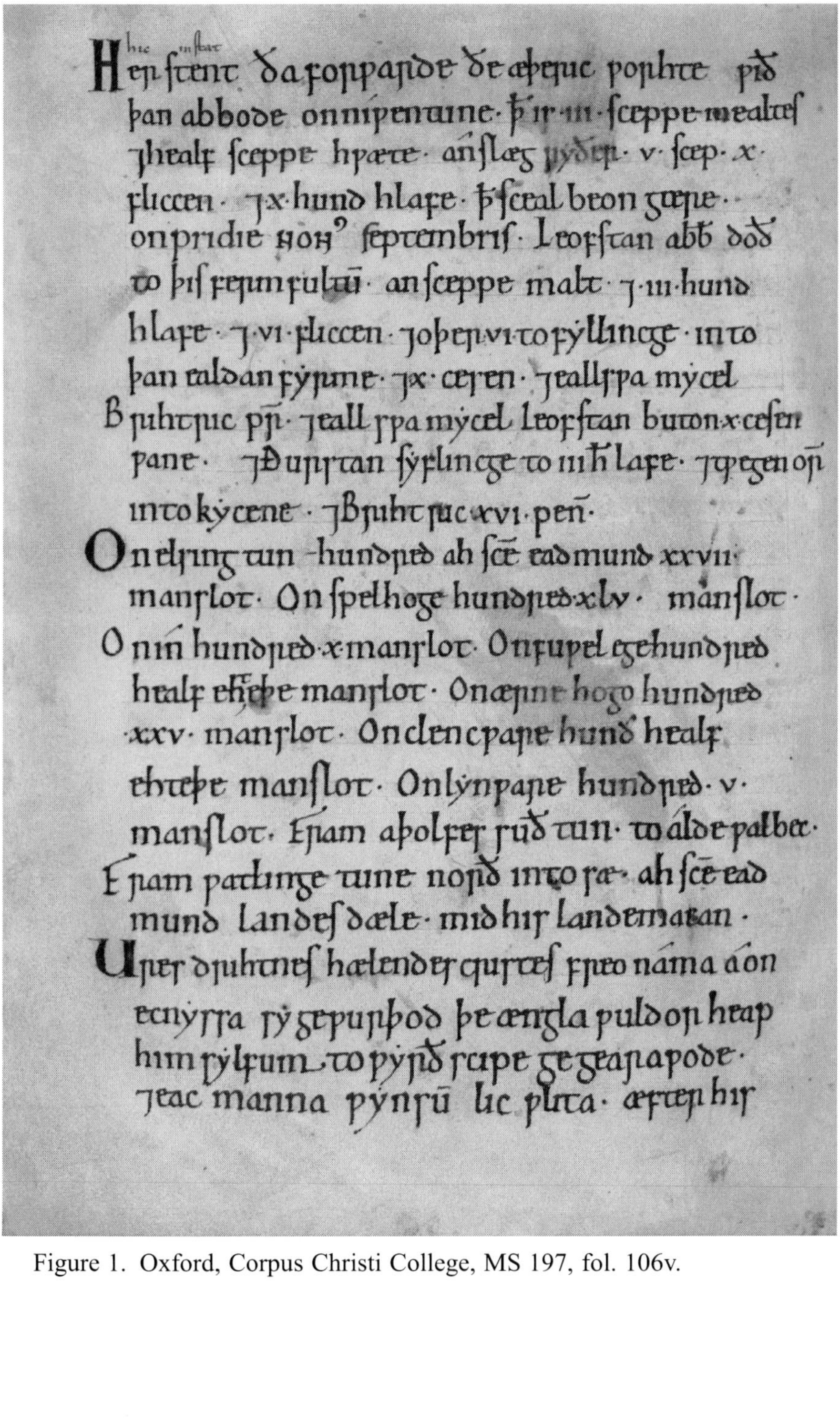
Her stent ða forwarde ðe ælfric worhte wið
þan abbode on niwentune. þ is .iii. sceppe mealtes
7 healf sceppe hwæte. an slæg wyðer. v. scep. x.
flicceń. 7 x. hund hlafe. þ sceal beon gare.
on pridie non' septembris. Leofstan abb dōð
to þis feormfultū. an sceppe malt. 7 .iii. hund
hlafe. 7 .vi. flicceń. 7 oþer .vi. to fyllincge. into
þan ealdan fyrme. 7 x. ceseń. 7 eallswa mycel
Brihtric wr. 7 eall swa mycel leofstan buton x cesen
wane. 7 Ðurstan fyllincge to .iii. hund lafe. 7 twegen or
into kycene. 7 Brihtric .xvi. wen.
On elmingtun hundred ah sce eadmund .xxvii.
manslot. On spelhoge hundred .xlv. manslot.
On nin hundred .x. manslot. On fuwel ege hundred
healf ehtefe manslot. On ærpinge hogo hundred
.xxv. manslot. On clencware hund healf
ehtefe manslot. On lynware hundred .v.
manslot. Fram awolfes rūð tun. to alde walbec.
Fram watlinge tune norð into sæ. ah sce ead
mund landes dæle. mid his landemæran.
Wites drihtnes hælendes cristes freo nama áon
ecnyssa sy gewurþod þe ængla wuldor heap
him sylfum to wyrð scipe gegearawode.
7 eac manna wynsū lic plita. æfter his

Figure 1. Oxford, Corpus Christi College, MS 197, fol. 106v.

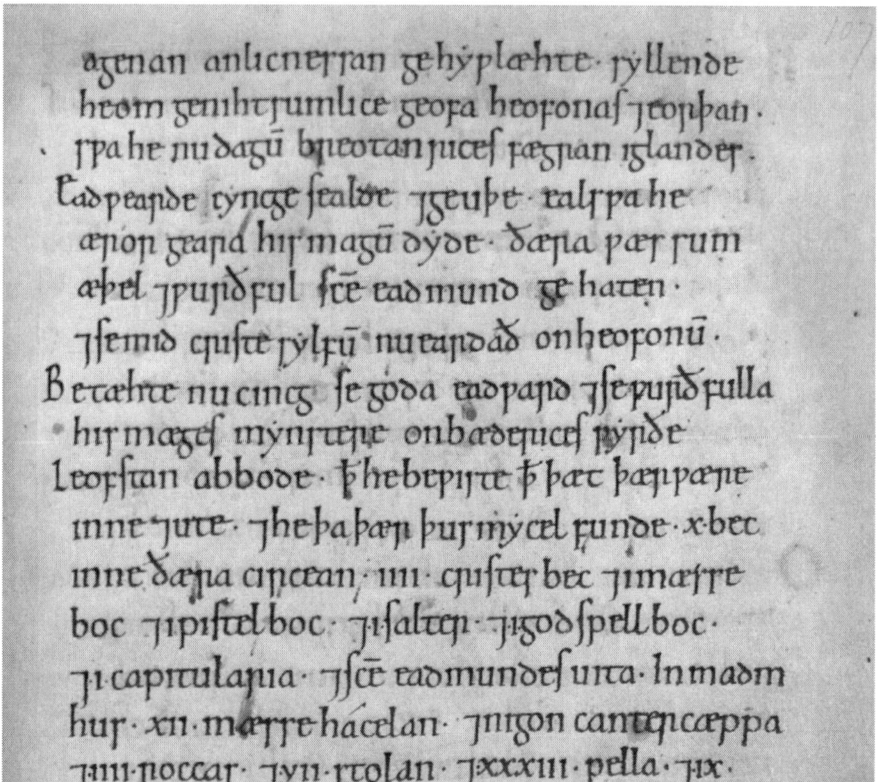

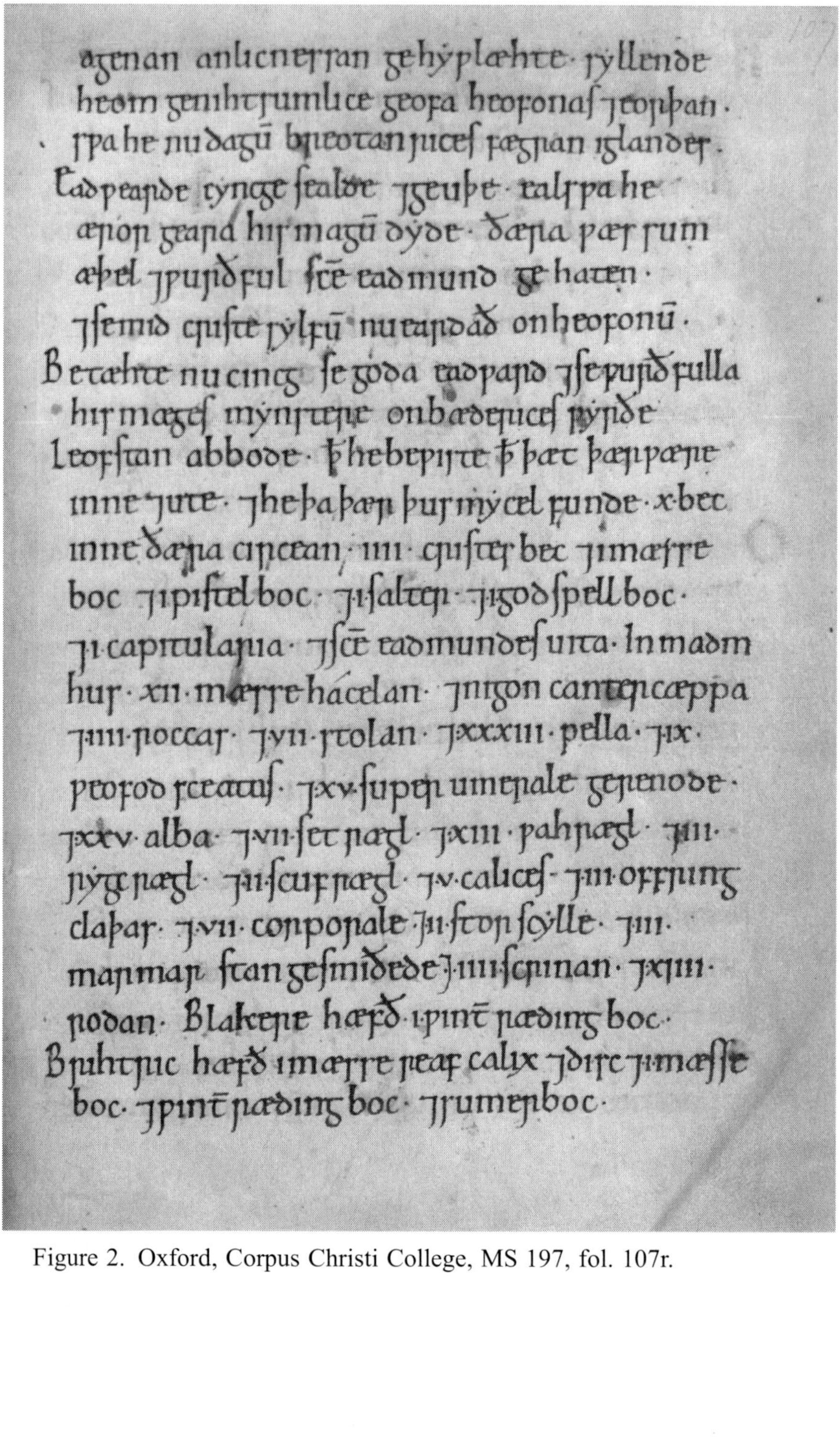

agenan anlicnerpan gehýplæhtc ꝛyllenðe
heom genihtrumlice geofa heofonaꝼ �986toꝛþan ·
ꝛpa he nu ðagū bꝛꞇotanꝛuceꝼ ꝛæꞅꞅan iꝛlanðeꝛ ·
Eaðꝛeaꝛðe tynꝛe ꝛealðe ꝛꝛeuþe ꝛalꝛꝛa he
æꝛoꝛ ꝛeanꝛ hiꝛ maꝛū ðýðe · ðæꝛa ꝛæꝛ ꝛum
aþel ꝛꝛuꝛðꝼul ꝼćē eaðmunð ꝛe hacen ·
ꝛ ꝛemð cꝛuꝼce ꝛýlꝼū nu eaꝛðáð on heoꝛonū ·
Beꝛælꝛꝛe nu cmꝛ ꝛe ꝛoða eaðꝛaꝛð ꝛꝛeꝛuꝛðꝼulla
hiꝛ maꝛeꝼ mynꝛꝛꝛe onbaðeꝛuceꝼ ꝛꝛꝛðe
Leoꝛꝛꝛan abbode · þ hebꝛꝛꝛe þ þæꞇ þæꝛꝛꝛꝛe
mne ꝛuꝛe · ꝛ he þa þeꝛ þuꝛ mýcel ꝛunðe · x · beꝛ
mne ðæꝛa cꝛꝛeꝛan · mꞇ · cꝛuꝼꝛeꝛ beꝛ ꝛ maꝛꝛe
boc · ꝛ ipꝛꝼꝛel boc · ꝛ ꝛalꝛeꝛ · ꝛ ꝛoðꝛꝛell boc ·
ꝛ ꝛ capꞇꞇulaꝛua · ꝛ ꝼćē eaðmunðeꝼ uꝛꞇa · In maðm
huꝛ · xꞇꞇ · maꝛꝛe hacelan · ꝛ mꝛon canꝛeꝛ cæꝛꝛa
ꝛ mꞇꞇ ꝛoccaꝛ · ꝛ uꝛꞇꞇ ꝛꞇolan · ꝛ xxxꞇꞇꞇ · ꝛella · ꝛ ꝛx ·
ꝛeoꝛoð ꝛꞇeaꝛuꝼ · ꝛ xu · ꝛuꝛeꝛ umeꝛale ꝛeꝛꝛenoðe ·
ꝛ xɛꝛu · alba · ꝛ uꞇꞇ ꝼeꝛ ꝛaꝛꝛ · ꝛ xꞇꞇꞇ · ꝛaꝛꝛaꝛꝛ · ꝛ mꞇꞇ ·
ꝛꝛꝛꝛ ꝛaꝛꝛ · ꝛ mꝛ ꝛcuꝛꝛ ꝛaꝛꝛ · ꝛ u · calꞇeꝼ · ꝛ mꞇꞇ oꝛꝛung
claþaꝛ · ꝛ uꞇꞇ · conꝛoꝛale ꝛuꝛ ꝼꝛoꝛ ꝛꝛꝛlle · ꝛ mꞇ ·
maꝛꝛmaꝛ ꝼꞇan ꝛeꝼmꝛðeðe ꝛ mꞇꞇ ꝛꝛꞇnan · ꝛ xꝛꞇꞇꞇ ·
ꝛoðan · Blakeꝛe hæꝛð ꞇ ꝛꝛꞇē ꝛæðꝛnꝛ boc ·
Bꝛuhꞇꝛꞇc hæꝛð ꞇ maꝛꝛe ꝛeaꝛ calꞇx ꝛ ðꝛꝛe ꝛ maꝼꝼe
boc · ꝛ ꝛꝛꞇē ꝛæðꝛnꝛ boc · ꝛ ꝛumeꝛboc ·

Figure 2. Oxford, Corpus Christi College, MS 197, fol. 107r.

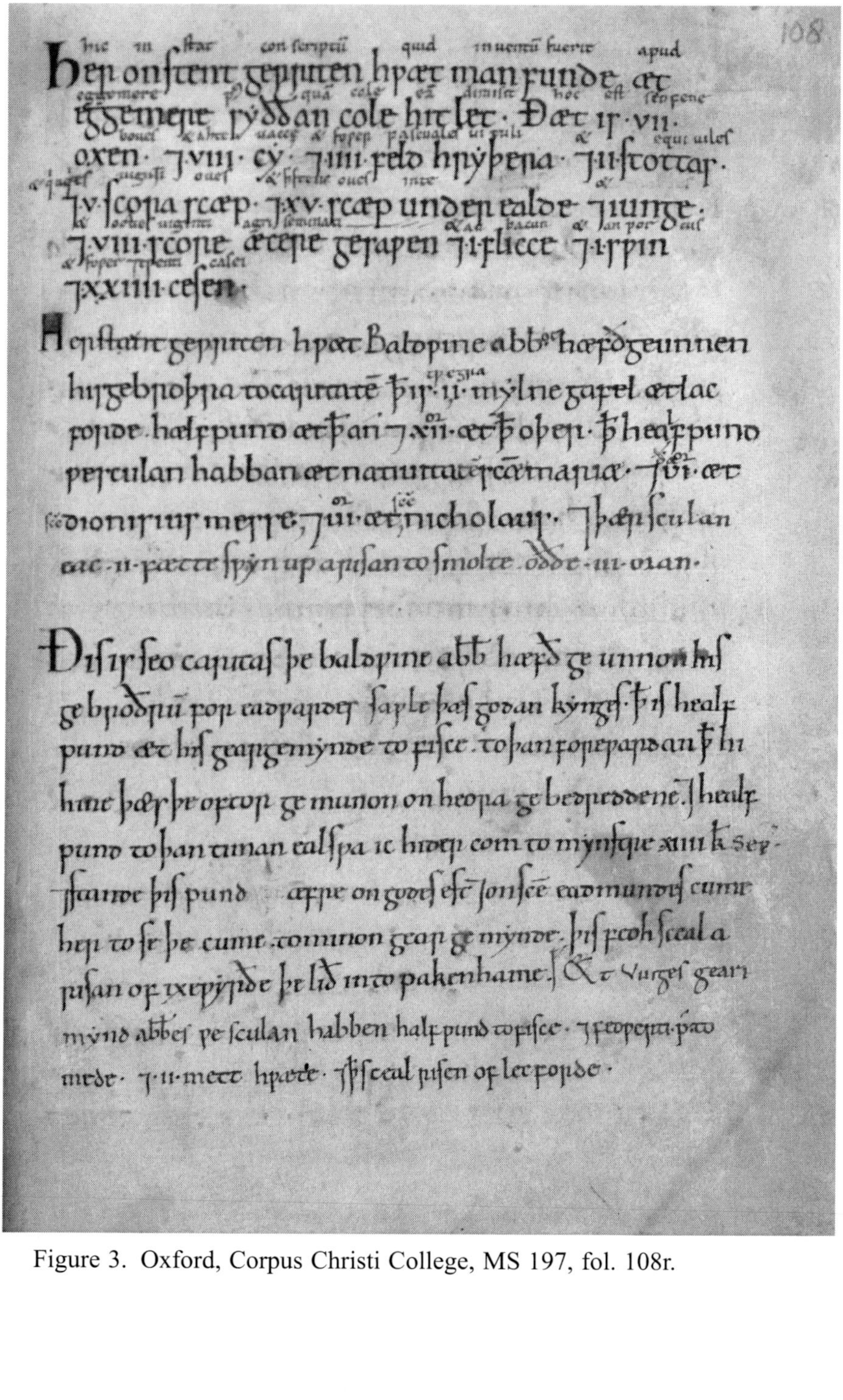

Figure 3. Oxford, Corpus Christi College, MS 197, fol. 108r.

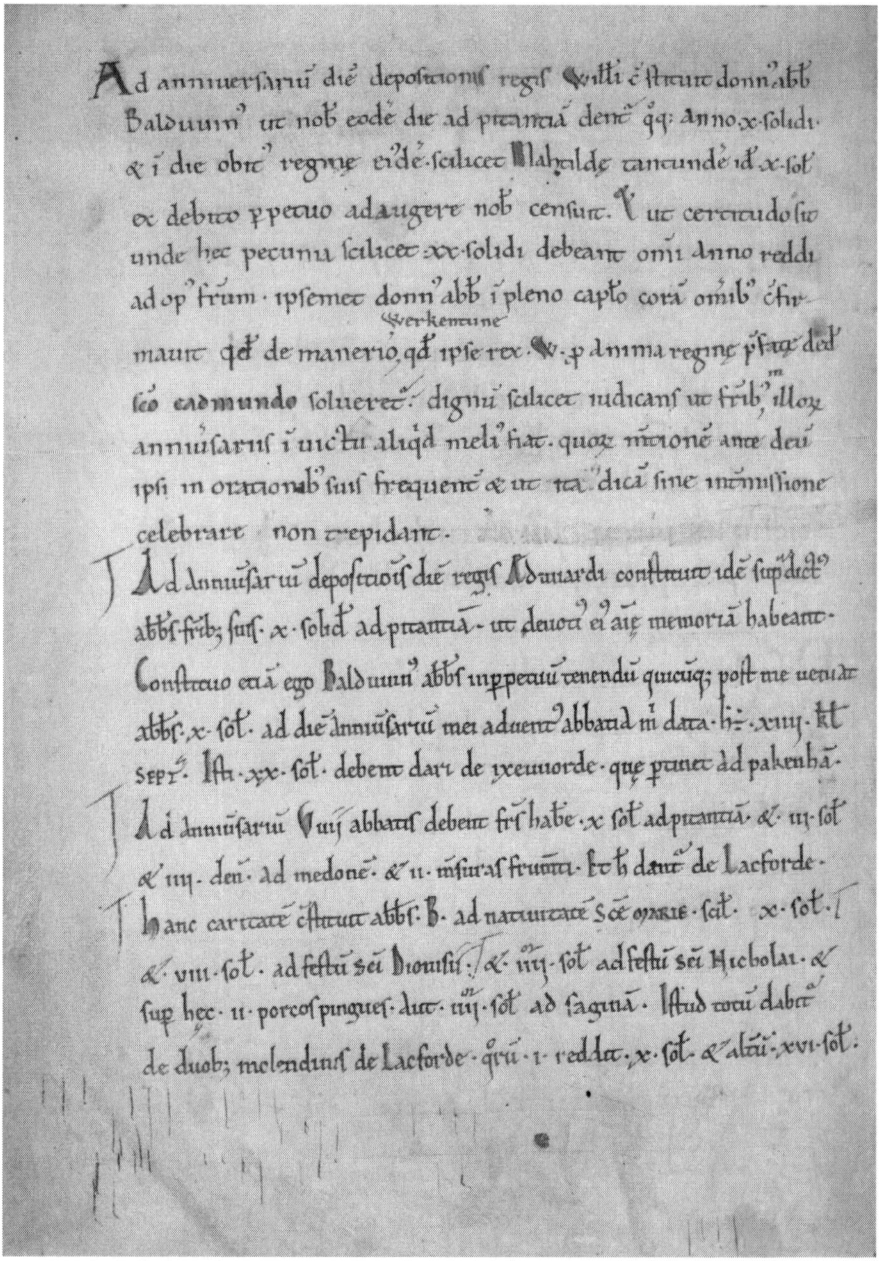

Ad anniuersariũ diẽ deposicioniſ regiſ Ƿilti ẽ ſtituit donn̄ abb̄
Balduuin̄ ut nob̄ eodẽ die ad pitantiā denr̄ q̄q̄ anno x soldi
& i die obtr̄ reginę eide ſcilicet Mahtildę tantunde id x ſot
& debito ppetuo adaugere nob̄ censuit. ¶ ut certitudo ſit
unde hec pecunia ſcilicet xx ſolidi debeant om̄i anno reddi
ad op̄ frum̄ ipſemet donn̄ abb̄ i pleno capto corā om̄ib̄ c̄fir
mauit q̄d de manerio q̄d ipſe rex Ƿ p anima reginę p̄ſatę ded
ſc̄o eadmundo ſolueret dignũ ſcilicet iudicanſ ut frib̄ illox̄
anniuiſariuſ i uictu aliq̄d meli fiat quox̄ ṅratiōe ante deũ
ipſi in oratiōab̄ ſuiſ frequentr̄ & ut ita dicā ſine intmiſſione
celebrare non trepidant.

Ad anniuiſariũ depoſitioiſ diẽ regiſ Admardi conſtituit ide ſup̄dc̄o
abb̄ſ frib̄; ſuiſ x ſolid ad pitantiā ut deuotu et aiẽ memoriā habeant
Conſtituo etiā ego Balduuin̄ abb̄ſ inppetuū tenendũ quicũq; poſt me ueniat
abb̄ſ x ſot ad die anniuiſariũ mei aduentuſ abbatia ĩ data hẽ xiiij kt
Septr̄ Iſti xx ſot debent dari de ixeuuorde quę pitinet ad pakenhā
Ad anniuiſariũ Ƿui abbatiſ debent frēſ habe x ſot ad pitantiā & iij ſot
& iiij den̄ ad medone & ii m̄ſuraſ frum̄t Et ħ dant de Lacforde
Hanc cartate c̄ſtituit abb̄ſ B ad natiuitate ſc̄ē oxarie ſcił x ſot
& uiii ſot ad feſtũ ſc̄i Dionisiſ & iiij ſot ad feſtũ ſc̄i Micholai &
ſup hec ii porcoſ pingueſ duc iiij ſot ad ſaginā Iſtud totũ dabit
de duob̄; molendinſ de Lacforde q̄rũ i reddit x ſot & altũ xvi ſot

Figure 4. Oxford, Corpus Christi College, MS 197, fol. 108v.

Appendix

Memoranda regarding Food Rents and Charitable Gifts from Bury St Edmunds

Oxford, Corpus Christi College, MS 197, fols. 106v–109r (AD 1045 x 1065, s. xii[1]); ed. and translated in A.J. Robertson, *Anglo-Saxon Charters* (Cambridge, 1939), no. 104.

Hand a (s. xi[mid]), see Figures 1 and 2.

1   [fol. 106v, lines 1–11] 'Her stent ða forwarde …' OE agreement of Æthelric with Abbot Ufi (1020 x 44) over a food rent at Newton (Sf), increased by Abbot Leofstan (1044–65).

Here stands the agreement which Æthelric made with the abbot at Newton (?Sf). That is three measures of malt and half a measure of wheat, one cattle for slaughter, five sheep, ten flitches of bacon and one thousand loaves which are to be ready on September 4th. Abbot Leofstan adds this help in obtaining provisions to the old levy: one measure of malt, and three hundred loaves and six flitches of bacon, and another six in completion, and ten cheeses and Brihtric, the priest (*pr*) as much, and Leofstan as much less the ten cheeses. And Thurstan relish for three hundred loaves, and two ores to the kitchen, and Brihtric sixteen pence.

2   [fol. 106v, lines 12–20] 'On Elsingtun hundred ah Sce Eadmund …' OE list of small-holdings in the Marshland area of Norfolk.

3   [fols. 106v, lines 21–107v, line 5] 'Ures drihtnes hælendes Cristes freo nama a …' OE statement about the appointment of Abbot Leofstan to Bury (1044) with an inventory of moveable goods, including books and vestments.

May the noble name of our Lord the Saviour Christ be honoured for ever for eternity, who formed the glorious assembly of angels for His own company, and also fashioned the pleasant countenance of men after his own image, furnishing them abundantly with the gifts of heaven and earth. Likewise in these days He gave and granted King Edward the fair island of Britain, just as He previously did formerly to his kinsmen, one of whom was called the noble and honourable St Edmund, and he now dwells with Christ himself in heaven. The good and the honourable King Edward has now entrusted his kinsman's monastery at *Beodricesworth* to Abbot Leofstan so that he may take charge of everything there, both inside and out, and he has found this much: ten books in the church (four gospel-books and one mass-book and one epistle-book and one psalter and one evangelistary and one capitulary, and the Life of St Edmund). In the treasurehouse, twelve mass-vestments and nine cantors' copes and four surplices and seven stoles and thirty-three cloaks and nine altar-cloths, and fifteen adorned amices, and twenty-five albs and seven seat-coverings and thirteen wall-hangings and three mantles and two veils and five chalices and three offertory cloths and seven corporal-cloths and two censers and three marble stones mounted in metal and four chests and fourteen crosses. Blachere has one winter lectionary. Brihtric has one mass-vestment, chalice and paten and one missal and a winter lectionary and a summer lectionary. Siferth has one mass-vestment and one missal, and Leofstan one manual, Æthelric one missal and capitulary. Thurstan one psalter. Oscytel has one mass-vestment and one missal and one *Ad te levavi.*

4   [fol. 107v, lines 5–21] 'On sce Edmundes byrig …' OE statement about arable land at Bury followed by an OE list of twelve estates that each pay one month's food rent to Bury.

5   [fol. 107v, lines 22–4] 'Her syndon .xxx. boca …' OE notice of the thirty books in Leofstan's possession additional to those held by the monastery [perhaps displaced from §3] with notice of a food rent from Pakenham (Sf) [belonging properly to §4].

6   [fol. 108r, lines 1–6] 'Her onstent gewriten …' OE survey of an estate at Egmere (Nf), with a Latin gloss (s.xi/s.xii).

Here stands written what was found at Egmere (Nf) after Cole left it: namely, seven oxen and eight cows, and four grazing bullocks and two plough-horses and one hundred sheep and fifteen underage and young sheep and one-hundred-and-sixty sown acres and one flitch of bacon and one pig and twenty-four cheeses.

Hand b (s. xi²), see Figure 3.

7   [fol. 108r, lines 7–12] 'Her stant gewriten …' OE memorandum about a charitable gift of Abbot Baldwin (1065–97) with an addition in hand c.

Here stands written what Abbot Baldwine has granted to his brethren as a charitable gift, namely the rent from two mills at Lackford, half a pound from the one and twelve ores from the other. We are to have the half pound at the nativity of St Mary, and the six ores at the festival of St Dionysius and six ores at [the festival of] St Nicholas, and there are also to be two fattened pigs produced for lard, or three ores.

Hand c (s. xi/xii).

8   [fol. 108r, lines 14–23] 'Ðis is seo caritas …' OE memorandum about charitable gifts of Baldwin to be given at the anniversary of the burial of King Edward and on the anniversary of Baldwin's arrival at the abbey, to be paid from Ixworth manor (Sf). An added note in hand d (lines 21–3), records a similar gift payable from Lackford on the anniversary of Abbot Ufi.

Hand d (s. xi/s. xii), see Figure 4.

9   [fol. 108v, lines1–11] 'Ad anniuersarium diem depositionis regis Willi …' Latin memorandum about a charitable gift of Baldwin made on

the anniversary of the burial of William I (d. 1087) and on the day of his wife Matilda's death, to be paid from the manor of Warkton (Nth).

Hand e (s. xi/s. xii).

10 [fol. 108v, lines 12–16] 'Ad anniuersarium...' Latin version of 8.

11 [fol. 108v, lines 17–18] 'Ad anniuersarium Vuij abbatis ...' Latin version of the added notice to 8 (s.xi/s.xii).

12 [fol. 108v, lines 19–22] 'Hanc caritatem ...' Latin version of 7.

Hand f (s.xii[1]).

13 [fol. 109r, lines 1–13] 'Ðis is Sce Eadmundes ferme on Byrtune ...' OE memorandum specifying the nature of the one month's food rents payable from various manors. [Lists the same manors as §4 above but probably dates from Baldwin's time, not Leofstan's].